Rude Awakening

Rude Awakening

Perils, Pitfalls, and Hard Truths
of the Spiritual Path

P. T. Mistlberger

BOOKS

Winchester, UK
Washington, USA

First published by O-Books, 2011

O-Books is an imprint of John Hunt Publishing Ltd.,
Laurel House, Station Approach, Alresford, Hants, SO24 9JH, UK
office1@o-books.net
www.o-books.com

For distributor details and how to order please visit the 'Ordering' section on our website.

Text copyright: P.T. Mistlberger 2010

ISBN: 978-1-84694-609-7

A CIP catalogue record for this book is available from the British Library.

Design: DKD

Printed in the UK by CPI Antony Rowe
Printed in the USA by Edwards Brothers Malloy

We operate a distinctive and ethical publishing philosophy in all
areas of our business, from our global network of authors to
production and worldwide distribution.

Contents

The image on the cover is of the 5th century CE Buddhist monk Bodhidharma, traditionally held to be the founder of Zen in China. The rendering shown was made by the fierce 18th century Japanese Zen master and calligrapher Hakuin. Bodhidharma's eyes appear wide and wild because according to legend he became so fed up with his drowsiness in meditation that he tore off his eyelids to ensure that he would never fall asleep again. Bodhidharma is the ultimate symbol of the resolute determination to stay awake no matter what, even in the face of the most challenging onslaughts of the mind, the trickiest traps of the spiritual path, and the most difficult hardships of life.

Better not start on the spiritual path.
But if you start, you had better finish.
Chogyam Trungpa Rinpoche

Introduction

Spiritual Awakening is Harder than You Thought (Which Only Makes It More Valuable)

Mark Antony: They say I'm a coward. What say you?
Lucius Vorenus: You're no coward. But you have a sickness in your soul.
Mark Antony: How do you know?
Lucius Vorenus: Because I have the same sickness.
From the HBO series *Rome*

The idea that the human race has a 'sickness of the soul', hard to dispute for anyone who studies history or looks at a daily newspaper, lies at the basis of all spiritual teachings (and their fossilized remnants, organized religion). There is a cure for this sickness – what has traditionally been known in the world's wisdom traditions as a path leading to 'self-realization' or 'awakening' or 'enlightenment' – but for some strange reason, it is almost never approached, let alone walked, and is still a barely known quantity in mainstream society.

The major theme of this book is that to the extent that the path of awakening *is known, it is not* well understood, and has been cheapened by endless side-paths, 'instant' approaches, and half-baked alternatives that do not lead to any appreciable transformation. Further, even among those who find out about this 'cure' to the sickness of the soul and set about trying to achieve it, they mostly fail. That is the hard truth for any who look closely and honestly into the matter. There are many, many reasons for this. The book you hold in your hands is dedicated to examining these reasons with a sharp, unflinching, and uncompromising light.

In the main this is not a polite, politically correct, or 'feel-good' book. It is not intended for those looking for a light read, something with which to idle away time on an airplane or as a distraction or escape from life-issues. The book is intended for sincere or long-time spiritual seekers. It may be especially helpful for mature adults who have come to realize that the whole journey of life – and in particular, the inner journey of awakening – has turned out to be much tougher than they thought it might be. An alternative title for this book could be *Falling Off the Wagon*, because the hard truth is that most spiritual seekers sooner or later fall off the wagon – that is, they return to negative habits and other pointless, useless, and self-destructive ways.

That said, this book can also be read with benefit by newcomers to the search for higher truth, regardless of age, because the sooner we become aware of the *hard* truths of the inner journey and face them, the better.

The basic premise herein is that *authentic* personal transformation or spiritual awakening, while possible, is in fact very rare. We live during a time when teachings concerned with 'personal growth' or 'spiritual development' are widely available – so much so, that most have been diluted, watered down into a palatable form that is easier to digest. The general result of this more superficial, 'feel-good' approach is, I argue, ineffectual inner work that, for the most part, does not result in significant or lasting changes for the one using it, either inwardly or outwardly. It has the effect of cheapening the whole idea of awakening or enlightenment, reducing it to the impact of a fad, trend, or the latest diet to try.

A second premise implicit here is that the majority of books dealing with the matter of spiritual realization are written in such a way that many problem areas are glossed over. Most teachings and writings on transformation are very polite and the focus tends to be on the positive – 'Do this to get that' – rather than looking at the blocks that are in the way of genuine inner or outer change.

To cite but two examples: firstly, books on meditation generally provide basic '101'-type instruction, along with mention of the benefits that arise from such practice, but rarely do they delve into (to any significant degree) the *resistance* typically thrown up by the mind as we encounter blocks to further and deeper practice; or more specifically, what to do when the unconscious part of the mind ejects difficult material, as sustained meditation practice will often cause it to do. And secondly, manifestation techniques teaching us how to bring our desires into tangible reality – how to 'get more things' – have flooded the market in the past few decades. While many of these books present valid teachings, few of them take a hard, deep look at the reasons why these manifestation techniques often *fail*. For every success story cited in such books, many more failures are not.

Of course, the methods, whether of meditation or manifestation, are not the problem; the problem is the nature of our mind, and its remarkable ability to sabotage efforts of inner work – whether these efforts are intended to manifest outer changes, or to break through into deep personal awakening.

This book takes a close look at the ways we sabotage our growth and awakening, and in particular, how we fall off the main road to enlightenment (or fail to understand what this road means), settling for more comfortable or consoling side routes. Many of the myths, fallacies, and fairy tales of the spiritual path are unapologetically uncovered and deconstructed. Although some who read this book may be heartened or even consoled, others may have their buttons pushed. The book is not meant to give one the 'warm fuzzies'; it is intended rather to function as an alarm clock.

Some may also see an irony or underlying humor within these pages, and that would be correct. As we all know, seen from a certain perspective life can appear absurd and deeply funny, and the spiritual path all the more so. There is a reason why psycho-spiritual practices (of all types) are often fodder for comedians and make for easy parody. There is indeed something ridiculous about the very effort to change ourselves; and the fact that so many gurus and teachers (to say nothing of religious authorities or clergy or academic educators) have been humbled via endless scandals has only added to the doubt and cynicism with which much of the public views the matter of 'personal growth' or 'enlightenment'.

Nonetheless, there *is* a legitimate 'path' and many have walked it – successfully – throughout history. The main point stressed herein is that making the journey requires an extraordinary sincerity and willingness to be deeply honest. Not a humorless sincerity, but one rather that is full of passion and a relentless willingness to face *anything* in the way of realizing our greatest potential of being.

Naturally, one might wonder who can write about the pitfalls and perils of the spiritual path without sounding like a hypocrite or a mere arrogant preacher who probably doesn't walk their loud talk. It goes without saying that I've personally fallen into many of the traps outlined in this book (I could not write of them if I didn't have some acquaintance with them) and have stumbled on my face so many times that I've internalized, out of necessity, Ram Dass's famous mantra, 'It's not how often you fall down in life, it's the way you pick yourself up that matters.'

As I write these words I'm in my early 50s and have been 'on the path', at least consciously, since my late teens. During these ensuing decades I have participated in much of the entire panoply of wisdom traditions made accessible to the average Western seeker growing up during the wildly exploratory decades of the 1960s, 70s, and 80s: *raja yoga*, the Gurdjieff Work, tantra, Tibetan Buddhism, Zen Buddhism, Theravadin Buddhism, depth psychology, *A Course in Miracles*, Reichian therapy, bioenergetics, Primal Therapy, rebirthing, Gestalt Therapy, tarot and astrology, Native Indian teachings, shamanism, ritual and ceremony, high magic, psychic exploration, the Enneagram, the Kabbalah, Gnosticism, Hermeticism, Taoism, martial arts, Sufism, spiritual alchemy, Advaita Vedanta, and others I'm doubtless forgetting. I have studied and participated in all of these traditions to varying degrees of depth, and have taught several of them. I'm a trained counselor, meditation teacher, and transformational workshop facilitator (since 1987), have co-founded one spiritual school, and founded two others that I ran for many years. I have lectured and taught in a number of countries and cities around the world. Over the decades I've had several thousand clients and students.   15

All that may sound impressive, but I'd be the first to admit that my life has been, in some respects, a sham. Not an intentional sham – I've been a sincere seeker and teacher, and have been reliably informed by many that I have helped them on their way. By 'sham' I mean the simple reality that I am both a 'spiritual guy' and a 'human guy'. Rather than denounce myself for failing to match some arbitrary standard of moral or character perfection, I've instead opted to make my life a teaching, to work with the raw material of *struggle* (and all that that entails) rather than giving up in the face of it. All my warts – my anger, my arrogance, my fear, my control, my laziness, my irresponsibility, my self-doubt, and so on – make up the fodder and fuel for my process of truly employing the Socratic maxim, 'Know thyself.'

There is of course nothing unique about having 'stuff' – the raw material of our personality and its endless messy manifestations – to work on. Everyone has it, just as everyone eats, sleeps, craps, and dies. A key to moving deeper into honest self-assessment is recognizing our sheer ordinariness. As much as we all tend to suspect that our 'stuff' is somehow special, we can rest assured that it is not, and that in fact it is so commonplace as to be, well – *boring*. (A devastating realization, as deep down most of us suspect *we* are special – either positively, as in 'better than', or negatively, as in 'less than' – thinking that our stuff *makes us special; that is,* defines who we are.) However, we can't see that our stuff is *not special* – which is ultimately understood to be a great relief – until we first become honest about our stuff. We have to dismantle pride as much as possible in order to go beyond fear and deeper into truth, into life, into Reality. (And for those of you out there who think you have 'no stuff' to look at, you are either lying to yourself or you are a saint in which case you can toss this book aside now.)

The book is divided into six parts: the first three deal directly with some of the major misconceptions and 'rude truths' that we sooner or later have to face on the spiritual path. In the fourth section seven steps toward awakening are outlined. The fifth section is a brief study of the lives and teachings of seven sages that I see as being vivid examples of uncompromising, radical, and passionate awakening. The last section presents concise practical pointers.

Two Premises

The book proceeds on the basis of two central premises.

The first is that a key problem with spiritual seeking is the assumption that one finds endlessly repeated in book after book, and in teaching after teaching, that we have these 'two parts' – a great spiritual self, usually called a 'Higher Self' or 'True Self' or 'Real Me' or 'soul'; and we have a regular self – the crappy, ordinary me that eats, burps, farts, and has all the warts and problems of the regular human. It's understandable how this formula …

Ordinary self → True (Higher) Self = Awakening

… arose, because it does provide some sort of light at the end of the tunnel to orient ourselves toward. The problem, however, is that the formula is typically misused. Inevitably what happens is that the old religious viewpoint of regarding our basic human condition as sinful or flawed or otherwise *not good enough,* simply creeps in the back door and we become 'spiritual fundamentalists'. We simply find a new way to condemn ourselves, and others as well while we're at it. Given enough time it becomes obvious that we've failed to 'transform' our regular self, or to escape it (as if such a thing can be done) and we become phony holy – preaching principles that we don't truly live by, promoting values that we have not truly attained to.

The second major premise is that there *is* an absolute truth (an unpopular notion in these relativistic, postmodern times). In the book this version of truth is generally indicated by the term 'highest truth' or 'highest potential', and on occasion by the word 'Reality', with capitalized first letter. (And when the word 'truth' is otherwise used, as in 'truth-seeker', it obviously refers to the ultimate truths of the spiritual life.) This refers, essentially, to the core principle of 'non-dualism', a fancy-sounding word that simply means that the universe (and *all* possible 'universes' or 'infinities' for you mathematicians) is ultimately One, a singular totality that is not truly divisible, except in our own mind.

Now any of you sharp cookies out there may think you see a contradiction between the two premises, as I seem to be saying that the separation between the ordinary self and the spiritual self is false, and yet I am also saying that there *is* a higher reality. In fact there is no real contradiction there. The essential paradox of awakening is this: we have to stop being phony and get real – and especially, we have to stop using spiritual principles to project a false image or, conversely, to reinforce self-rejection and self-loathing – while at the same time orienting our life toward a greater Reality. Not an easy task, not for a moment. But that is what makes self-realization the most valuable thing we can aspire to.

Part I

Hard Truths

Death carries off a man who is ~~gathering~~ flowers,
and whose mind is distracted,
as a flood carries off a sleeping village.
Dhammapada, 4:47

Chapter 1

Spiritual Posturing: The Regular Self and the Idealized Self

Hard Truth #1: The spiritual path – the idea of awakening to our highest potential – is extremely difficult. The odds are heavily stacked against us that we will be able to complete this journey successfully. That does not mean that we should not embark on the journey, or give up if we've already been at it for a long time. (On the contrary – it is precisely because spiritual awakening demands so much of us that it is supremely valuable.) But it does mean that to truly proceed – or pick ourselves up if we've fallen down yet again – we have to see to what degree our life, and in particular our spiritual life, has been a sham, a going through the motions, a type of posturing.

To be 'awake' is to see the truth. Naturally, we cannot see any 'truth' without first learning to be truthful with ourselves. If we're going to do this we need to begin by recognizing our falseness. We have to stop pretending. It takes a great deal of energy to pretend because in doing so we are fighting against something. Granted, sometimes fighting *against* something is necessary, just like sometimes 'going with the flow' is stupid (especially if the 'flow' is going, lemming-like, to hell in a hand basket). But more often than not, our fighting is a waste of precious time and energy.

What are we fighting against? Put simply, against *ourselves*. The main problem with the so-called spiritual path is *pretending* to be spiritual. (The very word 'spiritual' admittedly becomes somewhat repulsive if used repeatedly, but for now I beg the reader's indulgence. It remains the best word to describe the whole idea of 'work on self', individual transformation, or 'awakening'.)

By 'pretending to be spiritual' I need to be clear about what I mean. This 'pretending' is not usually consciously intentional. It is more what we can call unconscious pretending. It comes about by trying to inhabit a role – the role of the 'awakening person'. As a result, the spiritual path gets used by most in a way that unintentionally results in a kind of split within. The split is eventually comprised of two sides: the 'regular self' and the 'idealized, spiritual self'.

The idealized or spiritual self is the man or woman who undergoes some therapy, meditates, prays, does rituals or ceremonies, reads and collects spiritual books (like this one), works on self, participates in transformational work with others, does retreats or workshops, attends lectures or meetings run by famous teachers or authors, tries (even if only sporadically) to be 'conscious' in relationships, and perhaps attempts to perform some 'green' or related activism on behalf of the planet (even if only recycling their bottles or cereal boxes).

The regular self is the man or woman who has embarrassing faults and shortcomings, who has unpaid debts, who falls out with people and holds grudges, who can't function sexually, who eats too much (or eats junk), who has bad breath in the morning, who cuts corners on meditation (if he or she in fact meditates), who is mentally and physically lazy, who buys spiritual books but never reads them (or doesn't get past page 3), who watches shallow TV programs, bad movies, or raunchy porn, who gives the finger to the driver who cuts them off, who gossips pointlessly or destructively, who *still* refers to a need to 'kill time' (arguably our most precious commodity), and who recycles jack shit.

The idealized, 'spiritual' self is, essentially, a fabrication, and is ultimately much less real than the regular self. That is because this idealized self is mostly the result of a collection of temporary habits that we've acquired in our time of spiritual seeking – *habits we've acquired because of how strongly we've been trying to get away from something.*

What have we been trying to flee? The *regular self.* But as hard as we try, this is a project doomed to failure, because it is based on a misunderstanding. The misunderstanding is the idea that we can safely 'divide time' between the idealized and regular self, something like how we can divide time between work in the day, and evenings of leisure; or being alone weekdays and our time with the kids on the weekend.

Inevitably, in our desire to be spiritual, we become hypocrites. We do this because we're always feeling guilty about something, even if we can't put our finger on what that 'something' might be. (Although in truth, most people who have lived enough years *can* put their finger on more than one 'something' they feel guilty about.) This does not mean that we are 'bad' people – on the contrary, the vast majority of us are actually perfectly ordinary. The problem, however, is that most people get a wrong idea about what spirituality entails, thinking that it is something that can be attended to periodically, like church or synagogue or mosque or temple or monastery. Or we can do a workshop or retreat on occasion. Or sit down to meditate on occasion, like we might sit down for a fine meal once a month.

It may seem harsh to find fault with all that, but we have to be honest. Such 'seeking' – more accurately, *dabbling* – does not lead anywhere. It instead *reinforces* the inner division, the spiritual self 'working on' the regular self. This dynamic is really more akin to a somewhat pretentious superior bossing around his or her underling. 'Do this, or else … you will not be spiritual.' *Do this or you will not get paid.*

If we persist in this divisiveness between our 'spiritual' idealized self and our 'unconscious' regular self, our relationships in life gradually begin to reflect the split back to us. That is, we acquire 'spiritual friends' and 'regular friends' – or perhaps more precisely, 'spiritual friends' and family. With time, however, our spiritual friends may drift away, or lose interest in their practice (or even, as happens on occasion, turn vehemently against the whole idea of consciousness growth, for any number of reasons). And our 'regular friends' (or family) will remain annoyingly consistent, as people in general commonly do.

The whole problem of the split between our 'holy' and 'unholy' parts is residing in our mind, and nowhere else. Waking up to our highest potential is not supposed to become an internal war, God vs. the serpent, the Roman Empire vs. the barbarians, the angelic Higher Self vs. the smelly lower *chakras*. It is supposed to be reconciliation, a joining of forces, an inner *unification*. But all too often it becomes a case of the 'inner spiritual priest' condemning the 'inner animal'. In our very desire to grow we become little more than moralists, spiritual intellectuals, or spiritual posers, never truly walking our talk. We gain new ideas to boast about, or to beat ourselves up about, but we fail to truly live these ideas.

Summary

False spirituality involves developing an 'internal inquisitor' who casts judgment on our human self, with the result being that we become a hypocrite, a mere preacher of spiritual principles who does not truly live them – a talker, not a walker. In our very effort to wake up, we tumble into a very common pitfall: we confuse 'Know thyself' with 'Divide thyself'. In so doing, we do not truly transform or change anything within us, we simply run away from it. We turn *ourselves* into the enemy.

Chapter 2

Eastern Fundamentalism

Hard Truth #2: Eastern pathways (yoga, tantra, Buddhism, Taoism, martial arts, etc.), while containing many excellent teachings, can be misused as easily as Western religions or any other teachings. We misuse them by becoming a fundamentalist – one who subscribes to doctrine and dogma without deep personal understanding.

Some discussion of this topic is important, because for Westerners it tends to be hard to see. Western religious fundamentalism is both obvious and tiresome for most Western truth-seekers. To mention the easiest example: many of us are well familiar with the standard Christian fundamentalist views on redemption, the admonishment to 'accept Christ' (all too often accompanied by insufferable righteousness) in order to avoid dire consequences, and the lamentable doctrine of eternal damnation. We are also well acquainted with intolerant forms of Islam, and its related darker elements of extremism. Fundamentalist Judaism is less obvious (and Judaism is tiny in membership compared to Christianity and Islam), but is alive and well and has more than its share of rigid dogma.

Part of the counterculture movement of the 1960s involved a large-scale rejection of Western religions, and accordingly, a natural tendency to embrace the East. By 'East' we mean here mainly two traditions: esoteric Hinduism (essentially, yoga, and to a lesser extent, tantra); and Buddhism. In the 1950s–60s it was chiefly yoga (in various lineages) that became popular in the West; by the 1970s–80s yoga had been joined (and in some cases eclipsed) by tantra and Zen Buddhism. By the 1990s and into the early 21st century, Tibetan Buddhism and Advaita Vedanta (a philosophically advanced school within Hinduism) gained many adherents, and yoga made a strong resurgence, becoming widely popular (to the point of trendiness), especially in urban settings. Along with all these, other traditions like Theravadin Buddhism, Taoism, and oriental martial arts (including its softer forms like tai chi and qi gong), have remained quietly popular and familiar to most Westerners.

In the rush to embrace the East certain elements get overlooked, foremost of which is what we can loosely call 'Eastern fundamentalism'. If by 'fundamentalism' we mean strong attachment to religious doctrine – strict adherence to 'word' along with an inflexible righteousness – then in the case of 'Eastern fundamentalism' the tendency will be to become either unrealistically hard on ourselves, or too soft and lazy. A classic example of this involves the case of the word 'bliss', the English translation of the Sanskrit word *ananda*, a term that crops up commonly in Hindu scriptures. Teachings can be easily found in yogic doctrine that state that a natural result of inner awakening is to experience bliss. This soon becomes the idea that if we are not experiencing bliss all the time (or at least most of the time), then our spiritual practice must be faulty, or we must not be awake in any real sense. If we are not happy, something is wrong with us. 'Don't worry, be happy' – a phrase which, incidentally, Bobby McFerrin borrowed from the Indian guru Meher Baba – becomes 'If you are *not* happy, you should be worried, for you need to be *fixed.*'

The downside of the emphasis on states of mind like bliss or a 24/7 smilie face is that it eventually encourages denial and repression. The need to be seen as 'spiritual', as one committed to practice and the path, becomes the need to be seen as one *befitting* that path. The moment we seek to fit an image, whether in the eyes of others, or (even more problematically) in our own eyes, is the moment we have stopped being natural. We are simply developing a *spiritual persona*. In most cases such a persona is not forced or obvious, but subtle, which is why it can be difficult to detect. The rough Western equivalent would be a fundamentalist Christian or

Jew or Muslim who outwardly may indeed be upstanding, helpful, well adjusted psychologically, and showing a measure of peace and wisdom – all the while concealing a condescending view that regards non-Christians or non-Jews or non-Muslims as 'lost souls'.

A particular type of Eastern fundamentalism can take the form of ideas that seem (conveniently) to be opposed to Western values that Westerners may find themselves revolting against – such as, for example, the typical idea of a 'work ethic'. An example of this would be the Taoist idea of *wu wei*, which literally means 'no effort' or 'without action'. Another one would be the idea (found in several Eastern traditions) that 'you are already enlightened, you just don't realize it', which often gets interpreted as 'There is no need to practice.' All of these ideas are highly convenient for one who is lazy or resistant to being responsible in general. (As Gurdjieff used to say, 'If you are irresponsible in life, you will be irresponsible in the [inner] Work.')

The Western mind is, generally speaking, work-oriented, rooted in the idea of individualism and of proving oneself. Westerners in particular tend to conceive of things in terms of struggle, following a progressive, time-conscious, linear route to personal accomplishment and success. This is in part due to conditioning from scientific materialism and Western religions, both of which teach that we have only one life to live, have only a very limited amount of time in the bigger scheme of things, and so we had better hurry up and get done what we want to do, *now*. (This 'hurry up' mindset was once well illustrated in an anecdote related by the famed Swiss psychologist C.G. Jung, who was spending some time with Pueblo Indians in the American southwest. One of the Pueblo chiefs said to him that they had concluded that 'white people' were insane, because they looked troubled and restless and they always seemed to be in a hurry, seeking something that was not in the present moment.) Even our spirituality is hyped and marketed as a progressive yellow-brick path that presumably leads to some Land of Oz where everything will be wonderful and we will finally realize fulfillment. Then along come certain Eastern teachings in which seekers are taught essential ideas of non-effort, non-doing, and realization *now*, in this moment. These ideals are very tempting, because they oppose the Western idea of working hard to attain something. They appear to be an easy way out. Unfortunately for us, there is no 'easy way out' to spiritual awakening.

Fundamentalism is the tendency to take teachings too literally, and to apply them in an inflexible fashion to justify agendas. In that respect, Eastern religious fundamentalism has two forms and two general consequences. One is the tendency for seekers to abuse certain of its teachings, such as 'non-doing' ('Don't resist, just go with the flow') and non-duality ('Everything is really One'), by indulging in laziness, or failing to understand the role of boundaries and material reality in our overall experience. 'We're already One in spirit' can easily become 'What's yours is mine' if appropriated by the greedy ego. 'I need do nothing' easily becomes 'The world owes me a living, so I need not be responsible' if appropriated by the lazy ego, seeking to justify its resistance to making efforts and growing up.

The trickier face of Eastern fundamentalism is the emphasis on the idea of the 'illusoriness' of the personal self or ego, without properly understanding what this means. When the illusoriness of the personal self is over-emphasized there can easily occur a kind of false realization, a type of sickness in which one begins to feel a deep sense of futility with life, a pointlessness in doing anything or relating to anyone (since after all, if my ego is an 'illusion' and 'I do not ultimately exist as a distinct personality' then 'Others do not truly exist either, so why bother with cultivating personal relationships, forgiving people, or other related time wastage?'). This is a shallow understanding and is a common example of using a spiritual principle to avoid facing a deeper psychological issue (such as, for example, depression, resulting from a negative self-image).

The main issue to remember with fundamentalism in general –

whether it be of the Eastern or Western variety – is that it is basically the tendency to parrot a doctrine, to use a teaching that really amounts to little more than repeating by rote what some 'authority' has said, without truly understanding the words ourselves. Fundamentalism gets very troublesome when it is used to disguise a psychological weakness – for example, the 'All is One' idea being used to avoid fears of being deeply intimate with *one ordinary person* and repressing one's desires to be 'special' to one other. Or, probably even more commonly, using spiritual ideals to avoid dealing with actual relationship issues. 'I'm a spiritual person, I'm beyond this silly relationship crap. *You* need help, not me – I already meditate' (or get therapy, do yoga, etc.).

Summary

We misuse Eastern teachings by condemning others who do not live up to the ideals of Eastern teachings, or by beating ourselves up because *we* are not living up to their ideals. In so doing, we simply substitute being a Western religious fundamentalist with being an Eastern religious fundamentalist.

Chapter 3

Sex and Hypocrisy

Hard Truth #3:
A. You are a sexual being. Period. The path of awakening is not about denying this, or running away from it, or 'rising above' it. Sex is simply the lower musical notes of Spirit.
B. You are also more than just a sexual being. Your sexuality does not define the vast spectrum of your entire being.

A chapter like this practically writes itself. Here in the early 21st century we live in an era of so-called 'transparency' (part of the new smartphone zeitgeist in which half of what you say or do is being cached somewhere). Famed personalities from all walks of life are seemingly humbled on a monthly basis, and their 'fall' is almost always connected to sex (and occasionally, money or power).

There are few things in life as potentially embarrassing as sexuality, because of its sheer primal force – a force as powerful as the urge to breathe, eat, or sleep. Long ago a connection arose in the minds of many between chastity and religiousness; between purity and spiritual values. This connection was reinforced for centuries by celibate priesthoods and by ancient myths associating sex with a type of rebellion against God (as with Adam and Eve). To this day the lower parts of the body are still associated with the 'unclean' and despite the fact that the sex life of a certain percentage of the human race can now be viewed on Internet 'amateur' porn sites, sex itself remains a topic of discomfort for most. In Chapter 1 we discussed the notion of the 'idealized, spiritual self' vs. the 'regular self'. Needless to say, the prime elements of the regular self are the survival instinct, and sex. Nothing defines the basic humanity of the average person as clearly as the search for security, and the impulse to mate (in whatever form).

The spiritual impulse is often associated with freedom; with, as Plato described it, escaping from a cave. However, for the spiritual seeker, the idea of 'pure freedom' usually gets reduced to a more commonplace version. The very urge to become a 'spiritual seeker' frequently gets tied up with the desire to rebel against one's conditioning, to differentiate from one's biological family – to be different and unique. The historian James Webb wrote about this in a broader sense in his *Flight From Reason* (later titled *The Occult Underground*), where he suggested that many who seek out alternative forms of spirituality are part of a collective rebellion against the starkness of the 'age of rationality'. Many fear losing themselves in the sheer impersonality of the scientific worldview, which appears to eliminate both the need of a First Cause (God), and the cosmic importance of humans (as Copernicus and Galileo first demonstrated four centuries ago by showing that the earth is not the center of the solar system, let alone the universe).

There is doubtless truth to Webb's idea, but the urge to be free, or to rebel against what one perceives to be limiting values – whether those of family, or broader educational or social factors – easily gets distorted into a rebellion against one's lower nature. There is a difficulty in all this because it is true that entry onto the spiritual path often involves some sort of rebellion, or breaking away, from a more conventional life path. It is difficult to be interested in enlightenment (let alone authentically move toward it) without being at least a bit of a rebel. Mainstream society in practically all countries does not support an interest in matters like self-realization. The heavy focus is on survival, materialism, and becoming established in a conventional manner.

Adam and Eve were, in myth, the original rebels. But they also ended up experiencing shame after they ate the fruit of the tree of the knowledge of good and evil and 'opened their eyes'. This shame caused them to cover their naked bodies with fig leaves. The myth is a powerful metaphor for the link between rebellion and shame.

As we rebel from our conditioning and clarify our individuality, it becomes possible to set out on a spiritual path – because *only an individual can go beyond individuality and glimpse deeper truths*, let alone the Oneness of existence. However, in our urge to grow it's all too easy to rebel not just against the more traditional values of the world or our family, but against our own 'lower nature' as well. In our urge to flee from the prison of mediocre values, we all too commonly seek to flee our own 'mediocrity' – that is, our own survival impulse and sexuality. We confuse the idea of 'spirituality' or 'awakening' with the idea of escaping this world, including the domains of the 'lower *chakras*' – that is, the right use of power, sexual energy, and financial responsibility.

This accounts for a distasteful quality found among some practitioners of inner work, and it is a type of subtle smugness or self-righteousness, the belief that one is a member of the esoteric elite, and 'above' the lower domains. Puritanical tendencies crop up among the 'spiritual' almost as much as among the conventionally religious.

Any sort of movement against natural forces and practical responsibilities, such as the urge to sleep, eat, and have sex, is bound to end in failure. Human biology (and its primary drives) is millions of years old. Our spiritual impulse, our pull to move toward enlightenment, is minuscule in comparison to the power and age of our 'lower nature'. To attempt to deny this lower nature is invariably to end up a hypocrite.

What is to be done then? Are we then to indulge our lower nature, worry-free about whether or not it is diluting or distorting or overpowering our spiritual practice?

Some go this route. Some use modern teachings like Western versions of 'tantra' and trumpet them as legitimate avenues for inner work. But in most cases modern Western versions of tantra end up being gross simplifications, watered-down versions of a difficult and highly disciplined method of transformation. 'Tantra' in the West is often little more than a means to legitimize sexual desire.

The whole basis of awakening is reconciliation of opposites, and in particular, those of self/body with selflessness/spirit. As long as sex remains an area of fear or shame or exaggerated inhibition, we will almost certainly end up hypocrites in our efforts to 'be spiritual'. The other side of the ledger is equally problematic. If we indulge sex to the point where our 'spirituality' is a thinly disguised excuse to legitimize lust – for example, by participating in inner-work communities mainly to pursue potential lovers – we are also being two-faced.

Summary

A classic error is to confuse spiritual ideals with conventional religious morals. In this confusion, sex (and the lower *chakras*) is deemed 'unspiritual' and to be avoided; or as a potent force to rebel against. Almost none of us are able to 'avoid' such a basic facet of human life and so we become hypocritical if we fail to know, embrace, and deeply accept, our sexuality. (And yes, Jesus probably had sex, as did the Buddha.) *well...*

On the other hand, the spiritual path is not meant to be a disguise for 'chasing tail' or seeking a mate. Tantra and similar forms of inner work are not vehicles for legitimizing lust.

No: Sidd. Gautama did; the Buddha did not.

Chapter 4

New Age Fluff, Feel-Good Spirituality, and the Enlightenment Industry

Hard Truth #4: New Age or 'Feel-Good' spirituality – where the emphasis is on 'light' and 'ease' – is very prone to ignoring the entirety of the human being, and accordingly, very prone to becoming an escape for those who do not want to be responsible for the entirety of themselves and their life.

This is not an entirely enjoyable segment to write – certainly not because it is hard to find examples of superficial spirituality among New Age teachings – but because the original idea behind the New Age itself was actually noble, worthy, and important. Essentially, that original idea was one of syncretism, the cross-referencing of particular universal teachings found in most (if not all) significant wisdom traditions. The idea behind a 'New Age' was to get beyond the destructive prejudices of older ages, and in particular, the ignorance commonly held by a member of any given spiritual or religious tradition about *other* traditions.

For example, many, if not most, major wars have been (and still are) based on ignorance of the cultural ways of other people – basically, the fear and suspicion of that which is, culturally and especially religiously, *different*. Religious programming in particular penetrates deeply into the psyches of most, in large part because it is based on the promise of overcoming mortality. We humans live with the ever-present knowledge of our mortality – as someone once bluntly put it, we are all born with a death sentence – and this impending death seems to render pointless all of our efforts, trials, and tribulations. What has it all been for if one day we are simply to disappear, ultimately to be forgotten, as if we had never actually existed? Most of us become very good at forgetting such questions, or convincing ourselves that we don't really care. That is, we adapt psychologically to our condition – the reality of our limited life-spans – and proceed as if death were not a reality for *us*. That is of course both 'normal' and necessary for any semblance of contentment with our lot. It can be argued, however, that the fear of death simply becomes repressed, not truly overcome. This is where most religious traditions come into the picture, as most offer elaborate doctrines explaining the nature of the 'afterlife' (and all taking it for granted that such an afterlife exists in one fashion or another). In most cases, religions work to relieve the individual of the fear that their life is a meaningless blip in an infinite expanse and that each individual is utterly without significance.

Accordingly, religious conditioning is extremely powerful, and in particular for the 'mass man' who has no special interest in mysticism or philosophy. As a result, nothing throughout history has created greater divisiveness than religious dogma when wielded as a weapon against those subscribing to a *different* dogma. Whether it has been Islamic hordes crushing Buddhist temples, or Christian crusaders attacking Islamic communities, or Islamic and Jewish governments at each other's throats, or Hindu and Islamic cultures squaring off, or Christian persecutions of Jews and Pagans, the overriding theme has been a type of doctrinal perversion in which the original ideas of a spiritual leader have been shaped into a political (and military) tool.

The so-called New Age, which has older roots but which is really a child of the late 19th and 20th centuries (a magazine called *The New Age* was being published as early as 1894 in England, although its focus was more literary and social), was in large part an attempt to reverse that. In the course of developing its ideas, however, it inevitably fell prey to the Achilles Heel of syncretism, which is a tendency to dilute things too much.

The matter of this chapter, 'New Age fluff', refers to the weakest area of this syncretistic diluting. By 'fluff' is implied too much emphasis on values and qualities associated with 'light' and 'ease', and a corresponding tendency to shy away from 'dark' and 'effort'. That both 'light' and 'ease' have their place, and importance, in human experience goes without saying. Much of our past is colored with darkness and struggle. However, if these brighter qualities are emphasized to a degree that involves the repression of dark, and a resistance to appropriate effort, then we are simply inviting a different sort of imbalance.

To go beyond duality (the ultimate aim of awakening) is to resolve opposites by integration, not by the denial of one side of the polarity. We do not go beyond the dualism of the subject–object split by denying that objects (the universe) exist, or by denying that the subject ('I') exists. Either denial is a type of insanity. The idea is rather to master the relationship between both – that is, to truly learn how to live 'in the world' while at the same time maintaining a sense of self, of subjective presence (what Gurdjieff, for one, called 'self-remembering'). Higher awakenings and mystical realizations of Oneness cannot happen without this foundation of the balancing of opposites – between self and other, between spirit and flesh, between spiritual practice and worldly responsibilities.

Some New Age teachings have understood the idea of the resolution of opposites, but many have not – especially those involving a focus on the so-called 'subtle' or 'higher planes' of consciousness. These teachings and practices, which require considerably sensitivity, often come more naturally to those who are already in fear of the darker shades of life – and especially the darker shades within themselves. They literally 'seek the light' and tend to focus on such areas as 'psychic healing', angels, spirit guides, native spiritualities, nature spiritualities, and so forth. Not that there need be anything wrong in any of that, but very often such fields of practice and study are populated by delicate types who dislike confrontation in general (though of course, there are always exceptions). To confront someone (or something) requires the right usage of personal power. Many who seek the ethereal realms are avoiding the issue of looking at personal power, instead seeking to replace it with 'spiritual power', or even the power of 'other entities' (as in certain forms of psychic or mediumistic work), such as 'guardian angels', 'spirit helpers', and the like.

A useful map here is the idea of the seven *chakras*, the Hindu term for 'subtle energy centers' that correspond to psycho-spiritual states. There are many versions of this model, but usually the seven levels are considered to be: 1st (survival, grounding); 2nd (sex, emotions); 3rd (personal power); 4th (heart); 5th (communication); 6th (psychic sensitivity, intelligence); and 7th (wisdom, connection to the infinite). Many New Age teachings encourage a leaning toward the higher *chakras*, and an avoidance of the lower. For most, that likely does no good; like a totem pole that is weak on the bottom, sooner or later the whole pole will topple over – regardless of how exquisite the carvings may be at the top – if the lower part is not solidly grounded and properly attended to.

More insidiously, New Age accentuation of the 'light' closely parallels the stilted morality of organized religion in general. (Arguably, this distortion of New Age thought is simply Christian morality in a different guise – something made all the more probable by the frequent references to 'the Christ' or 'angels' in many New Age teachings.) The new era of 'transparency' has resulted in countless examples of priests being exposed, and most such scandals have involved the revelation that the priest is a sexual being (particular actions notwithstanding). The New Age practitioner who focuses on the domains of the higher *chakras* to the point that their own lower nature is being neglected or repressed, is not much different from the celibate priest, monk, or nun who has not truly transcended their own sexuality (or their repressed desires for power, wealth, status, and so on).

Relieved of Anxiety: Inwardly Free or Just Free of Responsibility?
A difficulty with modern spiritual pathways has been the tendency

of many teachers to emphasize a type of path of 'least resistance'. This usually amounts to just hanging around the teacher, with the implication being that because the teacher strove heroically for his or her own awakening, we need not do the same – that in effect, the teacher has already done the dirty work for us, and so we can just relax and absorb the good vibes and our awakening will be forthcoming. Implicit in all this is the expectation that those who hang around the teacher will also support him or her, energetically, financially, and by recruiting new students.

There is a naturalness to all that and in one sense it need not be a big deal. The problem arises when the idea that the teacher has already done the work for the follower gets over-emphasized, to the point where it becomes quite similar to conventional organized Christian tradition, which is based on the underlying dogma that we need only surrender inwardly to Christ, and we are automatically 'saved'. Christ did the dirty work for us by getting crucified and resurrecting, so we get a free 'piggyback pass' to inner purification and immortality simply by 'accepting' him.

Any sort of deep surrender, or explicit and implicit demonstration of trust, has consequences, and some of those will feel very good. They feel good because in surrendering we have been relieved of the anxiety that comes from the fear of facing up to our responsibilities. It is very easy (and extremely common) to confuse 'awakening' with the state of 'no-anxiety'. Not that there is anything wrong with feeling anxiety-free, obviously. However, we have to be watchful and honest about why we are feeling anxiety-free. Is it because of genuine insight into our true nature, or is it because we have been conveniently relieved of responsibility?

The whole essence of 'feel-good' personal growth is *relieving anxiety*. Group consciousness can be very effective for this (the proverbial 'group hug'). Accordingly, many end up joining a spiritual community because it meets their social needs, or becomes a surrogate family. The group-mentality easily creates a sense of comfort, lack of anxiety, and accompanying sense that one is indeed on the right track. These can be helpful but they can never replace the need to do our inner work ourselves – to be truly responsible for who we are and how we live.

The Enlightenment Industry

It is no great secret that the matter of personal development or personal growth, as well as the loosely (and often vaguely) defined field of 'spiritual enlightenment', has become big business. Much of this began with Werner Erhard's famous 'Either you are enrolling life, or life is enrolling you' mantra, which became the ultimate credo of the self-employed personal growth teacher. Erhard – whose birth name was Jack Rosenberg, and who changed his name to 'Werner Erhard' while on a plane – essentially initiated the phenomenon of public workshops for large groups of people, in the early 1970s (similar personal growth workshops had of course been around long before, but not of the size of Erhard's, which commonly had as many as five hundred people gathered at a time). He had originally been a highly successful encyclopedia salesman. In the 1960s he'd participated in some of the Encounter therapy groups and transformational workshops at the famed Esalen Institute in northern California, and he'd made an in-depth study of Zen and much of the work of the key transpersonal psychologists of the mid-20th century. A natural autodidact, he became extraordinarily successful as a teacher of transformational principles in no small part because of his skillful ability to market himself and his ideas.

Erhard's original teaching principles, based largely on a synthesis of ideas from Zen Buddhism, Maxwell Maltz's psycho-cybernetics, and other teachings, were essentially sound in theory; and although controversial as a facilitator, he clearly had the natural skill to evoke 'openings' in people, and to 'work a room'. Inevitably, as his highly successful network began to expand, he had to train teachers in order to handle the workload. Some of these teachers in turn went on to become very successful; some even broke away and founded their own independent lines of transformational work, and these in turn went on to train yet more workshop facilitators. By the 1980s and early 1990s, which arguably was the peak period for the flourishing of transpersonal, transformational, New Age, and more esoteric schools and communities, more and more facilitators were being trained in a broad variety of growth and healing disciplines. In addition to Erhard's original 'est' trainings (which grew into 'The Forum' and later on, 'Landmark'), numerous schools based on inner work from systems such as *A Course in Miracles*, 'Rebirthing' (breath-work), the 'Enlightenment Intensive' (Zen adapted for the West), women's and men's groups, the Enneagram, neuro-linguistic programming (NLP), and almost endless other types of group psychotherapy and meditation modalities, became widespread. All of these produced professional trainers from within their ranks – trainers who in turn opted to support themselves via the business of teaching the principles and methods they'd been trained in.

The problem in all of this boils down to the issue of mixing transformational work with business. That is not to say that the inner work that went on, and goes on to this day, in many such schools is not effective and valid on certain levels. But when someone becomes trained as a teacher or facilitator of such work, they inevitably invest their life in it, and essentially become a 'professional guru'. That is not such a big deal; indeed, most priesthoods are effectively professional, and even independent gurus in cultures that traditionally support such teachers indeed need to be supported. The difficulty arises when all sorts of manipulation tactics are employed to 'enroll' would-be students, and teachings themselves inevitably become diluted in the need to make them marketable and palatable for greater masses.

Ultimately the very notion of spiritual enlightenment becomes cheapened through all of this. One author, in commenting on this issue, reported a story of a woman who had returned to her workshop facilitators demanding a refund because the weekend workshop that she'd invested several hundred dollars in had failed to deliver the promised 'enlightenment'.

It's tempting to laugh at such stuff, but the point is clear. We live during a rare period in history, in the midst of an enormous population spike, with the result being that most everything has proliferated – including spiritual teachings and transformational teachers of almost every conceivable caliber. As a result, there is a tremendous amount of junk out there, and a real need for the serious seeker to acquire and exercise discernment.

Farther Out Stuff: 2012 Prophecies, Chemtrails, Crop Circles, Conspiracy Theories

A further issue connected to New Age teachings and networks involves alleged conspiratorial matters, as well as prophecy in general. This is a lengthy topic, of course, and in a mid-sized book like this only a few remarks can be made. Suffice to say, the main theme with prophecy, as seen through the New Age lens, is usually radical and wholesale global change, typically catastrophic. The latest of these has been the 2012 phenomenon, based largely on 'Mayanism', a general term used to define New Age views about ancient Mayan records, the most significant of which has been to interpret some Mayan teachings as suggesting that a wholesale and potentially destructive planetary change will occur in late 2012. Other more subtle views speak of a wholesale shift in consciousness to occur around that time.

The problem with all these ideas is that they put the matter outside of us – literally, 'far out'. The term 'far out' is slang for 'unconventional', something that is in fact very often part of the path of inner awakening in some way. However, where typical New Age thinking gets this wrong is in mistaking mere *anti*-conventional or *anti*-establishment views and attitudes for genuine inner awakening. Things like the 2012 phenomenon and prophecies about wholesale changes often become simply disguised ways of rebelling against authority. And in the context of inner awakening, they entirely miss the point. Wholesale *inner* change is possible now, and is not dependent on a Mayan calendar date, some galactic alignment, or whether Democrats or Republicans control the White House.

Maya is not just the name of an old and once relatively advanced Central American culture – it is also the Eastern term for the 'veil of illusion' in which we typically become entangled. Most such illusion is commonplace, the usual affairs we get utterly lost in. New Age *maya* is a bit more sophisticated, because it appears (for many) to be some version of truth, or at least a way to truth. However, it is just a more elaborate distraction. The same holds for other phenomena – everything from crop circles, alleged 'chemtrails', 9-11 conspiracies, moon-landing conspiracies, or David Icke's ideas about royalty concealing lizard-tails. The issue about whether or not any of these things are objectively real is utterly beside the point. The point is that pursuing such matters only converts a 'truth-seeker' into a 'dream-seeker', chasing endless rainbows in search of some pot of gold containing the Great Answer.

Genuine awakening has nothing to do with any Great Answer provided by a prophecy 'coming true' or the 'powers that be' suddenly dropping their drawers and showing us their pitiful goods or revealing their evil agendas. There has been a reason that traditional seekers of enlightenment sought out seclusion or environments with a minimum of distraction, because of the mind's endless capacity to spin webs of *maya* out of nothing.

For a modern Western seeker – living in a time and culture that has no strong wisdom-tradition and is daily bombarded with all kinds of superficial crap and pointless information – the challenge is to stay awake through all this by remembering what awakening is *really* about.

Summary
'Fluff' and 'feel-good spirituality' are terms indicating an approach to awakening that is based more on a *desire to be comfortable*. Meditation in this regard can easily become *medication*, and ultimately not much different from a recreational drug. The key sign that indicates when we are out of balance in this area is when we notice that our spirituality has become more of a social activity,

that our good feelings depend entirely upon our community, and that despite our participation in such teachings we are not really becoming more responsible. Additionally, if we ever find that our meditation practice is making us feel more 'spacey' or 'airy' and more disconnected in general, then the chances are good we are medicating, not meditating.

Other forms of New Age spirituality, especially its more extreme forms such as those found in prophecy and conspiracy theories, is usually motivated by an agenda to rebel against establishment or authority. The most common problem with this is that it becomes an elaborate distraction from doing the deeper, harder work of honestly facing into ourselves and taking responsibility for what *we* are contributing to human civilization and our planet here, now.

We need to become discriminating in these times of supermarket spirituality and endless flakey forms of fringy high strangeness. Being gullible usually leads to a wastage of time. The antidote is to *long for the truth*, and not to be satisfied with distractions.

Chapter 5

Dysfunctional Masculine Spirituality and Dysfunctional Feminine Spirituality

Hard Truth #5: The spiritual path appears to promise some sort of ultimate equality – after all, 'One in Spirit' does not make any mention of opposite sexes. But the vast majority of us are not living 'One in Spirit'. We are living in bodies and we have a gender. In these bodies, men and women are not 'equal' – they are different. From these differences great lessons can be learned, but not until we face the peculiarities of our gender, and in particular, the neurotic and dysfunctional stuff that commonly surfaces when we attempt to walk a spiritual path and carry on intimate human relations at the same time.

Few matters in life trigger stronger responses than those related to gender issues. It is a particularly touchy subject for two main reasons: first, the history of civilization is dark with gender discrimination, and it is no secret which gender has been discriminated against more. The second is that for most people, the opposite sex – or in the case of gays and lesbians, the romantic partner – represents (if only in theory) *fulfillment*, the inner and outer completion of our life. They represent our greatest possible happiness, and accordingly, our greatest possible misery as well. As such, any sort of criticism directed to this subject is often reacted to strongly, if only because most people deeply relate to the struggle to understand (let alone enjoy) the opposite sex or romantic partner. More to the point, most of us identify strongly with our gender, and any sort of criticism directed toward it is often difficult to look squarely at. But we must, if we are to become free of the pitfalls and delusions that cause us to waste valuable time on our path.

A few remarks about what follows. I offer some critiques of the ways I've noted over the years that masculine and feminine 'spirituality' becomes dysfunctional. By 'masculine' and 'feminine' it should be understood that these refer to tendencies found within both men and women. It is true that 'masculine' applies mostly to men, and 'feminine' mostly to women, but it is also true that men have a feminine component, and women a masculine component. And so for a man who identifies with some of the remarks on the dysfunctional feminine found below, he can think of that as his 'inner feminine'. A woman identifying with some of the critiques of the dysfunctional masculine in the next section can think of that as her 'inner masculine'.

Dysfunctional Masculine Spirituality

The dysfunctional masculine has been both loud and obvious throughout history. It takes many different forms: the abusive man or tyrant, the killer, the wimp or Momma's boy, the Machiavellian opportunist, the perverted priest/monk, and many others.

Perhaps the main current Western version of masculine dysfunction in spiritual work is a somewhat new phenomenon: the 'spiritually feminized man'. Many modern Western women complain that men during these times are too polarized: either they are too feminine, accommodating, sensitive, understanding, catering, and dreadfully dull; or they are obnoxious overly masculinized jerks. It may be safely said that of those fitting into this broad spectrum, the great majority, probably 90%, are of the first type. The true 'bad boy' is becoming something of an endangered species, and this is accentuated among those involved in transformational, spiritual work. Many women who meditate or do yoga or transformational workshops look for their men outside of their personal growth communities, and often complain about 'dull spiritual men' – the SNAG ('sensitive New Age guy'), who perhaps should be more properly called the SNAMB ('sensitive New Age momma's boy').

The overly feminized man (to the point of dysfunction) is a

product of four main causes: a poor father-link, a 'too close to mother' connection, feminist values he has become allegiant to (often as a way to 'get even' with his father) and in particular the modern-day taboo of criticizing these feminist values; and centuries of accumulated generational guilt (the heavy legacy of men subjugating women). The first – the nature and quality of his relationship with his father – is probably the most important. There is an idea found in some psychoanalytic schools of thought that I've found useful to help get a hold on understanding this. The idea is as follows: as a young boy is growing up, he's initially very close to his mommy, as all young children are (or should be). Boy or girl, for the first three to five years or so of life in a typical family, Mommy is #1, Daddy is #2 (notwithstanding obvious exceptions). For a little boy, however, a time inevitably comes when it begins to dawn on him that he is different in some essential way from his mommy. Put simply, she is a girl, and he is a boy. (If he has a sister, this difference may become obvious more readily.)

It's at this point that the boy begins to break free in some ways from his mother (very gradually, of course), and begins to identify more with his father. He becomes a little lad as encouraged, guided, and supported by his dad (or perhaps older brothers or uncles, if he has them). If, however, this father-guidance is lacking, or of poor quality – which typically happens if Dad is 'not available' (or, needless to say, non-existent), whether physically by being on the road, or mentally/emotionally by falling asleep in front of the TV, or being generally self-absorbed or not very interested in his son – then the necessary separation process from the mother happens in a less than ideal fashion.

This faulty separation process typically ends up taking one of two faces: the boy grows into a man who is either too soft or too harsh; either too spineless, or having hands of iron. Psycho-spiritually, the faulty separation process from the mother can be seen as reflected in a 'disconnect' between the 2nd *chakra* (sex) and the 4th *chakra* (the heart). The boy becomes a man who is either too much in his sex-center or too much in his heart-center (or too much in his head). When he projects this outwardly, he tends to see any woman as one of two essential types: she is either a whore to be fucked, or a mother-figure to be adored, worshipped, catered to, and above all, never to disappoint. In short, he becomes deeply conflicted around women, and all his intimate relationships with them reflect this love/hate dance.

Men in this boat (and there are many in current times) tend to become 'loyal' henpecked workhorses who have affairs or who lose their vitality, serial daters, loners, porn freaks or any combination of the above. They never quite satisfy their women because there is always the sense (for the women) that something is missing; the guy either does not have enough money, or he is not edgy enough (i.e., too boring), or he is too edgy, and so on. For the men, the problem is compounded because his need to examine his relationship with his parents (father, yes, but mother also) is not reinforced by the world that surrounds him. It is not somehow 'masculine' to examine oneself (unless one is a therapist or monk), because it is not action-oriented. So it all becomes doubly confusing: somewhere the man knows he needs to work on himself to heal his relationship with his 'inner masculine', but the very act of such healing is judged (by most) to itself not be masculine. In his very desire to become less wimpy, he simply becomes a new kind of wimp: the spiritualized wimp. The spiritual itself is often associated – inaccurately, I might add – with the feminine. Long ago I participated in a large workshop for men, during which the experienced seminar leader declared that more or less all shamans, Native 'holy men', were gay. This in fact is not true – many of the famous American Indian medicine men had wives – but it reflects a prevailing fear of the spiritual dimension in many men, precisely because this dimension appears to run counter to male instincts such as action, dominance, competition, and so on.

The male ego is especially given to competition. The 'peacock instinct', the need to preen and show feathers, or to growl louder than the next guy, to be stronger, cooler, deadlier, to make more money, to be more influential or successful, a better fuck, a bigger dick, funnier, more clever, and so on, runs very deep in the male psyche. This can become a major roadblock on the path of awakening because it creates problems in relationships, especially with other men. The mystical impulse is to recognize the unity behind all forms; the masculine ego's drive to compete, to rise above the next guy, is diametrically opposed to the mystical impulse.

Competitiveness need not be done away with completely, however. The man waking up to his higher potential need not throw away his sword. Rather, his challenge is to redirect this sword toward the inner blocks standing in the way of realizing his potential. In short, he must become a warrior for Truth, rather than a warrior to battle the next guy in order to have his women, his land, or eat his heart. The warrior's fierceness is actually an essential element of the awakening process. As in the legend of the first Zen patriarch Bodhidharma, who tore his eyelids off to stay awake in meditation, the transforming man must be fierce in making a stand against his own ignorance and sleepiness.

In short, the awakening man needs to perform something of a balancing act. He needs to develop the ability to put aside his competitiveness, especially when it interferes with important relationships on his path (which includes, crucially, his teachers – more than one male seeker has aborted his development because he has failed to see how his competitive instinct has wrecked his relationship with his teacher or mentor). But along with all that, he has to be on his guard not to become overly feminized, because if he does, he will lose the sharpness needed for his inner discipline.

Other forms of the neurotic masculine are of course common, with an interesting version being the 'controlling tyrant' type who becomes a spiritual guru. This is a person who often accumulates a significant following because he has the extremely attractive combination of wisdom and a powerful masculinity that has remained intact. Accordingly he often attracts many followers – in particular, adoring women who then drag their men along with them to be with the guru. This need not be a problem – many of the greatest spiritual teachers or philosophers in history were very masculine men – but it can easily go awry if the guru has not yet *Bih* worked out his own competitive compulsions. A competitive male guru will often fall out with any male disciples or students who appear to be growing too powerful and becoming a potential threat to the guru's position. He may also be prone to sleeping with female students, in such a way that ends up sabotaging his position and all his previous efforts. (I am not here commenting on the moral angle, rather I am pointing out the stupidity that is often a part of the male-tyrant type, a 'blind spot' foolishness that typically leads to the sabotage of his work.)

Dysfunctional Feminine Spirituality

Some of the problematic issues around feminine spirituality were already covered in the last chapter. This is because much of the New Age movement, especially the more recent version that arose in the late 20th century as shaped by such popular figures as Louise Hay, Shakti Gawain, Shirley MacLaine, Marianne Williamson, etc., has been feminine in slant. Earlier roots of this matter were evident in elements of the human potential movement as it developed chiefly in the 1960s. After centuries of hierarchical, rigid, patriarchal religion, a natural counterforce was birthed in the human potential movement as launched by such psychologists as Abraham Maslow and Carl Rogers. This more feminized approach has had a much greater accent on feelings, as opposed to action. A community I once participated in during the 1980s (during the height of the most recent New Age wave) expressed the idea well in a cartoon printed in their monthly newsletter. The cartoon showed a Popeye-like man flexing his muscles, with the caption reading, 'I like a man who can flex his *emotional* muscles!'

That a balance between the capacity to process feelings and emotions consciously, and the ability to be outwardly active and decisive in one's life, is important, is a given. However, just as imbalance can occur in over-emphasizing action to the point of neglecting awareness of feeling (the neurotic masculine), so too can imbalance result from over-emphasizing (wallowing in) feelings at the expense of action (the neurotic feminine).

At exactly what point we are 'indulging' feelings can be especially tricky to detect, but a good general rule of thumb is that whenever there is a sense that we are getting excessively caught up in *drama* and *story* – which almost always is crafted to manipulate others in some way (for example, by securing their sympathy) – then we are wallowing. To detect 'wallowing' or 'raging' (dramatizing anger) can be hard for one who was raised in a family with poor communication skills or with a father (or mother, for that matter) who was remote, self-absorbed, seemingly indifferent, cold, severe, or simply unavailable (or non-existent). This is because for one raised in such conditions, the urge to connect with adults later in life who are both willing and able to share more private inner thoughts and feelings, including those of the most vulnerable sort, can be strong, seeking to fulfill a need that has never been met.

However, when we become out of balance in this regard – raging, wallowing, dramatizing, and indulging in our 'story' – our life often does not work well 'outwardly'. That is, we get bogged down in mundane matters, such as relationship drama, or in financial, other practical matters or in general anything related to responsibility connected to our physical survival in the world. If we are too weighted on the feminine polarity, we tend to be burdened with indecisiveness and a general lack of clarity about our life direction and purpose. We may even try to disguise this lack via some Eastern philosophies that appear to override such matters: 'Life is without purpose', 'Just go with the flow', and so forth. 'Going with the flow' can be an act of wisdom; it can also be an act of foolishness (see late 1930s Germany). Sometimes it is necessary to go against the grain, but for one heavily polarized toward the feminine (with too much rejecting of the masculine), and accompanying 'fashion-conscious' or 'trend-conscious' tendencies, this can be hard to see. (And by 'fashion' I'm not referring to clothing or shoes; intellectual, social, political – and yes, spiritual – matters are also prone to becoming fashionable.)

The feminine polarity can be strongly given to the 'pack mentality' and this is often accompanied by a deep insecurity around breaking free, or confronting the disapproval of peers or family. The feminine in general is more prone to feeling obligated to 'toe the line' and not break away too far from family, social, or peer-constructed values – in short, to remain 'normal' or, arguably, *mediocre*. This is very problematic in the area of spiritual enlightenment because the path of awakening is one deeply connected to the need to be an individual first and foremost, to break free of consensus values that (in our world) generally disparage the idea of inner freedom. (Very few fathers or mothers will approve of their daughter's interest in inner freedom or deep spiritual awakening – it is too threatening to the standard family-centered status quo and the expectation that each generation should uphold that.)

There are other elements of feminine imbalance on the spiritual path. One example is a tendency to get caught up in concerns with appearance, to the point where 'spirituality' gets diluted into mere vanity – 'looking beautiful' is inserted into the spiritual paradigm, and we end up going to our yoga classes mostly to keep our body trim. (Or, as one woman once told me, she was interested in doing a vigorous deep breathing meditation mainly to help her cheeks appear more flushed and sexy.)

A final element of feminine dysfunction on the spiritual path to be noted here is fixation on security, and the confusion that easily occurs when this gets mixed with the desire to be 'equal' with men. A woman is generally attracted to strength – be that physical, mental, moral, creative, or financial strength – but in embracing a spiritual path, ideas of 'equality' easily cross-reference with feminist ideas of equal opportunity (after all, we are all supposedly equal in Spirit). And so a relationship with a man deemed 'equal' may at first seem appealing, but quickly becomes unattractive and uninteresting once it becomes clear that the guy is not stronger than her in at least *some* ways.

That is an example of spiritual ideals clashing with biological programming. The programming behind this is natural and expected: a woman carrying a child to term needs to know that the guy who got her pregnant is both willing and able to stick around and help her, protect her, and provide basic security. Without this feminine 'mother-bear' hyper-vigilance directed toward security (and in current times, money), the human race would likely not have endured through millions of years of evolution in harsh circumstances. But the whole matter becomes a problem when the woman employs her spiritual philosophy in an effort to 'break down' her man – to make him less dominant, less edgy, more feminine ('Tell me how you *feel*, dammit!'). If he does this, and *becomes* this way, she will often lose her attraction for him, which becomes aggravating and confusing to both.

Anxiety related to security also breeds self-absorption (or vice versa). The feminine polarity can be prone to a degree of self-absorption that is so intense, and so conventionally accepted, that it makes it very difficult to spot – both for the woman, and for the man who is too busy trying to 'make' (or keep) her happy. This becomes even more so if those surrounding such a woman cater to it (especially as in 'Momma's boy' type men, who are so afraid of the disapproval of their women that they usually end up enabling their self-absorption).

Summary

The path of awakening involves going beyond the limitations of our gender-conditioning, but first we have to honestly see such conditioning. It is easy to find fault in the opposite sex. However, our real work is to see beyond the blind spots that prevent us from recognizing the neurotic and dysfunctional elements of our *own* gender. To aid the awakening process we have to stop pointing fingers and look deeply into the mirror. This is nowhere truer than with gender issues.

Chapter 6

False Awakenings

Hard Truth #6: Our 'spiritual experiences' are just more stuff to let go of. They do not make us special, for the simple reason that we are not special.

The matter of 'false awakenings' is, as with many of the themes touched on herein, a book-length study. Nevertheless it is important to look at, if only because of its wide prevalence. And we're not just talking about the stereotypical religious nut who believes that he's seen God and bears a crucial message for humanity. (Perhaps the funniest example of this was a story I heard of a Christian who conveyed that during a vision he'd been taken down to see hell, and dutifully reported that he saw the Buddha there.) What we're really talking about are more subtle delusions brought about by altered states of consciousness and related experiences.

Some of you may have heard of the (true) story of three men, each convinced via mystical revelation, that they were the Second Coming of Jesus. They were placed in a padded room together. A few hours later, when they emerged, one of the men was still Jesus, and the other two were now his disciples. The story illustrates an important point: a subjective experience, wedded to a charismatic personality, can be a potent and potentially troublesome combination, because it often has the power to sweep others into its worldview.

False awakenings are often connected to unresolved authority issues (see Chapter 19). This is because it is the job of a good teacher or guide to point out delusions as they arise in a seeker. But if one resists guidance of any sort – 'I'll go it on my own' – one is going to be prone to a type of blindness. We all have blind spots – the biggest one of which is sometimes called our 'chief feature'. If we can really see and work with our chief feature, we have the possibility of genuine awakening. However, a seeker must be *ready* to encounter their chief feature, because if they see it prematurely, it can have the effect of disturbing them too much and scaring them away from the path altogether. (I've personally seen a number of cases of this happening – often accompanied by the former seeker vehemently denouncing the path and all teachers.)

In other words, if we are too resistant to guidance, or to receiving pointed feedback, then the chances are good that we will move into denial, or slip into various levels of delusion, and assume that we are further along than we actually are. More problematically, we may even assume the position of guiding others, and inevitably reap the negative 'cause and effect karma' when we misguide these others. The question of how to tell if an awakening is valid or 'false', hinges to a large degree on one's willingness to accept some sort of guidance, or at the very least, to stay in relationship with other legitimate (committed) seekers and practitioners of inner disciplines.

This is admittedly a tricky area because all bona fide awakenings are by nature *self*-realized – they are not conferred on us by another person, no matter how great that other person may seem to be. We have to find the truth ourselves. Yet at the same time, we have to 'find the others', the birds of our plumage. We have to guard against too much isolation. We need some semblance of community, however small. Even monks live and meditate together, for the most part; even hermits will on occasion break bread with another hermit.

The basic hallmark of false awakenings, in addition to the tendency for them to occur alongside too much isolation, is that they are altered states of consciousness. They are *states* of mind. Authentic awakenings are not truly states of mind. They are glimpses (or direct realizations, depending on depth) of Reality, that which is beyond delusion and distortion of any sort. Awakening is synonymous with an utter naturalness, the direct and tacit understanding that all things are simply *as they are*.

The line 'all things are as they are' may sound like a standard Zen cliché, but in fact there is no better description of ultimate truth. The awakened mind does not struggle with the universe. That does not mean that it is passive; only that it ceases to reject the unfolding of Reality moment by moment. The Sufi mystic Kabir alluded to this when he wrote 'The fish in the ocean is not thirsty.' There is a seamlessness realized between consciousness ('me') and the world ('that'). Deeper realizations yield the insight that there is no true distinction between consciousness and world, just as, in Kabir's metaphor, it is ultimately impossible for a fish in the ocean to be 'thirsty' (except in a deluded state of mind).

False awakenings are always based on some *experience* that we remain separate from. There is 'me' here, and there is this 'wow' experience over there. To use a crude analogy: many people like to go to fireworks displays. Standing there, looking up at the night sky, you can see these amazingly colorful and intricate patterns blooming and dissolving continuously, accompanied by loud booming or short crackling sounds. After a half-hour or so, when all the fireworks are used up, all that remains in the sky are wisps of smoke, and the show is over. You then leave (perhaps with some photographs of the event). Analogously, 'fireworks' arise within our inner field of experience, and then fade away. Most people like them because they are dazzling. They are entertaining, they distract us intensely. But never for a moment are we truly part of what we are witnessing. And so when the show is over, all that remains are 'wisps of smoke' that soon disperse – memories that within a few days fade, leaving nothing. So what was it really all about?

False awakenings – 'enlightenment experiences' – are very similar. They are, essentially, the fireworks of our inner world (along with related peak experiences, like falling in love, being moved by a great piece of music or art or literature, and so on). They are all fundamentally *experiences*. To 'have an experience' requires a subject distinct from the object or experience that it witnesses. Therefore, any experience requires duality, or separation. All authentic awakenings involve direct insight and awareness of deep interrelatedness, and ultimately of Oneness, non-duality.

At this point a natural question may arise: if we can taste Oneness, and then lose it, does that not render the 'Oneness' just another experience? Can we not simply say, 'I had an experience of Oneness, but alas, it has gone'? We can most certainly say that, but that does not mean that any separate self ('me') truly 'experienced the Oneness'. It simply means that we had a glimpse of non-duality – Reality – but that the conventional state of mind, the duality of 'me and my experiences', has returned. In order to make sense of this, the mind frames it as a memory – the memory of 'an experience that I had'. But this is not actually what happened. It is just the mind trying to reduce the matter to terms it is familiar with.

Another revealing quality of false awakenings is that they typically get used by the ego to bolster self-image. They easily result in self-aggrandizement, and moreover, a tendency to begin to see others as inferior, as less special. If a person has significant unhealed issues related to self-image, believing that they have been undervalued by their family, by others, by the world, and so on, they can become quite deluded if they use their spiritual experience as a crutch to boost themselves. 'I may have failed in all these other ways, but now I know that I am superior in *this* way, which is really the most important way because it is spiritual.' There is actually very little difference between this sort of view and the insufferable righteousness of many religious fundamentalists.

Often there is a fine line between false awakenings and outright mental illness. This is why it is almost always necessary to accept some sort of guidance, or at the least participate in some semblance of spiritual community, on the path of awakening. It doesn't matter if the guidance is of 'perfect' quality or not (almost certainly, it won't be); what matters is the demonstration of humility and willingness to move beyond our isolated ('I'm right!') view of reality. Of course, there is always some risk involved in being guided on the path (as there is risk involved in anything in life) but such risk is less than the risk of mistaking one's experiences of mere altered states of consciousness for genuine wisdom and liberation.

Summary

Reality, or the deepest truth of our nature, is not an 'experience'. No matter how exceptional our experience was, it was just that, an experience. It does not define who we are any more than our latest trip to the bathroom did.

Chapter 7

Bogged Down by Practical Matters: Whatever Happened to Truth?

Hard Truth #7: The most common reason for 'falling off the wagon' of the spiritual path is related to so-called practical matters, in particular domestic issues, and above all, raising a family. To deeply investigate awakening, we have to see the part of us that gets lost in practical matters as a misguided way to feel more meaningful and important, and to run from the fear of being nothing or not mattering to anyone.

Years ago I attended a reunion of sorts for a group of about a dozen people. We had all once been connected via an intensive spiritual practice we had undertaken together. This practice involved deep therapy, radical insight, meditation, ceremony, honest communication with each other, and so on. It was full-on inner work.

When I met up with the group again, I had not seen most of them for a few years at least. The evening was pleasant enough, but what was most striking about everyone's story at that point in their lives was how bogged down they'd all become in practical matters. In fact I wouldn't be exaggerating to say that they'd all pretty much fallen off the path. They were not seeking 'higher truth' anymore, were no longer making conscious efforts to understand themselves, and seemed to have resigned themselves to a routine conventional life. One or two of them had even developed a decidedly cynical tone in regard to the inner work. (And in case any of you are wondering, no, none of them was fulfilled, happy, or contented, so this was not some sort of 'I'm already enlightened so I decided to forget about seeking' thing. They had not 'transcended the seeker' – they had simply given up seeking, for various reasons.)

Of course, there is an argument that 'inner work' can become very self-absorbed, a type of refuge for the perpetually immature, and that sooner or later we just have to grow up and get on with 'real life' (especially if we have kids of our own to raise). There is a measure of common-sense truth in that. However, it is ultimately not a good enough justification. The deeper truth is that many people fall asleep in life because our man-made society – and how it has conditioned us – tells us that we are ultimately just slaves to a greater purpose. That 'greater purpose' is to keep the world running the way it has been for untold millennia. We are cogs in a machine and that is our lot in life, so we'd best simply get on with 'cogging', and give up all the navel-gazing and star-gazing.

The lie hidden within this sort of view is not too hard to see. The lie is that 'inner work', even something as straightforward as sitting meditation, is 'self-absorbed' and not compatible with a busy practical life. It is a falsehood because we know that the problem is not our views around self-absorption; the real problem is that we simply don't want to truly face *directly into* the matter of who we actually are. And so to put the label 'self-absorbed' on a truth-seeker is a type of cop-out. The label is usually assigned by those who fear looking within and taking responsibility for their own inner garbage.

The three main pillars of societal programming that for centuries have kept humanity asleep (and largely functioning as 'drones' to serve the system) are the socio-economic system, organized religion, and the nuclear family. The latter is a relatively recent phenomenon, at least in the West; prior to the 18th century or so, the 'extended family' was more the norm. A 'nuclear family' is the traditional modern family structure – two parents and kids living under one particular roof. It is more a phenomenon of the Industrial Revolution (since the 18th century, more or less). Of course, I'm not suggesting that there is a better alternative at present. The nuclear family structure does bring factors that are superior to the more disorganized extended family (or tribal culture). However, the nuclear family model has some serious problems as well, foremost of which is the tendency of the family to become too insular, and for children to become overly dependent on their parents (and thus, at least in potential, overly hostile to them – after all, we are most capable of resenting or hating those we have become most reliant on). The rise of modern psychotherapy is probably related to the need to deal with the unique neuroses brought about in part by the nuclear family structure.

'Bogged down by practical matters', in the case of a typical truth-seeker, often unfolds something like this. The person meets someone, gets into a committed relationship with them, and then lives with them. At a certain point in the relationship the romance-sex magic wears off, and deeper issues begin to surface. In the vast majority of cases, instead of both partners (or even one) making a real effort to look at their own stuff, to begin to examine who they are and how they are not contributing to the relationship in a healthy fashion, both begin to seek for something 'new'. That 'new' becomes, typically, one of two things: either to leave the relationship and look for a different partner, or to have a child together.

It may sound very cynical to suggest that most couples opt to have a child (or stumble into it) in part because their egos are beginning to surface, and they either want to run, or create a big positive distraction – the biggest possible, that being to start a family. But we don't have to theorize about this. We have only to look at the evidence. The vast majority of psychological dysfunction – everything from annoying quirks to serious mental illnesses – tends to be hereditary (the same way that much of physical health is – provided one does not grossly abuse one's body). Clearly, stuff gets passed down. If your grandparents and parents were mostly crazy people, it may be difficult for you to be otherwise.

Of course, there are always exceptions, shining examples of individuals who, by dint of sheer effort, rise above the dismal track record of their ancestors. But these are relative rarities. Most of us are chips off the old block, much as that is often unpleasant to consider.

In fact, sound arguments have been made that not only are we much like our parents, but we tend to be most similar to the parent we were the least close to. If we favored Dad, we have likely become similar to Mom in ways that are difficult to see (let alone face). If we were closer to Mom, then Dad's traits, at least to some degree, are likely alive and well in us. That these traits tend to be more part of our 'personality blind spots' – that is, others who know us well can generally see them, but we usually can't – makes it all the more difficult to face up to.

The problem largely begins with the mindset we have when we decide we want to produce children. (Granted, such a decision is often not conscious – 'It just happened' – but I'm suggesting here that even if it seemed to have been happenstance, intent was there at some level, however remotely detectable. And no, for the record, I don't include rape in this category.) If there is within our intent to have children any of the 'I want my kid to have everything I never did' refrain, then there is likely going to be a problem. The reason is straightforward: we cannot truly 'give' to someone something we do not have ourselves. I cannot give you a million dollars if I do not have this sum of money. Similarly, I cannot give you an outstanding character if I lack that myself. I can work hard to provide you with opportunities, true, but these opportunities will probably not amount to more than external factors. I may be a screwed-up millionaire, and out of the goodness of my heart, make you a millionaire also. But chances are you will also be screwed up.

Obviously, I'm not speaking against having children. There can be many good reasons to do so; speaking strictly personally, I would not be here to write these words if two people in my past had not made such a decision. Rather, what I'm calling attention to is the case of the truth-seeker (those of you reading this book) and the tendency to avoid deeper self-observation – particularly when the need for such becomes evident during relationship stress – by seeking distractions. The most powerful 'creative distraction' of all is to have a child, something utterly helpless and innocent to focus on. Having someone else to focus on can be a natural and healthy thing to do and is usually part of growing up (regardless if we are a parent or not). In the case of parenthood, however, it just as often becomes a potent excuse to turn away from our stuff, and to naively believe that bringing a little bundle of joy into the world will magically provide meaning and direction to our life. It won't. Once the magic wears off, the old unresolved patterns surface and it all simply gets passed down to our offspring. We don't end up giving them 'everything I never had' – we simply give them everything that we are. Even worse, it happens fairly commonly that the child becomes the 'dumping ground' of their parents' stuff. More than one 'problem child' has really been nothing but the bucket at the end of the family line, the unfortunate recipient of everything their ancestors opted not to look at or work on.

It's not the responsibility of children to make us feel better about ourselves, any more than it is the responsibility of a dog or a cat to make their owner feel more important in the cosmos. My main point here is that in the case of the truth-seeker, the decision to have children has to be weighed consciously, and not used as a means to avoid taking more responsibility for oneself. This can be a very tricky matter because the decision to have children may, on the face of it, seem like a decision to be more responsible, when lurking in the background may be the deeper motivation to gain power and esteem by becoming a parent and thereby not have to do the harder work of realizing, and facing into, the nature and degree of our unhealed stuff. To do so is to begin to break the chain of our negative family generational patterns, so that we can *truly* benefit our offspring, if we have offspring. To not do so is simply to pass the buck. Accordingly, to expect our kids to be less messed up than we are is not only unrealistic, it is irresponsible.

Outside of family and 'creating family' issues, the most common reason for 'getting bogged down in practical matters', such that we forget our inner awakening and our spiritual practices, is financial failure or success, and all related matters in between – everything from sheer survival to fat cat greed. The survival instinct is of course extremely powerful, and for perfectly good reason. We humans appear to be very good at adapting and surviving, at least according to evolutionary biology. We apparently came out of Africa millions of years ago, a continent with many large and powerful animals that, if meeting us one-on-one on a plain or in a jungle, would have no problem having us for dinner if they felt so inclined. Yet despite the relative frailty of the human physique (compared to powerful predators) we not only survived, we flourished and now more or less rule the planet (or tyrannize it, take your pick).

Our survival instinct is very well honed, shaped by millions of years of extraordinary success (in staying alive and having offspring, at least). Our spiritual impulse, our interest in awakening, is tiny compared to the behemoth of the matter of physical survival. Accordingly, interest in awakening can be easily crushed, rendered meaningless, or simply forgotten in the need to make ends meet, or the urge to protect, invest, and save for retirement (at which point one will probably not have enough energy to be a sincere seeker anyway).

Honesty is always the central issue. If we are more interested in being a millionaire than we are in becoming awakened, that doesn't have to be a problem, but we do have to be honest about it, else our inner work will lack authenticity and depth. It'll be more like passing the time with a nice but dull date, waiting for the 'real thing' – moola – to show up. Better to be an honest businessperson than a phony spiritual seeker.

Summary

Many are the ways to 'fall off the path', with family and security issues being near the top. As always, deep honesty is the key. We have to examine our motives, and what it is we truly want in life, what we see as *truly* being of importance.

Chapter 8

Online 'Enlightenment':
The Culture of Camouflage

Hard Truth #8: No, you won't get enlightened online. The Internet is good for information and quick communication, nothing more.

The outstanding problem with our modern-day online culture is lying. We humans by nature are strongly given to distorting, fabricating, exaggerating, and out-and-out lying, even if only in subtle ways, on almost a daily basis. Most people live with a fear of being exposed (which is doubtless why to have a dream in which we are naked is relatively common). The Internet (and related communication technologies like smartphones) is a near-perfect vehicle for hiding, while being present at the same time – much like going to a masquerade or Halloween party. You get to be there, but camouflaged. As such, Internet interaction gets wildly abused. Most online communication is mass catharsis, a would-be therapy program that is out of control and is usually anything but therapeutic.

Obviously there are some powerful advantages to the Web, such as an extraordinary means by which to access information rapidly or to connect quickly with others, often with people we otherwise would almost certainly have never met. But for the truth-seeker, online life presents a host of new problems. The main one is deception. That is true for online life in general, and it's no different for the truth-seeker who ventures online.

There are several ways deception plays out for the online spiritual seeker. One way, which is surprisingly prevalent, is that many surfers who visit or even post to so-called online spiritual communities are not actually truth-seekers. They may have stumbled upon the site, or more typically, they are attention-seekers, and at times, rabble-rousers – or as the online lingo has it, 'trolls'. Most common of all, they are simply lonely and are seeking companionship, or to have their relating needs fulfilled. Often such posters are very touchy and given to conflict – because they are not really there for deeper truth. They are there to relate and hopefully receive attention, love, respect, and so on.

The Internet is particularly prone to attracting cynical types who seek an outlet for their resentments. In the spiritual realm, this often plays out as online posters venting their distrust of anything involving teachers, guides, gurus, and the like. Some of this is connected to media-cynicism (which is highly influential in current times) and some of it to the growing popularity of atheism and the (understandable) mistrust of religion. The problem there for the truth-seeker is that the rampant cynicism can make it difficult if not impossible to remember what one was looking for in the first place (higher wisdom). The Internet is a major dumping ground for the sheer negativity that is part and parcel of the cynical, 'eye-rolling', sarcastic, *whatever* mindset of the current younger generations, and the burnt-out skepticism of the 'Baby Boomers'. The other side of the spectrum – religious fundamentalism and blind intolerance – is alive and well on the Web as well.

The deeper problem with online life for a truth-seeker is its addictive power. The Internet has grown to become something like a two-dimensional mini *'akashic* records' (an esoteric term for the idea of a library somewhere that contains all possible knowledge about everything and everyone). The end result is a tendency to spend a great deal of time online that otherwise could be spent in actual inner practice, or in actual contact with others. I say 'actual' because online communication is not 'real time' (even in the case of so-called 'chat'); it is delayed. This delay gives us the chance to say more accurately what we might want to say, granted, but it also relieves us of the need to be spontaneous, natural, and above all, authentic.

The word 'phony' actually originated with the rise of the telephone. To be 'phoney' was to relate only on the phone – and thus was seen initially as half-baked. (Prior to the phone, unless mailing someone, to connect with them you had to go to their house and knock on their door. Incredible!) We have gone past the phone, however, and found new ways to relate in a disembodied fashion. The Internet is like a big new dimension full of minds floating around without bodies – which could be fun if humanity was highly developed and mature – but alas we are not, and so online life is akin to souls relating on a 'higher' dimension when they have not yet learned how to be in the 'lower' (physically embodied) dimension. It is true that online communication can result in greater honesty, rather than less. Some will use it to express things that they would not feel the courage to do so otherwise. The Internet does get used at times for that more noble purpose. But that is more a rarity. The norm of online life is to distort the truth, either grossly, or subtly, simply because it is so easy to do so.

Summary

It is too easy to hide parts of our character in online relating, or online truth-seeking. The Web can be used to find out about things, but for deeper work on self you need in-person (embodied) relating, preferably with other genuine seekers or teachers. That is because you *have* a body.

Chapter 9

Most People Don't Really Want Enlightenment – Even Those Seeking It

Hard Truth #9: If you think you really want full enlightenment, you probably don't understand what it implies. If, in the chance you do understand what it implies, and you still really want it, there is a chance you will go far on your path.

This is another touchy subject, but for a truth-seeker it is arguably the most important one to look into. There is a connection between this subject and the issue of 'Eastern Fundamentalism' (Chapter 2) because the very idea of 'spiritual enlightenment' is singularly Eastern. Western religions don't talk about it, and even Western esoteric paths generally make little mention of it. (Other terms do get used – such as 'gnosis' – and while the final meaning is similar, the approach, and especially the emphasis, is different.) The word 'enlightenment' as used in traditional Western education is usually associated with the European intellectual movement known as the 'Age of Reason' that blossomed in the 17th and early 18th centuries with the birth of modern science (Galileo, Newton, Descartes, etc.). The idea of 'enlightenment' as some supreme spiritual state was imported from the Orient around the turn of the 20th century. It is as thoroughly Eastern as curry, kung fu, and sushi.

That, of course, has nothing to do with its quality or appropriateness for Westerners. But even if we have become clear that our interest in spiritual enlightenment is more than our passing interest in all things Eastern, we are left with the deeper issue of examining what exactly enlightenment represents. In short, we are left with two essential questions: do I understand what this enlightenment business is really about, and do I truly want it? (We might phrase this latter question as 'Am I truly ready for it?', but it amounts to the same thing.)

The issue of what deep enlightenment – or less severely, awakening – actually is, is one of the matters that marks serious inner work apart from 'feel-good' spirituality. As any realized sage will admit, the matter of awakening is serious business and the summit of awakening, enlightenment, is anything but easy to attain. (All clichés about how 'we are already enlightened' notwithstanding.) The reason why deep awakening is both a serious matter, and extremely difficult to realize, is because the vast majority of us are full of crap. I mean that in the best possible way – which, granted, isn't very good. By 'full of crap' I mean that our unconscious minds are loaded with all the unresolved stuff of far more than just our own small personal history. That alone is enough to present nearly insurmountable barriers for most people – but even in the case of one who has had a relatively functional background and was raised with a reasonable degree of love, support, and wisdom, they are still faced with the task of overcoming the collective history of their mother's and father's family lineage, the collective faults of their cultural milieu, and the collective scars of the entire human race.

To see this point we need not resort to somewhat arcane theories like C.G. Jung's 'collective unconscious' or similar models. We need only look at the history of human civilization and the world surrounding us today. Despite all our advances we remain to a large degree a barbaric species (more people were killed in warfare in the 20th century alone than in all previous centuries put together). Man's inhumanity to Man is legendary and remains alive and well today. We continue to progress scientifically (in most areas – our space travel has yet to surpass 1969), but our educational institutions still lack any sort of comprehensive means of teaching young people about how their minds work, and what they can do to train their minds more efficiently. The Zen teacher Philip Kapleau in his renowned book *The Three Pillars of Zen* lamented the fact that our schooling system focuses on the acquisition of knowledge, but teaches students scant little about how the mind itself can be trained to self-observe. He published his book in 1965; matters have not changed since. Scientific materialism has largely replaced the old religions and become the new religion. Its priesthood are the scientists, the ubiquitous 'experts' who are consulted on the important matters of reality, our modern-day 'sound bite sages'.

Obviously, science is important and has allowed for many wonderful things to come about. Science is not the problem. The problem is ignorance of our mind and of the nature of our being. Few people are raised to be self-aware, to have much of an inkling of what their minds contain. And so when we set out with an interest in awakening – or, in more rare cases, with an interest in full enlightenment – it is very common to be surprised, even shocked, at what we discover about ourselves along the way.

The first thing we have to get over, if we have any sincere interest in the matter of awakening at all, is the idea that we are in any way special, purely good, or otherwise lacking in undesirable traits. We all have plenty of undesirable traits (which is what I meant above by saying we are all full of shit). But this 'first barrier' is a very hard one to surmount, which is why most seekers soon beat a hasty retreat off the main path, and seek out gentler and kinder side routes that are more consoling and comforting (but rarely lead anywhere).

There is no free pass to enlightenment. It's not like a ticket we buy to get into something. It's not 'self-improvement' or 'getting more happiness' or living merrily ever after in some sort of 'fifth dimension' la-la land where we are surrounded by angels, white unicorns and rainbows. Rather, the journey of authentic awakening is closer to Dante's journey as sketched out in his *Divine Comedy*: first, we go to *Inferno*. Before anything, we make a trip to hell, which is symbolic of facing *into* our own inner darkness so as to take responsibility for it, as opposed to turning away from it in the hope that it will not be there anymore when we look again.

But to state the obvious: who the heck wants to go to hell? Hardly anybody (provided we are not pathologically self-loathing).

However, to cite but two famed examples, Jesus had to face Satan in the desert and Buddha had a showdown with Mara (the Buddhist Satan) just prior to his great awakening. The stories of most other radically awakening sages (seven of these stories are covered in Part V of this book) usually involve difficult confrontations with their own darker angels prior to their profound breakthroughs. And if these great sages had to pass through such a fire, what makes us think that we will be spared that? We won't.

Most would-be seekers flee the path when they meet their inner monsters (or even just get a glimpse of them). Sometimes this takes the form of getting feedback from a teacher or therapist or fellow seeker, feedback that they decidedly don't like; sometimes it takes the form of a relationship disappointment; sometimes it takes the form of a disturbing experience brought about by intensive meditation practice; or more commonly, it takes the form of realizing that one is just not up to the amount of work, and honesty, required for legitimate awakening. It's too hard, too much of an investment of time and energy (and often, money). And, to make the whole matter more difficult, our entire surrounding society in no way supports the movement toward individual awakening. On the contrary, it reinforces the opposite, the belief that our fulfillment comes from *things* – possessions, positions in life, and people (who are supposed to make us feel good about who we are).

And so, if we're very honest, most of us don't really want spiritual enlightenment. We want to be happy, or wealthy, or important, or loved, or fucked, or feted, or famous. Spiritual enlightenment, when we examine it closely, demands too much of us. More to the point, it demands *all* of us. Who among us is up to that?

The other matter that needs to be mentioned here is the mistaken view many have of what it means to be enlightened – the typical assumption is that it means 'bliss', 'fearlessness', etc. (some of which was covered in the chapter on Eastern fundamentalism), and that following this, our life will be perpetually delightful and easy. All evidence points to the error of that view. Awakening to our highest potential does not mean we abandon the world and retreat to some insular self-congratulatory realm. Awakening means that our heart opens to the terrible suffering in the world, and the clear understanding that our life is now dedicated to helping alleviate that suffering. That rarely means some life of effortless ease. It means baring one's soul to the heart of darkness of humanity, and facing fully into the matter of just how we got into this fix in the first place. In other words, *to be awake is to be a deeply responsible being* – and above all, responsible for who we are.

None of that is possible without first being open, in the true sense of that word. To awaken is to be cracked open, wide, and deeply sensitized to Reality – both in its absolute sense (non-duality), and in its relative sense (the 'world' as we typically know it). To be open to the world is to be open to its immense suffering. It was not visions of bliss that motivated the Buddha to seek his enlightenment – it was upon seeing a sick man, a cripple, and a corpse, that he felt the urge to solve the problem of human suffering. It was not visions of heaven that motivated Jesus to undertake his ministry and seek for 'fishers of men' to aid him – it was his deep compassion for the suffering of the multitudes that surrounded him.

Summary

We probably don't really want enlightenment. It's just a new toy for us to play with (until we find out that this toy has fangs and can consume us wholesale). But if we're certain that's not true in our case – *truly* certain – then we're truly on our way.

We may find out, one day, that *wanting* enlightenment keeps it away, but we'll see that when the time is right. For now, it is best to *want it as much as we can.*

Part II

Further Myths, Fairy Tales, and
Misconceptions about Spiritual Awakening

*Miseries, though belonging to the world of dreams, are certainly painful,
and do not vanish until we cease our dreaming.*
Srimad Bhagavatum, xi, xv

Chapter 10

More on the Denial of Darkness and 'Falling Apart'

The repression of negative emotion and passion is one of the most common stumbling blocks for those seeking growth and wisdom. Part of this tendency to repress ourselves is coming from a wrong motivation for awakening, which is an attempt to move toward the 'light' (usually represented by such values as love, peace, joy, harmony, etc.) primarily because we fear honestly facing the 'dark' within (anger, vengeance, control, fear, shame, competitiveness, jealousy, lust, etc.). Owing to the fear of negativity, the idea of 'spiritual growth' may at first seem appealing because we think that it will magically involve 'getting rid' of darkness – in particular, our own darkness. To 'transcend' means to go beyond, and is a term commonly connected to enlightenment. However, 'inner darkness', or what C.G. Jung called the 'shadow', is *not* to be transcended, it is to be *integrated*. The word 'integrate' stems from the Latin *integratus*, meaning to 'make whole'. To integrate an inner quality is to 'bring it home', to take ownership and responsibility for it, rather than rejecting or denying it. Sanity, healing, and wholeness lie in integration.

The opposite – 'disintegrate' – is to fragment, break into pieces, or as the colloquial expression has it, 'crack up'. We say a person 'cracks', 'falls apart', has a 'meltdown' or 'breakdown' when met by circumstances or stress that they do not handle well. In effect, what we are really saying is that they have not properly responded to something. They cannot properly respond because they are, in effect, paying the price for having rejected too many parts of their personality, and especially elements of their shadow side. An inwardly fragmented person – one who fears or who has not honestly faced their anger, or their sexuality, or their controlling tendencies, or their fear, or their jealousy, and so on – tends to handle adversity poorly. Such a person is frequently fearful and often responds badly to stress (either by becoming numbed out and disconnected, or overly confrontational, vehement and dramatic).

In our work on self, the idea is for our shadow tendencies to be seen, accepted, embraced, and absorbed, at which point these tendencies are revealed for what they really are: pure energy and pure potential passion for life and awakening. 'Absorbing' and 'embracing' do not mean, of course, *indulging*. We are not to indulge our laziness, or greed, or anger, unless we want more laziness or greed or anger. The key word here is *acceptance*. We accept these tendencies as a way of assuming responsibility for them. We stop lying by claiming to be beyond them, when we are not. We instead tell the truth about them, and get to know them. In so doing, we eventually stop being controlled by them, or expressing them covertly.

As mentioned in Chapter 1, most people walking a spiritual path sooner or later end up dividing themselves into two parts – the 'spiritual person' and the 'regular person'. The former is largely impersonal, the latter is deeply personal. The personal self has needs and desires, but is often a subject of fear, derision, condemnation, and eventually repression. Our 'spiritual side' becomes a judge, a type of righteous priest archetype. When we create this inner split, we end up unconsciously drawing to ourselves people who have the potential to trigger us and make us aware of the repressed sides of our personal self. More to the point, we are often attracted to such people, even if they seem to offend or repel us in various ways.

If we are seeking to awaken to our highest potential, it is very easy to slip into avoidance and denial once we get a glimpse of just how much psychological baggage we are carrying. That does not mean that such baggage must be exhaustively analyzed and examined, like unnecessarily taking apart our garbage and analyzing it piece by piece. But it does mean that we cannot awaken to the deeper reality of who we really are if we do not first recognize who we are *now*. We must get deeply and radically honest with ourselves. We must give up all pretense or putting on airs or in any way pretending to be 'spiritual'. There is little hope of attaining to true awakening if we do not become *authentic*, and such authenticity is made possible by being in touch with, and honest about, the shadow side of the mind. Such honesty then frees us up to truly witness these elements of the mind, and to deepen the understanding that we are *not* these elements. But we cannot go 'beyond jealousy' or 'beyond manipulativeness', for example, without first honestly recognizing our capacity to *be* jealous or manipulative.

Our 'darker' tendencies, if denied or ignored, will come back to haunt us in the form of behavior from other people (a classic one being our lover or spouse or children acting out qualities that we have repressed within ourselves). Whatever part of us we inwardly deny, we will unconsciously draw to us, in the form of someone or something that will provoke the denied feelings within us.

Myth: Spiritual awakening is rising above my inner darkness.

Clarification: Spiritual awakening involves seeing, embracing, and integrating our inner darkness, by being deeply honest and accepting of our negative character tendencies. This acceptance of them is *not* the same as indulging in them. It is directly experiencing them in the light of awareness and deep honesty. Only on the basis of such honesty is it possible to enter into the fuller levels of awakening. Eventually, we begin to glimpse the deeper truth: there is no 'light side' or 'dark side'. There is only the raw reality of who we are, now.

Chapter 11

Soul Mates and Other Romantic Fairy Tales

The notion of a perfect 'soul mate' and the idea of the ultimate romance, as well as the anguished longing to find one's perfect match, is ultimately based on romanticizing the pain of incompletion.

The underlying sense – the core-level pain – of feeling incomplete is always fundamentally *spiritual*, meaning it is originating in the contraction and 'closed fist' of fear and mistrust, and the profound sense of alienation and separation we experience from both life, ourselves, and our highest potential. With the introduction of the notion of ideal romantic love – the perfect soul mate – the pain of separation from our highest potential gets redirected into the pain of separation from our *true soul mate*. In other words, the idea of our highest potential gets reduced to an idealized, imagined other person, and moreover, a person who we imagine to be our potential ideal partner.

The soul mate culture is reinforced in modern times through the entertainment and advertising industries, which produce an ongoing stream of movies, songs, and images all dedicated to the notion of ideal romantic love, that is, of finding the ideal romantic mate. Once this mate is found, we are further told, we will then and only then experience fulfillment and completion.

The powerful intensity and intoxicating richness of intimate partnership can never be underestimated, but the conditioning that comes along with the cultural influences just mentioned should not be lost sight of either. For one, the idealized soul mate is not just credited with the power to complete us and make us forever happy, but also, by extension, they are credited with the power to psychologically destroy us as well. They can make, break, and un-break our heart, so we are repeatedly told.

From the point of view of the 'hard core' truth-seeker, romantic love is regarded as an elaborate expression of dependency, with so-called New Age/romantic notions of the 'soul mate' seen as just spiritualized, disguised forms of dependency, the belief that we *need* a particular person in order to experience happiness. And thus, that our Source of fulfillment and completion is *outside* of us, not within, and certainly not who we actually are – and, therefore, the ideal of the soul mate is ultimately just egocentricity sneaking in through the back door.

This is true from the absolute perspective, but we must be careful not to deny the personal self and its needs. It is difficult to go beyond our more conventional needs – needs for intimacy, physical contact, and regular relating – without first having experienced them to some degree. 'Experiencing them' does not imply relationship longevity. It is not necessary to have been married and monogamous for thirty years in order to cultivate a strong passion for truth. It is necessary, however, to be honest about our *personal* needs and desires, and to allow ourselves to experience them. If we don't they simply become repressed, only to manifest later as psychological disturbances or as an 'inexplicable' loss of interest in walking the path.

The great irony about intimate relationships is that the temptation to believe that our inner completion comes from outside of us is enhanced via interaction with our partner. And yet, that same relationship also carries the best potential to catalyze us into a sincere search for truth – once we have been disappointed enough with our quest for the perfect soul mate, or exhausted by our attempts to change our current partner into something *we* think they should be. In short, once we exhaust our urge to manipulate (as well as becoming fed up with being manipulated), we have, in some key respects, become ripe for transformation. We have begun to grow up.

The 'Perfect' Soul Mate Fairy Tale

In relationships, we tend to attract into our lives patterns that match or complement our own patterns. In short, like attracts like. That is, if we ourselves are not exactly perfect or not perfectly 'dwelling in our soul', no 'perfect soul mate' could ever locate us (even if they existed). Likewise, if we believe that we have already found our 'soul mate' but we carry issues that we do not truly want to face, then eventually the 'soul mate' will simply trigger this unfinished (and uncomfortable) business inside of us. At which point, we then decide that they are no longer our 'perfect' soul mate. Either way, we almost always get a good reflection of the patterns we are caught up in. It is not that we get what we deserve; it is rather we *get what we are.*

From the point of view of the spiritual idea of Unity or Oneness, because the self is understood to not exist in any *truly separate* fashion, all that is really going on in standard relationship dynamics is the *matching of patterns* (which we call 'attraction'). An example of a possible pattern-match would be a woman who is unconsciously looking to re-create her relationship with her father (for whatever reasons) and a man who unconsciously seeks to care-take or control (for whatever reasons), thus wanting a 'fatherly' role in a relationship. The number of possible pattern-matches is endless, but the factor that brings the two people together is the sense that through *this person* I can get something – whether that is healing, or love, or fulfillment, etc. – with the key piece being that *only* this particular person can do it for me.

Because patterns usually change (just like weather), individuals change in their feelings toward each other. If there really was one specific soul mate out there assigned to each of us, then we might expect that our feelings for each other would not change. But because it is the *patterns* that are attracting or repelling, feelings people have for each other do in fact change all the time. And this is why romance always wears off sooner or later. It is because we (and our partner) are in a constant state of change, even if such changes are slow and subtle.

The road to hell is paved with believing that our basic worth, well-being, completion, and happiness lies *in* one other special person, and in particular the way they think and act toward us. More specifically, it lies in holding to the position that their thoughts, feelings, and actions toward us will *never change*. It is fixation on permanency, and the fear of letting go and accepting change, that generates most psychological suffering. All of this shows us the deeper issue of interest here, the fact that our personality is largely nothing more than a set of conditioned patterns, minus any substantial individuality. We are entirely creatures of cause and effect, and our personalities are entirely interactive; that is, dependent on the personality manifestations of others.

The path to inner freedom and wisdom is in cultivating a deep interest in Reality that is beyond dependency. That does not mean that we set about avoiding relationship (which is pointless anyway). For most of us it's necessary to accept the deep desires to be with one specific other person. But unless this is balanced by cultivating a passion for truth and a sincere intention to realize our highest potential, suffering will sooner or later result, arising from patterns of dependency repeating again and again in a similar fashion. We may laugh at some famous celebrities when we read that they are on their fourth or fifth marriage, but we are not much different in our own relationship patterns, running up against the same disappointments time and again (whether we have been a serial dater or in a lifelong stable marriage).

Myth: We have a soul mate, and until we meet such a person, we will never be fulfilled.

Clarification: The idea of the 'perfect soul mate' is a fairy tale created by our desire to remain dependent and childlike (that is, not responsible for our own development). That of course does not mean that a deep and profoundly intimate relationship with a kindred soul, even lasting lifelong, cannot happen. The main point is that to commit to awakening is to commit to giving up fantasies, including the fantasy of living in *expectation* of the arrival of the perfect partner. We must practice with what is real, actually in our life here and now, and not live in hope of future fantasy-fulfillment (even if such hopeful thoughts arise in our mind, which they will almost certainly do from time to time; our practice is to witness them without clinging, or aversion). There are few things worse than to be in love with a promise, and yet this is how most people live – for, as the sports term has it, 'future considerations'.

Myth: It is not possible to become enlightened *with* an intimate partner.

Myth: It is not possible to become enlightened *without* an intimate partner.

Clarification: There is no evidence to back either of these up. Many authentically awakened sages did not, or do not, have a primary relationship partner. Equally so, some did, and do. It cannot be denied that for Westerners in particular the tendency to seek an intimate partner is strong. However, it is also true that most people fritter away huge amounts of time by simply walking the treadmill of repetitive relationship patterns, reliving again and again scenarios based on trying to get one person to love and accept them in a way that completely protects them from facing their inner fears and frailties – the heart of co-dependency.

There is nothing wrong with the path of intimate relationship with one specific person, especially if used as a vehicle to grow (by practicing deep honesty with each other, for example). But it's not a definite requirement for waking up to our greater potential. Equally so, it is possible and even common to avoid intimate partnership in the name of our zeal for spiritual awakening, when in fact this 'zeal' is partly a defense to protect against fears of becoming too dependent or of being abandoned in a relationship. This kind of 'spiritual zeal' is largely a cover for unresolved pain. In all cases, what matters is being deeply honest with ourselves and summoning the courage to look into our fears, so as to pass beyond them.

In addition to all this, a sound argument can be made that we have no real choice in the realm of intimate partnership, because free will is largely an illusion and we do not choose our attractions. They are either there or they are not. How we act (or not) on these attractions is also (in this argument) not controllable, because it is all simply part of the infinite chain of cause and effect. If we are 'meant to be' with someone, we will (owing to previous causal forces). This view – pure determinism – may seem especially bleak but it does provide for a certain clarity into the only essential matter that may have any element of 'free will': the intention to wake up.

Chapter 12

More on Altered States of Consciousness: *Makyo* and Glittering Illusions

Psychic 'Powers', the Paranormal, and *Makyo*

The growth of the Human Potential schools of psychotherapy (and related alternative approaches to therapy) in the 1950s–60s, as led by such forebears and pioneers as C.G. Jung, Alfred Adler, Abraham Maslow, Wilhelm Reich, Carl Rogers, Fritz Perls, Alexander Lowen, Arthur Janov, Leonard Orr and others, was also accompanied by a general revival of widespread interest in other fields of consciousness exploration, an area that may be loosely defined as the 'paranormal' or 'altered states of consciousness'. This field includes such areas as the exploration of psychic phenomena, including precognition (knowledge of the future), telepathy (direct mental communication without speech), clairvoyance and remote viewing (the ability to see into 'invisible realms' or beyond normal human sight), séances and 'trance-channeling' (communication with 'discarnate entities'), 'out-of-body travel', and so on. In the yogic traditions of India, these abilities are known as *siddhis*. This entire vast field has been accompanied by (especially since the 1960s) the emergence of widespread recreational drug usage, and occasionally interfaces with it.

Any one of the fields of 'paranormal' study may yield useful insights into the workings of the more subtle levels of the mind and into more subtle aspects of character. However, from the point of view of the *direct* path to awakening, the field of paranormal investigation and the exploration of psychic abilities is a sidetrack, and one that can easily wander off into tall cornfields from which we may not emerge for a long time, if at all.

This is not to suggest that paranormal exploration is to be

scrupulously avoided, but it is to point out that we should be clear about our motivation for exploring these things. The hard truth is that we are not going to achieve deep self-realization by exploring these realms. They can serve as stepping stones to the direct path to awakening, but they are certainly not the main route, and all too often they do not even lead to the main route.

In Zen Buddhism they have a term that describes the psychic visions and experiences that often occur for those who commit themselves to a disciplined spiritual practice such as meditation. The term is *makyo*, and it refers to the hallucinations, visions, and other paranormal phenomena that can occur as the subconscious mind opens up during sustained meditation. However, despite the sometimes spectacular nature of these experiences, which may even include prophetic visions or communications with long-dead ancestors, great saints, or historical teachers, the Zen practitioner is counseled to ignore them, let them go, and to continue witnessing whatever is arising in the present moment.

The reason for this is subtle and addresses the main trap within the exploration of paranormal phenomena for one whose aim is full spiritual awakening. The trap is this: because the path of awakening involves a gradual wearing down of the ego's apparent existence and its basis for sustaining its illusions – foremost of which is a personal disconnection from the totality of existence – anything that in any way enhances this central illusion is effectively working *against* awakening.

Part and parcel of ego-based separation is the belief in 'specialness', which in this case is a term to define the tendency to compare ourselves to others and always come out feeling either better than or less than (either 'positively special', or 'negatively special'). The trap contained within the exploration and especially the intentional development of paranormal abilities or psychic powers, is the tendency to believe we are now *special* in having such abilities. This becomes a form of what the Tibetan teacher Chogyam Trungpa called 'spiritual materialism'; that is, the usage of spiritual practices to reinforce egocentric tendencies, rather than deconstruct them. Another term for this tendency is 'spiritual narcissism', the usage of spiritual practice to increase self-importance, rather than diminish it. (By 'self-importance' what is meant here is forced, puffed-up posturing, as opposed to a healthy, legitimate self-confidence.)

Psychically sensitive individuals will commonly perceive negative qualities or energies *in others*. (As Sartre once put it, 'Hell is other people'.) If they have not done work on integrating their own shadow tendencies, the psychic perception of such tendencies in others is more likely a projection of their own baggage and will, typically, only serve to make them feel more separate from these others. It also carries the risk of providing others with useless or false information; information distorted by the psychic's own ego-filters.

Lucid Dreaming and Out-of-Body Experiences

Other types of altered states of consciousness worth mentioning here are those involving lucid dreaming (a dream where the dreamer realizes, to some degree, that they are dreaming) and its close cousin, the so-called 'out-of-body experience' (or 'astral travel', as the Theosophical Society originally called it). I don't particularly enjoy casting doubt on these types of experiences because they are valid within their context, and they may even foreshadow what awaits us if consciousness is continuous after the death of the body. But they are not necessary for direct awakening here and now, and as with all such spectacular experiences, they can lead one off down a rabbit hole that gets seriously disconnected from the greater purpose of self-realization.

When I was in my early 20s I gained some degree of 'proficiency' in these areas (in fact, it was lucid dreaming and out-of-body 'travel' that basically got me going on the 'path'). After several years of on-again, off-again, remarkably vivid lucid dreaming and 'OOBEs', one night I found myself in a lucid dream in which I suddenly realized I had no more interest in pursuing experiences in the dream, self-created or not. And so I sat down in lotus posture (not a posture I use in regular life – but the dream body is flexible!) and sank into meditation. I was having a lucid dream, with my physical body sound asleep in my bed, while I was sitting meditating in my dream body. After a while, I simply decided to wake up (into my physical body).

It was then that I realized that lucid dreaming basically meant chasing endless varieties of experiences, without truly reflecting on the one who is experiencing (consciousness itself). I won't say that that marked the end of my lucid dreaming, or even my interest in it, but I did see clearly that the way it is usually pursued does not have much to do with awakening in the greater sense. (There *is* a teaching within Tibetan Buddhism that utilizes lucid dreaming as a tool for deeper awakening, but this is an exception in what otherwise is a great deal of 'lucid dreaming for lucid dreaming's sake'.) Like all altered states of consciousness, it can be a stepping stone, but the sooner we realize that it is no more than a stepping stone, the better. This is because direct awakening is not about exploring *dimensions* of being or domains within the space-time field. It is about going to the very root and source of consciousness itself.

Drugs and Even Stranger Stuff

The related issue to consider briefly here is recreational drug usage. This can range from casual (though chronic) pot smoking, to the use of mild psychoactive substances like MDMA ('Ecstasy'), or stronger ones like mescaline or LSD, all the way to 'shamanic self-discovery' via powerful psychotropics like ayahuasca. Some of these drugs, especially MDMA, can mimic states of consciousness associated with stereotypical views of enlightenment (such as deep self-acceptance, peace, and lack of negative emotion or reactivity). However, the state of mind is dependent on the drug, wears off, and often leaves side-effects (in the case of MDMA, depression is a common after-effect among chronic users). 'Shamanic'-type drugs like ayahuasca are more problematic, because evidence is strong that legitimate psychological realizations and spiritual insights can be facilitated by the drug (as they can by other hallucinogens). However, the essential dilemma remains: the drug produces an altered state of consciousness, and enlightenment, being the end of all *states* of consciousness, is not captured by any drug. That does not mean that a drug cannot temporarily clear away blocks to reveal a deconditioned glimpse of Reality. But it will always be a temporary foray produced by chemicals that the user is in risk of becoming reliant on, at whatever level of dependency.

One particular (and peculiar) area of altered consciousness work – whether induced via 'psychic capacity' or via recreational drug usage – is that of interaction and communication with 'non-human' or 'non-physical' intelligences. These can take the form of anything from animal-spirits ('totems') to 'high spirit guides' to 'extraterrestrials'. Part of the fascination commonly held with the whole area of altered-state communications, especially with so-called spirit guides, is the assumption that the entities being communicated with are somehow perfected beings, or at least, beyond us in development. Allowing that such entities are part of a real subjective experience (putting objectivity aside for a moment), the fact that they are supposed to be non-physical should in no way imply that their spiritual realization is somehow complete, or even transcends our own. However, the tendency of the average person is to assume otherwise, doubtless in part because of centuries of religious conditioning, which teaches that the gods, angels, and spirits 'above' are more advanced than mere humans.

All experience of altered states of consciousness is *makyo*, a distraction from the route to the top of the mountain, a glittering sideshow in which to avoid the less dazzling work of self-observation. Occasionally drug usage can be useful for 'blasting away' certain 'large boulders' obstructing our journey up the path, but we must always remember why we blasted the boulders in the first place, and not get caught up in endless fascination with the sparkling, scattered, remaining shards of the boulder.

None of this is to imply that great wisdom cannot be found *out there*, from whatever source. But such outer wisdom remains useless in the service of awakening if we do not use it as a mirror to access our own inherent wisdom, and vigilantly avoid getting ensnared in the alluring dream-worlds of altered states of consciousness that can appear to so closely impersonate enlightenment.

Myth: Psychic capacity, paranormal experiences or 'powers' (like yogic *siddhis*), or other altered states of consciousness (including those induced by drugs), are part of the path of enlightenment.

Clarification: All or any of these may be part of our journey up the mountain. But none of them ultimately has anything to do with enlightenment, and most lead us astray from our ultimate destination. They are part of the realm of experiences that arise, and subside, *within* consciousness. Enlightenment, however, is beyond experiences that are transitory, impermanent. Enlightenment is not an 'experience', no matter how profound or spectacular.

Chapter 13

Reincarnation:
Food for the Spiritualized Ego

Reincarnation, the idea that a person – or at least, some part of them– not only survives physical death, but gets 'recycled' back into another body (usually held to be human) and undergoes another physical birth, has long been basic to Eastern wisdom traditions, as well as to some of the Western esoteric teachings. Reincarnation is not taught by the big three mainstream Western religions (Judaism, Christianity, Islam). It is in part due to a rejection of these faiths that many Westerners came to embrace Eastern (or Western esoteric) paths, and so embrace reincarnation in some fashion as well.

Reincarnation as a belief is easy to misuse. This is especially so if we seek to 'know our past lives' (most commonly via hypnotic regression) if we have current-time unresolved self-esteem issues. The temptation will usually be to seek identification with a 'past-life' personality that we see as being in some way more significant than the person we think we are now. In this way, reincarnation (however we explore it) becomes a distraction from facing directly into our present-time 'stuff'. If such information genuinely aids in the gaining of insight into our *present*-time conditions (thus becoming a type of Jungian psychoanalytic tool) then it can be of some help (by broadening perspective, mostly, and by recognizing how negative patterns simply repeat, whether in this life, or in many lives). However, all too often past-life information, however gleaned, ends up being simply a distraction: an esoteric ornament, a curiosity or discussion piece having limited practical ability to aid in individual awakening to present-time reality (regardless of the legitimacy, or lack thereof, of our 'past-life memories', none of which are falsifiable anyway).

Seekers involved with Eastern teachings have had something

of a love/hate relationship with reincarnation over recent decades. Traditions like yoga and Tibetan Buddhism seem to encourage belief in it, while more austere paths like Zen or Advaita Vedanta clearly discourage exploration of it. The classic non-dualist ('All is One') type response to the idea of reincarnation runs something like this: there is a profound problem with the whole notion of reincarnation, and it is that our True Self, being beyond form, space, and time, has never actually incarnated *even once*, let alone many times. It is only through the functions of identification and projection that we 'fall asleep', take physical birth, and identify with the body-mind complex we find ourselves in. But our true nature is not identified with a body, mind, personality, or limited form of any sort. Consciousness (the 'True Self') is limitless, formless, free and unattached. Our true nature is unchanging and constant. This entire life we are living, with our personality and body, is one big elaborate dream. Strictly and ultimately speaking, *it never truly happened*. Therefore, reincarnation is simply a redundancy: an illusion piled on an illusion. We are no more this personality than we were any other. As Ram Dass once concisely put it: 'Reincarnation is real to the extent that you think *you* are real.'

That is all very well, and may indeed be the underlying truth, but in our present condition we have little way of confirming it. For example, to state that our 'True Self' has 'never incarnated even once' is, for most of us, a mystical assertion, a *belief*, not something falsifiable. (See Chapter 2, 'Eastern Fundamentalism'.) It also skirts close to the 'Higher Self' problem in which personal, bodily reality tends to be rejected, or dismissed as illusion at best, in favor of a 'Higher Self' that lords over our mere humanity.

That noted, we can use common sense to see how reincarnation as an idea is so easily misused. The personal self, the self of identifications and projections, is always changing, even if slowly and subtly. Further, this separate personal self is highly interdependent with the physical body. To some extent it is both shaped by the body, and shapes the body. Given that, it is obvious that any two personalities dwelling in two different physical bodies – for example, one body now, and one body two centuries ago – will be two very distinct, and different, personalities. So, to say that '*I* was this person in that past life' is bound to be false, because who we are almost always referring to by 'I' is the limited, always-changing self of *this* body here and now, a self which is impermanent and tightly bound up with the physical body of *this* life.

From that perspective, we can never truly claim that 'I was Cleopatra, or Napoleon', etc., because the 'I' is a transitioning, ever-changing phenomenon. Anyone can verify this simply by revisiting old childhood haunts, or reconnecting with a friend that you have not seen in a very long time. With sufficient passage of time it becomes clear that in many respects you are simply not the same 'I' that you were then. Looking a little deeper, we can see that *something* has remained continuous, what we can call 'pure awareness', but it is very difficult, if not impossible, to attach any sort of 'I' to this pure awareness, any more than we can ask a mirror to do anything other than reflect what is put in front of it. The mirror has no identity as such – unlike the parade of bodies and personalities that pass before it.

Finally, there is the issue of psychological health: most people have more than enough on their plate with their actual life. Even if we could clearly recall past lives, it would probably be deeply upsetting, and would doubtless threaten some people's sanity. The history of humanity is dark with suffering; it follows that the average person, if they *had* past lives, has suffered a great deal in those lives, and committed many acts that they would be ashamed of. Real or not, it is no doubt better that most of us remember nothing.

Myth: 'I, Mary Smith, was So-and-so in my last life.'

Clarification: The 'I' that we are almost always referring to, is the *personality* ('Mary Smith'), and this personal self is interdependent with our physical body. If we had a different body, we'd be a different personality – Jane Smith, not Mary. (The argument can be raised here that if we transplanted parts of our body, etc., we would still be the same person. That is true only with more minor body parts. Change your face, and the personality will alter to some degree. And of course brain chemistry influences personality. Change significant parts of your brain – even conjecturing that 'you' could survive that – and your personality with new 'brain-parts' will certainly be different. But that doesn't mean that 'you' no longer exist, something that highlights as well as anything the contrast between personality and the simple 'I am' presence.)

According to many teachings, what we can call the true 'I' – pure consciousness – is not conditioned by personality (is not imagined, or shaped by beliefs or memory) and therefore can never be said to *be*, in any ultimate sense, a particular personality or body. We may believe in that or not (and we may have had a glimpse of it). But what is most important is detecting any tendencies we may have to use reincarnation as a crutch or an escape to avoid who we are here, now, in this life – and above all, our need to be responsible for that.

Myth: Remembering my past lives, with vivid clarity, would be cool.

Clarification: Not likely. More probably it would be excruciating, or at best, deeply humbling. It might even make us psychotic.

None of this is to rule out the possibility of reincarnation or even of recalling past lives. (For to do so would be merely another kind of presumptuous folly.) The essential point made here, however, is that we are better off attending to the one life we know for sure we are living in.

Chapter 14

Enlightenment Doesn't Care
If You Are Rich Or Poor

Renouncing the World vs. Material Prosperity

Though it can be said that higher truths are timeless, it is also true that civilizations change and evolve over time, which results in changing 'inner work' requirements for the people of these civilizations. Thus, spiritual paradigms change as well, despite the unchanging nature of ultimate Reality.

A classic example is that of the old idea of renouncing the world in the name of committing oneself to a spiritual path. In past centuries the common way to pursue a spiritual quest was to remove oneself from society and retire to a hermitage, or monastery, or ashram, and seek apprenticeship from a guru, teacher, or shaman who often dwelt in a remote area, and so on. Going along with all this, especially in the case of formal renunciations, such as in monastic vows or ashram habitation, would often be a vow of poverty of some sort, and a general renunciation of worldly things.

All of this constitutes part of our religious conditioning, and how we have been accustomed to view a life deeply committed to awakening. What this largely translates into is the belief that spiritual development somehow requires material poverty. Or, put another way, one who aspires to the deepest spiritual life has no right to be affluent, materially abundant, or outwardly successful.

From the point of view of committing to awakening *within* civilization, as opposed to fleeing from civilization in order to realize our deepest potential, it is clear that it would be useful to drop the old model of worldly renunciation as being *mandatory* for spiritual practice. From this point of view, it would be reasonable to claim that to be a 'spiritual householder' is the current paradigm, and even that what is called for now is for spiritual principles to enter the mainstream of society – rather than the odd person removing themselves from the world to practice spiritual principles. For this, the longstanding paradigm of individual awakening requiring the renunciation of material things, sequestering away in a monastery or mountain cave, or living in poverty, must be seen for what it is, an old model that can now be relegated to myth. The spiritual path does not require us to become an anti-materialist.

But to all this must be added an important caveat. It is one thing to commit to being a 'spiritual householder', and it is another thing entirely to be able to truly do it. There was a good reason for 'leaving the world' in the older traditions, and it is a reason that is still valid in certain respects. The main trap for householders doing inner work is growing superficial in their practice – where one's meditation or therapy or study becomes not much more than a 'Sunday church' routine – and eventually becoming consumed by practical matters. Potentially there is a great payoff in being a householder, because if we can stay true to the path of awakening while also handling our worldly responsibilities and relationships, then the chances are good that we could also do it living in an ashram, monastery, or hut. We have, however, to guard against self-deception creeping in, something that is much more difficult to notice in the marketplace than in the monastery. Realization of our highest potential is not like going to the yoga studio or gym a few times a week. It has to become seamlessly integrated with our daily existence.

The other part of this is the emphasis, something that is part and parcel of a capitalist society, on 'getting ahead', being successful financially, and materially abundant. Books and teachings about 'enlightened wealth' have become part of the current spiritual paradigm. Here again, the main problem is diluting spiritual principles in the name of attaining material wealth. All too often the spiritual principles become part of a clever backdrop to the deeper and truer intent, which is the desire for financial wealth. While there is obviously nothing wrong with financial wealth, it is not a prerequisite for inner realization. Here again, honesty is crucial. If being a millionaire is more important to us than enlightenment, that's fine for what it is; our only task is to be honest about that fact, rather than disguising our material ambitions or feeling guilty about them.

It is, of course, possible to be both outwardly and inwardly wealthy – realizing our spiritual potential does not mean we can't be an emperor. However, we need to be realistic. Walking the path of awakening is difficult if we are lugging two hundred pounds of gold in a backpack. We would be better off giving some of the gold away to lighten and simplify our journey.

Ultimately, the main issue is not how much money we have in our bank – it is our *state of mind*. A certain level of material comfort is needed (for most people) in order to not be consumed with distracting, anxious thoughts. Meditation or contemplation is difficult if the bills have not been paid. Radical honesty is equally difficult if we are struggling financially, because it will often involve us trailing off into hypocrisy (if I am to be deeply honest, I must first be deeply honest about why I am behind on my bills).

Similarly, once achieving a level of material comfort, it is tempting for many to pursue more, to the point where what passion for truth there was dissolves into passion for investment numbers. A new form of neurosis arises, that based on the need to maintain what we have, acquire more, and fear losing it all. Again, this invites mental agitation which blocks our journey and ends up with us finding ourselves entangled in some jungle of worry without ever remembering how we got there.

Enlightenment doesn't care if we are rich or poor. It cares only that we arrive.

Myth: I must be free of material encumbrances (including financial entanglements) to realize my spiritual potential. I must renounce my love and attachment to material things.

Myth: I must be financially prosperous, even wealthy, to be truly awakened. That spiritual poverty stuff is old paradigm.

Clarification: Abundance and prosperity, material or otherwise, are simply forms of energy. The presence or absence of this energy has no ultimate bearing on our realization of our spiritual potential. Historically, people have awakened while experiencing all extremes of material living, from affluent, physically comfortable conditions to those of extreme poverty or even homelessness.

A basic level of material comfort and financial integrity is needed. And obviously, there is nothing wrong with enjoying material things, or having material wealth. The real issue, however, is our state of mind, and in particular, being free of distracting mental agitation – that is, the real issue is *attachment*. It is not how much money we have in our bank that is the issue, it is the degree of attachment we have to this money – whether it be a billion dollars or our last twenty bucks. A person who is attached to their poverty is as neurotic as a person who is attached to their wealth, and vice versa.

Chapter 15

Gurus, Disciples, and Guru-bashers

The issue of false gurus and teaching prematurely has been touched on in Chapters 4 and 6. In this chapter we take a closer look at an equally problematic matter: 'guru-bashing'. Here in the early 21st century we are saturated with information. This is nowhere truer than in the 'self-help' field, or even in more obscure esoteric realms. There are no more secrets. All the previously hidden teachings are now more or less available, along with a surplus of others. Spiritual or personal growth bookstores are packed to the rafters with titles on every conceivable topic. Vast amounts of information (though less organized and of wildly differing quality) can also be found at a click on the Internet.

A side-effect of all this has been an increasing tendency to believe that one can walk a path of inner awakening with no real outer guidance – that teachers are not needed. We are told repeatedly that *the truth is within*; or that we should just *trust ourselves*. And with our trusty computer, interminable personal growth websites and our bookmarked Amazon stuffed with endless discounted spiritual books, we can do it all without leaving our chair.

This is mostly nonsense. Simply knowing that the 'truth is within' is useless for the average person, because when they turn within, they encounter little more than their noisy mind and their confused self. To expect to be able to meditate effectively without guidance from an experienced meditator, or to expect to be able to explore one's blind spots without a skilled therapist, or to expect to be able to think profoundly about ultimate matters without wiser elders, is like expecting to compose superb poetry, play the violin, or paint at the level of a Rembrandt or Leonardo Da Vinci on our first attempt. It just isn't going to happen, no matter how many 'how to' books we order, stack up on our night table, and read up to page 6.

The Sanskrit word *guru* translates as 'weighty one', meaning that the guru's counsel and teaching is weighty or powerful. In other words, when they speak, you listen; not out of fear, but because their words resonate with 'weight', i.e. truth and wisdom. In the East, especially the yogic and Buddhist paths, the guru has traditionally been an indispensable piece to the overall process of awakening. When the Eastern models of the guru–disciple relationship began to be transplanted to the West in the 20th century, difficulties were encountered in understanding this tradition, let alone accepting it. Because the guru–disciple relationship has traditionally been held so sacred in the East, it usually entails a demonstration of trust or 'surrender' on the part of the disciple, which often translates into behavior that a Westerner may interpret as submissive, or as is commonly expressed, as 'giving away one's power'.

While there is no question that many gurus have had significant character impurities that distorted their ability to teach, and that further to that, some gurus or teachers have misled or misguided their followers owing to these character traits, it is also true that the majority of gurus or teachers are legitimate, having something of value to impart, and usually operate in a manner of integrity. However, many Westerners, especially those with underlying authority issues, have been unable to view the guru phenomena without strong doubt or cynicism. In fact, in mainstream language, the very word *guru* has partly come to suggest humorous, parody-like connotations of a stereotypical exotic con man who demands worship (and money) of his brainwashed followers. In Hollywood movies the 'Eastern guru' is more commonly a character of comedy than drama.

Western cultural conditioning has its roots in Greek and Roman individualism, in which the 'hero' or 'rebel' (often fighting against odds or gods) is lionized and held as a standard to emulate. The West is much more concerned with individualism than the East (where, in general, there are stronger family bonds and a sense of responsibility to tradition before self), and thus there is a greater natural tendency in the West to question authority. Further, we live in a time of media-saturation, and the media is notoriously cynical about gurus and the traditional guru–disciple relationship in general.

As a result, the phenomenon of guru-bashing has developed, wherein centuries of painful collective scars connected to authority issues (and especially, religious authority issues) are commonly projected onto gurus. This is especially so if the guru appears to be asking for a strong commitment on the part of the seeker. This strong commitment is, in truth, absolutely vital for most wishing authentic transformation, but if the commitment in any way involves physical aspects (such as time, energy, service, and especially finances), which more often than not it must to at least some degree, then the commitment is seen with knee-jerk cynicism by the guru-bashers.

Being directly mentored, at least for a period of time, by a worthy guru or teacher or therapist is almost always an essential aspect of the journey of awakening. To locate a proper teacher–student relationship for oneself requires a balance of discernment and awareness of the traps inherent in guru-bashing, which more often than not are based on pride, resistance to (or unresolved anger toward) authority, attachment to independence, or media conditioning.

Myth: No one should follow a guru or teacher (so many of whom are corrupt anyway), as the true teacher is within.

Clarification: Ultimately, it *is* true that the true teacher is within, or more to the point, that the true teacher is our actual greatest potential self. But few of us can simply leap directly to this highest potential. This is due, in large part, to the existence of psychological blind spots, parts of our mind that are virtually impossible for us to see on our own.

For the vast majority of people, a guru, teacher, guide, mentor, spiritually oriented therapist – or even a strong 'soul friend', one who is both clear and honest with you – is a necessary thing to have on the path of awakening. This is partly owing to the connection with the guide, and partly to the community of practitioners that are sometimes connected to the guide, which more often than not ends up playing an important role in our awakening.

Of course, any community of seekers gathered together should never be assumed to be some utopia of harmony and flawless wisdom. Every spiritual or philosophical community has its share of issues and problems that happen when people try to interact together in truth, and especially when any degree of organization or hierarchy is present. (And reasonable arguments have been made that 'spiritual communities' are as much, if not more, dysfunctional than any other sort of intentional community.) However, the overriding spirit that should govern our participation in any such community is that of self-discovery. We get involved with gurus or teachers or mentors, and the students around them, purely in the service of our awakening, not to find some surrogate family. Keeping that in mind tends to prepare us for the disappointment that easily follows when we begin to see the typical social dysfunction that occurs in most spiritual communities, even if the inner work going on in their midst is authentic and useful.

Chapter 16

'Spiritual Growth' and 'Creating Our Reality'

Spiritual Growth: Is There Such a Thing?

It is sometimes said that from the ultimate perspective *all* spiritual growth is an illusion, if only because there is nothing to truly grow. The very idea that we are a discrete self, something to be improved, shaped, altered, and so on, is seen to be false from this absolute point of view, because the very entity we call 'me' is itself seen to *not actually exist* the way we've long believed that it does. Not that 'I' do not exist, but rather, my 'conventional self' is understood to be based on assumptions that are seen (from this absolute perspective) to be false – foremost of which is that 'I am an entity distinct from everything else'.

However, almost none of us are operating from this ultimate, absolute perspective. From where we stand – as a particular identity having a physical body – we have no choice but to regard 'spiritual growth' (or development, or realization, or awakening) as *real*. One day we may realize that the 'path of awakening' is stuff we just made up, but for now the path is real, as real as the sleep we need at night, the food we must eat to feed our bodies, and the air we must breathe to survive into the next moment.

To regard the spiritual path as unnecessary and 'work on self' as pointless is usually a type of spiritual sophistry; that is, a clever way of evading the real inner work that has to be done for one interested in enlightenment. Even for one who has been working on themselves for many years, having a sudden revolutionary insight that self-realization has been sitting under their nose all that time still does not mean that all their efforts have been fruitless. The efforts were essential because they aid in wearing out our attachment – and addiction – to *experiences*.

Some approaches to self-realization teach the following: The constant effort to change ourselves simply results in experiences – and experiences, by their very nature, are coming and going. Eventually, we begin to notice that the experiences do not define who we are. And no matter how much we meditate, or what kinds of spiritual techniques we employ in this attempt to grow spiritually, we sooner or later begin to notice that our actual nature is not created by all our techniques and practices. We cannot create what we already are; we can only discover what we already are.

All this carries much truth, but the essential point conveniently overlooked by those who emphasize the 'no-effort' philosophy is that we cannot reach the point of realizing the irrelevancy of 'spiritual growth' (and spiritual experiences) without first making sincere and significant efforts. The view from high up the mountain shows us many truths, reveals many illusions, and puts things in perspective. But only when we actually get high up the mountain! For that we need to give up our proud and lazy conceits, do the hard work of self-examination, cultivate the courageousness to face our ego-mind, and thereby actually climb the mountain. Otherwise, our 'spiritual growth' will be mostly imaginary (and yes, it is indeed possible to *dream that we are awake*).

In short, all efforts of work on oneself – spiritual growth – amount to wearing away layers of falseness to arrive at the true potential of who we are. Once clearly glimpsed, we understand that this truth can't be created or destroyed by our imagination – but it most certainly can be feared, attacked, ignored, disregarded, and plain forgotten. The only way to prevent this from happening, provided we have developed passion for truth, is via effort.

And thus while it is true that our best potential is not truly created – that is, it is not imagined into being – it is also true that we must make efforts to realize it, as these efforts are crucial to wearing away illusions. Hence the paradox: spiritual growth itself may ultimately be an illusion, but we have to walk the path anyway. There is no shortcut to truth.

Do We Really Create Our Reality?

Most so-called New Age teachings have been an eclectic mix of wisdom teachings originating from many old sources, such as are found in Eastern mysticism and the Western esoteric traditions, with a strong dose of Transcendentalist and 'New Thought' teachings that originated in the 19th and early 20th century mostly in America, with Emerson, Phineas Quimby, Wallace Wattles, Ernest Holmes, and others. What many of these teachings have held in common is the idea that our highest potential nature is identical to our 'spiritual source'. In other words, waking up to our spiritual essence is ultimately the same as realizing that our highest potential shares the same consciousness as the Source – simply because only the Source is ultimately real.

Two examples sometimes cited in these esoteric views are from Hindu and Christian doctrine. The first is often expressed as *Tat Tvam Asi,* meaning 'You are That'; this is sometimes phrased as '*Atman* (individual soul) is, in the end, understood to be the same as *Brahman* (ultimate Reality).' In other words, who I *really* am (free of ego) is One with God. The second is from the New Testament, where Jesus says, 'I am the way, the truth, and the life: no man cometh unto the Father, but by me.' (John 14:6, King James Version) The main difference of interpretation in the esoteric view is that here 'Jesus' represents our highest potential, not just the historical personality from Nazareth. From that point of view, it is indeed true that *only* via our highest potential do we 'cometh unto the Father', that is, join with ultimate Reality.

What these wisdom traditions also teach is that once standing in our true self (so to speak; the language for the various traditions of course differs) we can finally grasp how this consciousness is the same consciousness that is 'creating' the entire universe, generating its appearance at all moments, via the power of pure creative thought and reflective awareness.

This is, of course, a complex philosophical issue, and one

heatedly debated for centuries. Suffice to say that most mystical/ spiritual schools of thought come down on the side of some form of 'philosophical idealism', which essentially says that Reality is founded on ideas and consciousness, that mind precedes matter. This is the reverse of 'realism' or scientific materialism which teaches that the material universe precedes consciousness. To generalize, for an idealist consciousness is primordial, and therefore precedes the brain; for a realist, consciousness is an emergent property *of* the brain.

There is a crucial point to understand here, and it is this point that is often not properly grasped by many who look into (or seriously try to use) 'manifestation' teachings with the idea of improving themselves and their lot in life. The point in question is that the very awakening process described by the wisdom traditions has at its heart the understanding that the ego is dissolved – or *outshined* – by the light of higher consciousness. Put another way, the 'I' is eclipsed by ultimate Reality, much as how stars 'vanish' at dawn with the rising sun. So, to realize that my consciousness is the same consciousness that is 'creating' the entire universe necessitates that *me* or *mine* is an illusion. In other words, *I* cannot attain to ultimate Reality. The moment I join with Reality, I am no more – only Reality (or God) *is*.

Thus, we cannot have our cake and also eat it. We can certainly manifest things in life and even become quite skilled at drawing things to us. But for one interested in ultimate truth, the matter becomes literally 'out of our hands'. A clear distinction needs to be made between 'manifesting' or 'creating our reality' as they are typically understood, and the purity of enlightenment. While it is in fact true that we 'create our reality' in terms of our subjective perceptions and our apparent ability to bring about changes, the reality of enlightenment is such that our very *motivation* for bringing about changes is altered. Our more selfish ambitions and desires are dissolved and our actions are animated by a wholly different force, one that arises from a much bigger perspective. We literally think bigger, and in particular, about how we can serve the awakening of the human race. All 'manifestation abilities' become dedicated to that higher cause.

Myth: Spiritual growth is an illusion. You are already enlightened, and so there is nothing to 'grow'. Therefore, don't bother meditating, doing therapies, etc.

Clarification: There is no free pass to enlightenment. No matter how much one may seek to deny it, work on self is exactly that, *work*. For periods of our journey we may experience this 'work' as play, or as creativity, or as profound intimacy, or even as effortless understanding. But in almost all cases, these will be but temporary periods, 'rest stops' on our way up the mountain, from which we can enjoy the wondrous view. Once rested, however, the path continues uphill. Continuing uphill is important, because if we rest too long our 'rest period' will become sleep and dreams – from which we may not wake up for a long time.

Myth: We create our reality, and can control it accordingly. I can still manifest my desires *and* be dedicated to enlightenment at the same time.

Clarification: In *some* ways we create our reality, and in *some* ways we can shape it via conscious intention. For example, you can make significant changes in your life by learning the art of changing your personal 'frequency' – using intent ('acting as if'), visualization, and so on, to match the 'frequency' of what you desire (if wanting more love, then you become more authentically loving, and love will begin to seek you out; if wanting more abundance, then demonstrate abundance in generous thought or action, and abundance will seek you out, etc. – in accordance with like-attracts-like). However, the deeper you go into yourself, the more you see that your personal 'I' is something like a mirage covering a much vaster presence (your greatest potential self). This vaster presence acts with natural intelligence to do what is necessary – 'chopping wood, carrying water from the well' – simply, directly, without wasting time and energy in dreaming about castles and other fairy tales. From that place we may indeed both enjoy and accomplish great things, but all in the context of contributing to the evolution and awakening of the human being.

Part III

Yet More Annoying Roadblocks on the Way

Mesmerized by the sheer variety of perceptions, which are like the phantom reflections of the moon in water, beings wander endlessly astray in the vicious cycles of illusion.

Lama Jigme Lingpa

Chapter 17

Unclear Motivation: Ulterior Agendas

It is the most obvious point of all: in order to wake up to our greatest potential, we have to be clear that we truly *want* to. We must have the right motivation. Problems with 'right motivation' for spiritual awakening occur when our desire to 'wake up' is disguising other agendas. The most typical ulterior agendas usually have to do with unconsciously seeking to fulfill relating needs; namely, love and consolation. For example, it is fairly common in the case of spiritual or personal growth communities for a person to participate in the transformational practices or programs put on by the community, under the apparent intention to awaken and discover their higher nature. However, what is often the deeper, hidden motivation for participating in the community is the desire to find love, usually in the form of the so-called soul mate, but often in the guise of looking for a surrogate parent or family. The teacher and/or community around him or her then gets 'set up' in that role in the mind of the seeker.

This is an unclear motivation for awakening precisely because it is the same old pattern being rehashed and disguised as a spiritual quest. The old pattern is simply the usual search for a *personal* source of love. As the authentic spiritual journey involves getting a taste of an impersonal, collective, or more universal love, it follows that any attempt to hide the search for a *personal* source of love (soul mate, idealized parental figure, etc.) within a professed search for impersonal love is bound to eventually cause problems. Our negative relationship patterns will simply get transferred to our relationships in the spiritual community.

Another form of unclear motivation for awakening is based on a deep unresolved sense of guilt, usually connected to believing that we have failed someone, like an authority figure from childhood such as a parent or teacher. This 'guilt' is not about 'I made mistakes', but rather that 'I *am* a living, breathing mistake'. We then believe that if we can attain the approval of the current authority figure (guru, spiritual guide, or therapist) then we will have won the love and approval that we believe we never received during our early years. We will have recomposed the story of our early life and given it a happy ending, thereby redeeming ourselves.

This longing for approval from authority can have a religious tinge to it as well, where the image of 'God' takes on some sort of subconscious role in our mind that we later have difficulty separating from the role of our guru, teacher, or therapist. There is the assumption that God, and all so-called 'teachers of God', should be flawless beings with the ability to dispense unlimited compassion and approval. This particular strategy of ulterior motivation is usually unmasked the moment we begin to perceive 'flaws' in our human guide. We then usually experience resentment upon realizing that our new authority figure is not perfect. (Or if the guide we've been following for a long time is found out to be just a 'regular person'.) The resentment arises because the unclear motivation has been revealed. We never wanted inner awakening. We wanted a new (and better) daddy or mommy or lover. What is ultimately getting revealed in all of this is the need to take responsibility for our journey.

An even more subtle form of ulterior agenda occurs when we become a truth-seeker in large part as a reaction to our family of origin. If behind our quest for enlightenment is in fact a desire to establish our identity as *unique* – 'I want to do something that is the opposite of what my family thinks is right, or what my father did, or what my successful siblings are doing', etc. – then it will become clear in time that what we're really looking for is to be seen as a special person, to establish our identity, and while we're at it, to thumb our nose at our family. When this desire to be recognized as special fades as we mature and get humbled by life, then we may well find ourselves feeling deflated and losing interest in enlightenment. In any case, our motivation is revealed to have been immature. We then have the chance to grow beyond that.

A yet more subtle and complicated faulty motivation is the desire to attain spiritual awakening in order to attain spiritual status. In this case, we undergo all the trials and tribulations of the awakening process, but underneath it all lurks an ambition for *spiritual power* – arguably (and ironically) the greatest 'worldly' power there has ever been.

Lie Detector Questions: Are you on a spiritual path because you're still trying to get love in a backhanded way? Are you in any way seductive toward your guru, teacher, or therapist? Are you on the path in order to prove something to your family? Are you seeking spiritual awakening in order to gain worldly power? Do you desire to be recognized as someone spiritually great?

Of course, recognizing such desires is no big deal. They are very common. The idea is to see them clearly and honestly, so that we can get on with deeper, more important matters.

Chapter 18

Insincerity and Laziness

Laziness is one of the great impediments to accomplishing anything in life, and this certainly applies in the case of spiritual awakening as well. At its core laziness is a resistance to life, and in its strongest and most harmful form is essentially a kind of unconscious longing to return to the womb – the primal condition where nothing was required of us, all our needs were looked after, and we had no responsibility whatsoever.

Resistance to life in general – laziness – while superficially a type of resentment ('Leave me alone, I don't want to do it!'), is essentially deriving from a deep-seated sense of a lack of self-worth, and often conceals a great deal of pain. It is not so much the sense that 'I do not want to be here', but more, 'I do not have a *right* to be here'. It is an expression of a profound doubt in our personal value. Rather than feel the pain associated with our lack of self-worth, an attitude of passivity sets in. We resist taking risks of any sort or venturing into new territory – both outwardly, and more importantly, inwardly, because we fear making errors, of finding out that we can't truly do it, thereby only reinforcing the self-doubt.

The very essence of spiritual awakening is exploring new territory – generally speaking, territory of the inner sort, though on occasion, this may involve large changes in the form of our outer existence (such as changing or leaving an occupation, a primary relationship, a dwelling, or even a city or country). But more commonly this new territory has to do with the inner space of discovering hidden thoughts and feelings and aspects of our personality that have been repressed or denied, discovering capacities for expression and communication, and deepening our understanding and wisdom.

Waking up to our highest potential requires courage and sincerity. When we lack self-worth, we are always undermining movements toward courage and sincerity. We end up being cowardly and insincere. We literally don't take ourselves seriously. We then act this out by being lazy, because, after all, what difference does it really make? All this will manifest in particular as a *mental* laziness that will try to keep us tethered to useless, negative, energy-consuming patterns and habits. Moreover, we will not make sufficient effort to truly understand ourselves. We will 'pass time'.

To be lazy is ultimately to be irresponsible. True responsibility is directly connected to profound freedom, but this comes only out of *effort* and *action*. Such effort or action may be sitting on our meditation cushion for twenty minutes every day, or it may mean making that phone call we need to make, but either way it will be *movement*, whether of the inner or outer sort.

It is the essence of sincerity and right effort to prioritize our spiritual awakening. In the words of the Buddha on his deathbed, 'Work out your salvation with diligence, and be a light unto yourself.'

Lie Detector Questions: Are you willing to do something about it – *now*? If not, are you willing to honestly face your resentments and underlying belief in your lack of self-worth – and start to do something about *that*? Be honest. An honest 'No!' is better than a false 'Yes', because an honest 'No!' will help you to begin to confront and start to deal with the anger that is covering up the pain of belief in lack of self-worth.

Chapter 19

Unresolved Authority Issues

It is in the nature of things to be guided by someone else, from the moment of birth, through childhood, schooling, and later adult learning and activities. We learn from each other, and for any given thing that we want or need to learn, there is almost always someone who has the capacity to guide us in some fashion.

The teacher–student relationship applies across the gamut of life and certainly with inner awakening as well. Almost always, in order to learn and progress in the realization of our true nature, we need to allow ourselves to be mentored to some degree by a real physical person. This is not to deny that considerable progress is not possible through reading and absorbing the literature of the great awakened teachers of history (at least where this has not been unduly distorted and shaped into religious dogma), or that deep insight into the nature of truth cannot be gained by solitary practice. Both of these are important and effective for inner awakening – but in almost all cases, they are *not enough*. An actual living teacher, guide, or mentor of some sort is important.

In the course of entering into a relationship with a teacher, regardless of how long this relationship lasts, there will usually be a degree of authority-projection directed at the teacher. To some degree they will be put on a pedestal, with the inbuilt danger that the higher the pedestal, the heavier they can crash to the ground. The 'crash' of a teacher will, more often than not, be occurring only in the mind of the student, but still has the power to destroy the relationship and sabotage any learning achieved up to that point. (Of course, the reverse occurs commonly enough – faulty teacher damaging the student – but this topic has been covered extensively in recent times, almost to the point of being overworked. Our interest here is in identifying our authority issues that we bring to our relationship with a teacher.)

The most typical kind of psychological projection directed at a therapist or spiritual mentor or teacher is the parental kind, where a father or mother figure is initially seen in the warm, wise, powerful, and presumably charismatic figure of the teacher (part of a process known as 'transference' in Western psychotherapy). But it is not just any parental figure that is being projected here; rather, it is an *ideal* parental figure, what Joseph Campbell called the 'archetype of the Supernatural Aid'. Because of this idealism, a double-edged sword is fashioned, holding both the promise of inviting profound trust in such a person (which certainly can, under correct conditions, facilitate profound progress in *us*), and also the danger of creating an unrealistic fantasy-world that involves the expectation of receiving special attention and ultimate spiritual parenting. The danger is real because if at some time the mentor is perceived as no longer lavishing special attention (regardless of whether or not this 'special attention' had any basis in reality), or as no longer providing perfect 'spiritual parenting', then we may withdraw in resentment or even seek vengeance in some way – all the while outwardly looking for evidence of the teacher's imperfections. We will become a Sherlock Holmes with a magnifying glass, hunting for a thorn among dozens of roses.

Unpopular as it may be to say this (owing to the numerous scandals involving gurus in recent times), such a falling out with a teacher is, more often than not, related to unhealed authority issues on the part of the seeker. As mentioned, errors and abuses of power have been and continue to be perpetrated by gurus, spiritual teachers, or therapists. However, in the majority of cases the apparent imperfections of the guru, teacher, or therapist are more properly related to projections and perceptions on the part of the disciple, student, or client. In particular, if the needs for love, affection, attention, and approval were not sufficiently met via the upbringing the seeker received in his or her early years, then there will tend to be a lifelong quest, mostly at a subconscious level, to find someone who *can* provide this ultimate parenting, and so fill in the 'hole' that remains in the form of memories of deprivation and neglect.

However, because the essence of awakening involves growing beyond the childish fixation with getting love and approval from very *personal* sources and very *particular* individuals, the entire project of winning approval from these certain key people – no matter how elevated we may see them as – is doomed to failure, largely because it is not really *their* love and approval that is being sought, but the love and approval of a childhood figure (usually, a parent). Thus, the entire relationship with the guru or teacher or therapist becomes the acting out of a childish need for special attention.

Though this acting out will not result in awakening it can be seen as useful, in terms of it showing us where our liberation does *not* lie. This kind of realization is often very important because authority issues transferred to spiritual teachers – whether through 'falling in love' with the teacher or rebelling against them as in the need to 'surpass (make wrong) the master' or 'bring down the king' – often have the capacity to masquerade, if only for brief periods of time, as genuine awakening. More than one seeker has confused guru-infatuation or emancipation from the guru with awakening, when in fact both are usually our immature authority issues being rehashed.

Lie Detector Questions: Are you seeking truth – or an authority figure to fantasize about? To seduce? To fight with? Do you compete with your teacher? Do you punish them in subtle ways? Do you want to be a guru yourself?

Chapter 20

Excessive Intellectualizing
and Anti-Intellectualism

The intellect, being, in a sense, the 'navigation system' of our inner being, plays an immensely important role in our spiritual evolution. In this connection common problems arise in one of two general ways, what we can loosely call 'excessive intellectualizing' and 'anti-intellectualism'. Both can create significant problems when not clearly understood.

Excessive Intellectualizing

In current times, with the tremendous availability of written material on spiritual matters, both in bookstores and on the Internet, it is easy and tempting for those of an intellectual nature to overindulge in the study of personal transformation or enlightenment. *Some* study of the literature on awakening is generally necessary. But because of the sheer bulk of writings that can now be easily found on these matters – we live during not just the 'golden age' of spiritual publishing, we live in the *gluttony* age of spiritual publishing – there are two general by-products to deal with.

The first is that we are *always reading and never practicing*. Worse, even as our night table teeters with six or seven books perched precariously on each other, our reading becomes superficial. We get to page 12 of one book and soon are distracted by another. We become a skimmer, and more of a book collector than a close reader of what we are buying.

The second tendency is to get overly hung up on transformational concepts. Or worse, to get hung up on *one* particular teacher's understandings, to the point where a kind of parroting effect happens where we are simply memorizing or even preaching the words or writings of others, and at times even unknowingly mimicking the understandings of one particular teacher, when we ourselves have not truly realized this understanding. That is, we are seeing the matter of awakening via concepts, through the safe filters of our mind, but we are not truly *participating*. (As mentioned in an earlier chapter, during these online times it's even possible to find an online guru, and be strictly an online disciple – a collection of interacting pixels on a screen – and almost always, one who is not fully honest in any number of ways while engaging in such interacting.)

Obviously, there is nothing wrong with books (one of our greatest inventions) or words or concepts. The issue is how they are used, and specifically, hidden behind. For the truth-seeker the potential problem with them is in mistaking shallow intellectual understanding for genuine realization. Intellectual understanding is essential, and some argue, is in itself enough – *if* our comprehension is profound enough (for example, Shankara, the great Indian sage, maintained this). Most, however, find that a strong intellectual understanding is a necessary foundation, but must be accompanied by committed practice. 'Practice' basically boils down to three things: honesty with ourselves via self-observation and penetrating insight, meditation, and responsibility for our life.

In the context of excessive intellectualizing there is a noteworthy relationship between intellect and sex. When sex is too repressed, our minds tend to become overactive (in an ineffectual way). We spend a lot of time in our head, living in fantasy (and I refer here not to just sexual fantasy, but to fantasy in general). That does not mean that we have to become very sexually active to cure that. It means we need to pay attention to what we are doing with our sexual energy, and in particular, how we understand and deal with our sexuality.

In general, deeper awakenings that go beyond the mere parroting of words or living through borrowed ideas in beautiful books, shows up as comfort with being alone, as well as comfort in being with others. Excessively living through the intellect often results in hiding from the world, and hiding from oneself. Paradoxically, the more we hide in our mind, via attachment to knowledge, the less we truly *know* ourselves – because we are not encountering ourselves via interaction with others.

Anti-Intellectualism

The other side of the coin of 'living too much in the head' is developing an anti-intellectual position, which for the spiritual seeker is usually based on falling prey to the 'pre-trans fallacy'.

There is a great deal of confusion concerning matters of the transformational path when dealing with the issue of the ego, and the idea of going 'beyond' the ego. A common misunderstanding is that any kind of work on self involves a general return to a childlike state, a sort of 'back to innocence' or a 'return' to a divine source. This is not actually the case, at least not in the simplistic, linear-like fashion it is sometimes presented in.

The 'pre-trans fallacy' (popularized by the noted American philosopher Ken Wilber) is based on a straightforward idea. It is the idea that 'trans-ego' states of mind (spiritual states *beyond* the ego) can be confused with 'pre-ego' states (childlike states), resulting in faulty understandings about spirituality, and in particular issues related to responsibility (after all, if enlightenment means 'being as a child again', then who cares about paying bills?). Wilber maintained that Freud, for one, made this error, assigning all mystical states of consciousness to the memory of an infantile state of 'Oneness' with the mother. He also speculated that C.G. Jung made the opposite error, assigning certain pre-ego states of mind to a cosmic, 'trans-ego' spiritual state.

In many views of developmental psychology and spirituality, three basic levels are recognized. These are:

1. Pre-ego (roughly birth to age 2 or so)
2. Ego (roughly from age 2 on, with the development of language skills)
3. Trans-ego (possible in adults who commit to working on themselves)

Most who commit to a spiritual path (in whatever form) see themselves as basically attempting to go 'beyond the ego' (stage 3). But what does that really mean?

The ego is fundamental to individual development, necessary for both survival and individuation (recognizing who we are in distinction to others). Something can be *initially known* only in contrast to something that it is not. In the psychological realm, the ego is what provides this basic contrast. As children growing up, we had to learn how to separate from our parents (in particular, our mother, as we were originally joined with her body). This is sometimes called the process of 'differentiating'. The development of our ego was basic to the process, and thus it is important that a young person develops a 'healthy ego', which means, functional boundaries, solid sense of self, a measure of self-esteem, and so on. Problems with ego-development are, however, common, and often make it difficult for someone to truly embark on a path of awakening, because we cannot begin to go 'beyond' the ego if it has not developed in a normative fashion. This is why many who begin to work on themselves have to do some form of psychotherapy (whether spiritually oriented, or more conventional) in order to heal and integrate old wounds. Failure to come to a reasonable degree of healing with our past, and with our basic sense of (apparent) personal identity, increases the likelihood of falling prey to the pre-trans fallacy. That is, venturing into spiritual practices and beginning to confuse altered states of consciousness that can arise from such practices with early-life memories of 'Oneness' (like being merged with what was around us), along with an abandoned sense of responsibility, precisely because we desire to relive our childhood in a way that gets us what we didn't get back then. Spiritual states of mind do indeed include a sense of 'Oneness', but they do not abdicate our basic sense of identity. We do not lose the ability to recognize our own name, and thereby successfully answer the phone or reply to an email. More to the point, we do not abandon responsibility, and all the areas of life in which that is important.

Likewise, concerning the role of rationality on the spiritual path, there is similar confusion. Trans-ego, awakened states of being are non-rational (which is *not* the same as irrational), which can lead to the mistaken view that *all* rational states are therefore non-spiritual.

From there, it is a short leap to assuming that *all non-rational states are therefore spiritual*. This, however, ignores the fact that pre-rational states are different from trans-rational states. That is, the 'Oneness' felt by a child is not the same as the Oneness experienced by a mature, responsible, awakened adult. The former is best characterized as a state of fusion. The latter is a state of deep realization in which the ability to use the mind (or personal identity) is not lost.

The main difference between ordinary rationality and the rationality of trans-ego states is that in the latter there is less *identification* with the mind. It's not that the mind becomes non-functional or somehow 'disappears' (a misunderstanding of the Zen term 'no-mind'); it's rather that we come to recognize that we are *not* the mind (any more than we are the body). But recognizing that we are not the body does not mean that we abandon the body, mistreat it, or pretend that it is not real (much less, 'not spiritual'). The same is the case with the mind.

For those who are heavily identified with the mind (common with the intellectually oriented) there is a tendency to dismiss all spiritual states of being as 'pre-rational' (often deriving from a fear of them). That is also a pre-trans fallacy, in this case, confusing post-ego states with pre-ego states, and in so doing, dismissing all spirituality as a childish attempt to avoid being a responsible adult (or necessarily implying that one who pursues such matters is automatically self-absorbed – 'navel gazing' as it is sometimes derogatorily referred to).

Contrarily, it's common in New Age or personal growth communities to develop anti-intellectualism, by confusing pre-rational states with trans-rational, and thereby assuming that any non-rational state must be spiritual – even though many non-rational states are actually highly egocentric or narcissistic (self-absorbed) – that is, they are in fact *pre-ego* states.

In the natural development from ego to trans-ego, the mind and sense of individuality, along with the capacity for responsibility, are not abandoned. Rather, they are included on the journey, even as we deepen our sense of who we really are and orient ourselves toward greater wisdom, compassion and skillful ability to help others.

Lie Detector Questions: How many books have you bought over the years and not truly read? How afraid are you of meeting so-called gurus or teachers or other seekers? How much do you avoid relationship in general? How much do you content yourself with an online life for your 'spiritual growth'? How much have you used spiritual notions of 'going beyond the mind' as a reason to denigrate intellectuality and intellectually oriented people? How much have you done this owing to doubting your own intellectual capacity?

Chapter 21

Relationship Drama

It scarcely bears mention: nothing in life, with the exception of health, financial issues, or large-scale catastrophes like natural disasters and wars, consumes the attention and energy of the average person as much as relationship drama. There are of course endless forms of relationship, but here I'm talking more about so-called intimate, romantic, or 'primary' partnership.

The outstanding feature of such relating, in the vast majority of cases, is *repetitiveness*. In Buddhism they have the metaphor of the 'Wheel of *Samsara*', which contains the essential idea that awakening to our true nature involves nothing like any sort of standard ladder-like 'progress', but is rather more akin to simply getting off of a repetitive cycle (a 'wheel') altogether. (After all, where is there to 'progress' to on a wheel?)

The neurosis of relationship drama is in some ways a modern-day phenomenon, at least to a degree likely not known in previous ages when, for instance, most marriages were arranged, or when the notion of 'serial dating', multiple partnerships, and certainly multiple marriages was more or less unknown. Relationship intrigue, along with such accompanying themes as loyalty, betrayal, triangles, infidelity, and so on, have long been around, of course – but not to the degree they are in the modern, industrialized world. There are many reasons for this but they would form the basis of a long sociological study, falling outside our immediate scope.

What concerns us more at this point is recognizing the link between absorption in relationship drama and falling asleep to our greatest potential in life. This all gets especially important to understand for one interested in higher growth, because many modern transformational teachings are relationship-inclusive. That is, they involve methods that attempt to use relationship itself as a vehicle for awakening. These include teachings from 'modern tantra', *A Course in Miracles*, and many forms of group therapy and couples counseling with a transpersonal or spiritual platform. There is even a form of modern Westernized Zen, called 'enlightenment intensive', adapted from traditional oriental Zen Buddhist *koan* work, that is designed to be done in 'dyad format' – two people facing each other, asking each other, over and over, *koan*-type questions such as 'Who are you?' (This latter method, devised by Charles Berner in the 1960s, is not, strictly speaking, 'relationship work', and has a proven track record for creating deep openings for many sincere seekers. However, like all other methods that involve interaction between two people, even if at the most austere level, it runs the risk of being corrupted – as for example, when used by two people with motives other than awakening, as discussed in Chapter 17.)

It is arguable that all transformational work involving 'relationship processing' does not ultimately 'work'. That is something of a severe statement and requires close explanation. The first thing to acknowledge is that, as discussed in our earlier chapter on 'feel-good' spirituality, many seekers confuse awakening with a state of 'no-anxiety'. Relationship methods, when used in a standard transformational workshop or seminar setting, can and most commonly do result in a lowering of anxiety – that is, in a temporary fix. The term 'fix' may seem unnecessarily dismissive, and indeed it is difficult to argue against relationship methods when the results (forgiveness, emotional healing, more harmony and peace, etc.) are so appealing. However, unless the core issue behind all the relationship dysfunction is addressed, nothing ultimately changes. It merely *cycles*, eventually to arise again, Phoenix-like, in some future relationship drama, even if with a different person. Like a fix that eventually wears out, we sooner or later need a new working part – or to try to fix the old part yet again.

What is really going on here? Why is relationship drama so

difficult to escape from, and why is it so powerfully persistent – even to the point that most well-meaning psycho-spiritual techniques designed to address and work with it, in a nitty-gritty 'in the trenches' fashion, fail to yield any profound transformation in the *individual*?

The answer to that question is two-fold. The first part we have already touched on, that being the issue of motivation. Any relationship drama, or relationship 'spirituality', will simply be an exercise in useless repetition, ultimately a lot of 'sound and fury signifying nothing', if the essential truth is not exposed: we are not truly interested in awakening, we want to be *recognized and loved by someone else*. The very need to be loved by the other, demands that the other *exist*. And it is herein where we gain insight into the second answer to the question. Relationship drama is so difficult to escape from for the simple reason that we *do not want* to escape from it. We do not want to escape from it, because it is the most effective way to perpetuate the illusion that we exist as a distinct person, in contrast to others. To give up relationship drama would be to surrender the very core of the ego and its dualistic perception of the universe we exist in.

In short, we're having too much fun with this whole game, this entire cosmic dance of separation and interrelatedness, to abandon it. Only very rare individuals, here and there throughout time, reach a point of genuine completion with the dance of 'I and Thou', of distinct entities, and of the whole kingdom of 'me and mine'. When we are at that point, we will know it. And until we are at that point, all talk we make about 'Oneness', about the 'illusion of the individual', and so forth, is mostly empty talk – spiritual bullshit.

Is there, then, any point in even concerning ourselves with awakening, enlightenment, or a 'spiritual path'? There is. All is not lost (although the previous paragraph may seem to be implying that). The mere fact that we even go through the motions of walking a spiritual path indicates that we are responding to some sort of ancient 'call', like a bird that has strayed far from home and is sensing a distant beacon calling it to return. We may not understand all the implications of this call, but somehow, we hear it; somehow, we glimpse its dim and distant glow in the vast dark of our world. Not all of our inner being – in fact, not even a small percentage of it – may be 'on board' to make this long journey, but that doesn't matter. The greatest treasures are those found against seemingly insurmountable odds. We are compelled to go, because we are *called*.

Lie Detector Questions: Is your search for truth, or for love? To the extent that you think it is more for the latter, do you believe you know what love is? How capable are you of loving another in such a way that truly supports who they are? How much do you truly love Truth?

Part IV

Awakening: Seven Steps up a Challenging Mountain

Note to the Reader

This part of the book is based on the idea that the path of spiritual awakening runs through five essential stages, which are further elaborated on in the section following, in 'Seven Steps up a Challenging Mountain'. (In the five-fold scheme below, the stages of 'Preparation' and 'Purification' are broken down into two steps each, resulting in seven steps overall).

A good argument can be mounted that to try to define the awakening process in such a linear fashion is ultimately contrived or even arbitrary. My main point in doing so, however, is to stress the idea that an awakening experience in and of itself means little. The real test is what follows it. An awakening experience is akin to being handed a flashlight in a dark mansion. Now that we have some light, we get down to the nitty-gritty work of sorting out our house. This is why Awakening is designated as only 'stage 2' in the scheme below, to be followed by essential levels of purification and integration, and only later by the possibility of a deeper, stabilized and mature awakening, that I define by the terms 'enlightenment' and 'illumination'.

1. **Preparation**. It is here where we first set foot on the path, motivated (usually) by some sort of disappointment with our life. This 'preparation' almost always requires of us that we *let go* of something, in order to allow for something new to enter. At the same time, we need to develop a degree of willingness to embrace the unknown, because what awaits us (provided we keep going) is a new way of viewing reality, one which we have not been taught before.

125

2. **Awakening**. It is common on the path to have some sort of 'awakening' experience at a fairly early stage on our journey. (In fact, in rare cases, this awakening may precede the 'preparation' stage, via accidents, illnesses, or other spontaneous and entirely unexpected circumstances that may create inner openings. But even when this is the case, we must typically 'backtrack' and cover the 'preparation' stages.) This awakening can have a wide range of depth and quality – everything from a minor opening or glimpse of higher truth, to a major breakthrough in understanding that seemingly turns our world upside down. All wisdom traditions have names for these awakenings, but all more or less agree that such an experience does not mark the end of our journey; on the contrary, it is usually just the beginning. However, it is common at this stage to misinterpret the experience (in an almost endless number of ways) and to cease our efforts in walking the path. Many possibilities occur at this point, but the most typical way to go astray is to *reduce the experience to a memory* – something to lament the passing of, or something to boast about. A less common but more problematical result is to set oneself up as a teacher prematurely, something that usually results in considerable suffering later on (mostly, for the teacher, although on occasion for the teacher's students, sometimes in catastrophic ways).

3. **Purification**. The initial awakening experience (regardless of degree of quality, or even if it occurs several times) is almost always followed by a period of hardship (sometimes considerable) in which a natural purification is occurring. Other terms for this phase are 'integration' or 'deliverance', although 'purification' is simplest and clearest. What is happening here is that the rest of who we are has to catch up with our awakening and whatever new perspective it has generated.

A good analogy is as follows: our entire being can be thought of as something like a mansion with many rooms. For a long time it lacked working lights and was mostly in darkness, with many rooms we'd never entered (as best we can remember). With awakening, the house now has power and some lighting. After enjoying the fascinating quality of light and our ability to *see* (at least to some extent), we then set out exploring our mansion. What we discover, almost always, is that some of our rooms are a mess, and need considerable work to clean up. This cleaning process is often unpleasant. It can also go on for a very long time.

It's during the third stage, Purification, where many fall off the path. There are all sorts of ways to go wrong at this point. But most of them boil down to a failure to be deeply honest with ourselves. 'Falling off the path', in this context, can be very tricky – because it's entirely possible to *fall off without realizing it.* The Purification stage is far more important than most realize. As a respected Zen master once said, 'Zen is character.' It's a potent statement because we tend to associate awakening with something that transcends our behavior in the world; that is, that insight trumps action, that realization trumps character, when in fact both are equally important. The essence of the Purification stage, alongside the need for radical honesty, is the matter of 'joining opposites' – that is, the need for us to become a whole person, no longer divided and at war with ourselves. To the extent that we resist the needed resolution of opposites, we will find our 'purification' to be very rough.

It is possible to teach in the Purification stage. In fact, the vast majority of spiritual teachers are in this stage. Further awakenings commonly occur in this stage as well.

4. **Enlightenment.** This is the preliminary stage of bona fide self-realization, in which one begins to manifest a true inner consistency and wisdom that arises from having passed through most of the rougher ordeals of purification. In truth, few make it this far. Most of us who have had a bona fide 'awakening event' spend the rest of our lives in stage 3, purifying and integrating, and deepening. (Paradoxically, it is here, in the fourth stage, where the illusory nature of 'stages' begins to be understood; that our essential nature is 'unborn'.)

5. **Illumination.** This is a deeper and fuller stage of enlightenment.

The candle of awareness and wisdom burns consistently at this point, no longer going out or even flickering. This is the domain of the great sages. All that remains at this point in terms of interest in 'others' is compassion and the intention to help. Needless to say, very few make it this far.

***

What follows are seven chapters describing the journey of awakening by on occasion using the metaphor of climbing a mountain. In general I try to stay away from specialized 'spiritual words', as I find that these are too easily misunderstood. But in some places such a word is necessary in order to point toward the peak of possibility. Herein I use the word 'Reality' for that, first letter capitalized. This can be taken to represent the highest principles of life, and our greatest potential.

Chapter 22

Preparation I: Abandoning Ship

It is scarcely possible to recognize the deeper truths of Reality, or experience the fruits of such recognition, without first letting go of what does not work.

There is no growth, no awakening in life, *to* life, without first seeing and acknowledging our existing *disappointment.* By 'disappointment' is not meant our usual, day-to-day grievances about the common matters of life – rather, what is meant here is that core-level disappointment, that gnawing sense that something is missing, that something is out of focus in our life at a very fundamental level – that so much more is possible, even if we are very unclear as to what that 'so much more' might be.

As long as we don't see this essential disappointment, or remain in denial of it, we live a life of mediocrity. We spend much, if not all, of our lives settling for 'the lesser of evils'. We get stuck in routines, living in quiet desperation, accepting something limited, something lacking in life, in juice, in brilliance, in depth, in quality, in power. In short, we play small.

Why do we play small? We do so because deep down we do not believe we are worth anything more. A low, or poor, self-image is practically a universal trait. Those with what we label 'self-esteem issues' do not disguise this (often because they lack the ability to do so). Those who appear outwardly confident or in control (the 'successful' in the world) are all too often 'puffing up' to guard against seeing and feeling the reality of their doubts and fears and insecurities. They are just more insulated, more cleverly defended, than those with seeming lesser confidence.

Why do we suffer from a generally low opinion of ourselves? Because we know, at some hard-to-define depth, that we are not living our greatest potential. If we are especially sensitive, we may even suspect that we do not even actually *exist* the way we assume we do – that we are living in a strange kind of dream-world – and that the only reason we've come to accept this 'dream-world' is because we've been taught that it is 'reality'.

The Personality and the Potential Self

To go further into this idea, we are going to use two terms here: the personality, and the potential self. You may recall that in the Introduction and in Chapter 1, a fundamental problem with a similar type of conceptual division – between 'ordinary' and 'great, spiritual' self – was looked at. The issue examined there had to do with misusing the concept as a means of escaping the deeper and necessary work of honest self-examination – essentially, copping out from looking at ourselves by hiding behind spiritual ideals. Once clear that we are not falling into such a basic trap, we can begin to re-examine the idea from a fresh angle, as a means to seeing deeply into our essential nature.

By 'personality' we mean all of our personal tendencies that are part of the 'front' that we show the world – the *persona* (which aptly comes from the Greek word for 'mask'). This 'front' is in many ways an elaborate act. However, we become deeply identified with it – we do not think of it as an 'act', and most people feel offended if the idea is put to them that their personality is basically false, a conditioned form of acting. Taking offense is understandable, as our sense of 'me' is largely tied up in the personality. Most have no idea of who they are (or might be) outside of personality.

In the context of awakening to our highest possibilities, the personality is seen to be largely a product of conditioning and usually an obstacle to higher truth. The personality is brought about by external forces upon us – family (and other societal influences) shaping and molding us the way they desire us to be – or the opposite, us reacting against family forces or other external influences and intentionally developing traits opposite to how *they* are. Either way, the personality evolves largely as a result of family conditioning. Through the personality we become simply an extension of our family. We 'carry the torch' – and even if we rebel and seemingly become 'opposite' to our family conditioning, we are still at the mercy of it, and so still, essentially, are molded by it.

The idea of the potential self is that it represents a consciousness and a way of living that is essentially free of cruder external influences. The vast majority of people are not living to their best potential, nor do they even have an inkling of its nature. The vast majority of people live their entire lives in a strange kind of dreamland (or nightmare). Occasionally this dream-world gets rudely or painfully disrupted, at which point a 'mini-awakening' of some sort might occur. This may be brought about by a crisis involving an accident, relationship breakup, health problem, or other unexpected and difficult circumstance. What most commonly happens, however, is that the 'mini-awakening' is quickly forgotten as we learn to cope with the unforeseen change in our life. We adapt (as we humans are so good at doing) and soon go back to sleep again.

What does it mean to be 'asleep'? Typically we spend about 30% of our lives in bed, slumbering, living in dreams. But in fact most, if not all, of our life is lived in a kind of dream-world, thoroughly asleep to our higher possibilities. The essence of this sleep is being *identified* with that which we are not. We are like a character playing a role in a theatrical play. Having played the role for so long, we have come to believe that we *are* that character. As Shakespeare once wrote:

> We are such stuff
> As dreams are made on; and our little life
> Is rounded with a sleep.

The process of waking up to our higher potential begins only when we recognize, however vaguely, that we have been asleep. We cannot escape from jail without first recognizing that this is in fact where we are. We cannot stop suffering in the role we are playing within the drama of our life without first recognizing that we are in fact *playing a role*.

In order for this to happen – and this is true for the vast majority of people – we need to get humbled in some fashion. Our pride, our arrogance, our attachment to 'being right', needs to be dented or broken in some way. For many people this happens via relationship heartbreak or health issues; for others, by personal failures, financial struggles, social embarrassments, or other humiliations. Here it is useful to remember that all setbacks, failures, and especially the feeling of embarrassment, are keys to inner growth, because they cause our pretensions, our pride, to be stripped away (even if only momentarily), leaving us exposed, defenseless, and vulnerable. In other words, adversity in life, if it is strong enough to stop us in our tracks, can bring about deep honesty. Such honesty, directed upon ourselves, is a golden key to wisdom.

Prior to our arrogance, our stubborn attachment to insisting we are right about everything, being broken or at the least sufficiently shaken up, we are too proud, too full of ourselves to allow anything greater to arise from within. We cannot awaken to our higher possibilities if we are too much in control. Our control needs to be derailed, our grip on our attachments needs to be loosened, and our hold on the role we are playing needs to be disrupted in some way, in order for a shaft of light to enter our life.

It is one thing to say that we have been living a false life, even inhabiting a false self – and that there is, in reality, a greater potential self, something much deeper, vaster, and more powerful, awaiting us. It is another entirely to cultivate a willingness to begin to grow beyond our personality – our repetitive behavioral patterns and routines. This willingness only comes about when we are truly ready to let go of the romance we have been having with our delusions, our dreams, and our suffering.

We have been living a false life with illusions and dreams because that is what we have *wanted*. We are always doing what we want, at the deepest level. We play small, and live in dreams, because it is comfortable for us, like old shoes that fit snugly and easily. If we are in hell, it's because, underneath all our posturing and pretensions and complaining, that's where we want to be. (This viewpoint should not be conflated with 'victim-bashing', but taken more as a challenge to examine our underlying motives and agendas in the face of our most difficult life circumstances.)

We want to be asleep not only because it's comfortably familiar, but because we are *interested* in it. In order to have a romance with something, we need to be deeply interested in it – fascinated, bewitched, mesmerized, hypnotized. Like a child that never grows out of his or her childhood toys, we remain hooked on our suffering, on our limitations, because we have not yet grown sufficiently tired of them.

The main problem with all so-called 'work on self', or the 'spiritual path' in general, is a failure by many of those involved in it to find it *sufficiently interesting*. For many it seems to lack juice, vitality, drama, fullness. It is something like church that must be attended once a week. We cannot quite relate deeply to ideas of 'enlightenment', the 'divine', 'ultimate truth', or 'Reality' – even if we already seem to be involved in seeking, however tentatively, such things. For many who embrace these ideas, they remain *ideas*, and are rarely lived. Other matters, 'mundane' reality, have a stronger grip on us. And so the rub: we may think we want to grow, to wake up to our higher potential; however, in all but the rarest of cases *we do not really want this*. We want to continue our romance with our suffering, with our limitations, with playing small. This is where we are more at home and ultimately prefer to remain.

The Gates of Hell
In Part I of Dante's famous work *The Divine Comedy*, called *Inferno*, he described an inscription at the 'gates of hell' which read: 'Abandon all hope, ye who enter here.'

This is a powerful metaphor, but the way we are considering it is not the way that Dante intended it. He meant it to refer to those who are entering hell. What we suggest here, rather, is that it is in fact the most important 'magic formula' for *escaping* from hell.

What is hell but ignorance of our highest possibilities? As mentioned, ignorance of it exists because we are not sufficiently interested in it. We are more caught up in the lesser forms of 'salvation' offered by the world. And so, until we truly begin to grow tired with our routine life and our personality – and more to the point, begin to *abandon hope* that these can ever bring fulfillment – we will never leave our world of dreams and nightmares.

The process of abandoning hope is begun when we stop resisting the deeper movement of our inner being. We are like a wondrous figure locked inside a block of marble, formless and blind, and Reality itself is attempting to carve this block of marble to free the wondrous being – to free *us* – so that we can escape and begin, for the first time, to truly live. But we are our own worst enemy. We continually frustrate the movements of existence to free us from the block of marble, because we have convinced ourselves that to leave the marble – to leave prison – is almost certainly to die.

And so we continue to have hope, we continue to cling to our rotting ship, which actually long ago sank to the bottom of the ocean. In fact, we dwell in the bottom of the ocean, having adapted to its insufferably heavy pressure, its deep darkness, and its bare hint of freedom. Like ghosts wandering in some deep-sea castle, we move about in sluggish mediocrity, all the time resisting a natural 'up-current' that would bring us to the brilliant clarity of the surface.

How do we allow this natural force that seeks to liberate us to operate in our lives? How do we stop interfering with our own natural movement toward truth?

In fact, the process has already begun. We would likely not be reading these words and considering these matters if that were not the case. From one perspective the process of awakening began in us long ago; it only seems vague, or entirely forgotten, because of our fascination with the objects of the universe. The universe is an infinite

playground of forms and objects, all dazzling and breathtakingly engaging, like the gems of a necklace or crown. These gems sparkle and pull us in, capturing our attention and becoming our lesser gods and goddesses. We serve them with deep devotion and, above all, with genuine interest in their existence and nature. We are, however, so much more than a mere object, even if it be a precious gemstone. We are an infinite potential, a pure creative space, an unblemished vastness.

Vastness, alas, by its very nature is intimidating. We fear getting lost in vastness. And so we compensate by clinging, by attaching ourselves to what seems to make up our immediate realm. We establish our own private 'empire', our own personal reality show, in which we 'rule' and star. We become the architect of our own prison, the screenwriter of our own melodramatic play – regardless of how pathetic that play may be, and our role in it.

The day inevitably comes, however, when we begin to gain overwhelming evidence that the reality we have constructed is somehow flawed. 'Glitches' in the program begin to show up. Something is wrong, something is missing. We begin to sense that we've been duped, or if we are a bit more sensitive, we begin to suspect that we've duped ourselves.

It is at that point that our first key presents itself. This key is the decision, however vaguely formulated, to *abandon ship* – to get out, to make a U-turn, to drop a weight we have been carrying. That 'weight' may appear, at superficial glance, to be something in our life that is not serving us, that is clearly in the way of our expansion into something greater – such as a relationship caught in a deeply negative rut, or a dead-end vocation, or a social circle that is suffocating and limiting; or more to the point, an attitude, view, or position we hold that is slowly choking us with self-righteousness. But beyond that, we begin to glimpse the deeper issue, which is that we have been clutching onto security our whole life, clinging to the known, clinging to our limited self-image, because of a deep-seated fear of the unknown.

And so we make the most crucial of all decisions in embarking on the path of awakening: we decide to embrace the unknown.

Summary

1. Our journey toward Self-discovery and Reality only truly begins when we honestly recognize our core-level disappointment – the sense, however vague, that something essential is missing.

2. We 'play small' in general, and fail to recognize greater possibilities, because deep down we do not think highly of ourselves. At root, this is because we know, at some level, that something is fundamentally 'off' in our being, and with our existence. We are, in a sense, living a kind of lie. We are living in a type of self-constructed dream-world.

3. This dream-world is generated by our personality. The personality is founded largely on fear, guilt, attachments, and the need to control our life and minimize anxiety.

4. The dream-world begins its gradual process of dissolving when we recognize, even if only in glimpses at first, that we have been dreaming. This often involves our pride – or our self-image – taking a hit in some way.

5. We begin to see that the reason we have been lost in dreams (and nightmares) is because we have found them *interesting*. No matter how much we may complain about them, they have captured our attention, for whatever reasons, and that is why we have remained in our dream-world, stuck in repetitive patterns. *Because that is where we have wanted to be.*

6. We proceed further by allowing ourselves to *lose hope* with what clearly does not provide answers. We demonstrate this by *giving up*

something that is in the way of our proceeding further, in order to make space for something new.

7. Deep honesty must be summoned here. We are not to 'give up' a relationship, for example, as a way of 'getting more free' if really we are just running from something, or shirking responsibility. We must get clear on what is truly appropriate to let go of, and then do it. Often what we need to let go of is not an external matter, but rather an attitude, position, or view.

Chapter 23

Preparation II: Embracing the Unknown

We Are All Control Freaks

Our journey to Reality becomes sincere when we develop *courage*, and specifically the courage to face ourselves. Without this type of courage there is little hope of ever waking up in any authentic fashion. This courage is crucial in order for us to begin the process of becoming free of our conditioning. To do this we must decide, once and for all, not to shy away from the unknown. We humans generally seek to control our world because controlling makes us feel safe. It seems to give us some degree of security in which to defend ourselves from the lurking sense that we are frail, mortal creatures with a limited life-span and limited possibilities.

In the pre-industrial age, just a few hundred years ago, people in cities or towns rarely went out after dark because they feared the streets in the night hours. And for good reason: not only could they be robbed, they could fall into a ditch or stumble on a rock on the unpaved roads or be accosted by an animal. In modern times our streets may be illuminated at night but the primal fear of the unknown remains, always causing us to seek what is known and familiar in life. In short, we usually prefer even the known hell to the unknown. And that is why we repeat negative patterns over and over, continually banging our head against the same brick wall, each time hoping that maybe *this* time, the wall will break down and we can get to where it is we think we want to be.

There is a simple formula for growing in courage, intelligence, confidence, aliveness, and inner clarity, and it this: whenever possible in life, when presented with a choice between the known and the unknown – providing such a choice does not violate common-sense discernment – *choose the unknown*. This is because every time we walk down that 'dark street' toward the undiscovered, barely able to see what is around us, we are becoming more fearless, more willing to see that our wings are actually bigger than we thought they were. We become sharper and more present to life, to the power of this moment, as we venture into new territory and as we gather the courage to stop living a life of endless routine.

It is interesting to note that the word 'routine' derives from the same Latin root (*rupta*) as the word 'rupture' – meaning to 'break' or 'open by force'. For example, to break open a path in a forest leads to the path becoming a *route*. To follow the route regularly, back and forth, makes one's actions a *routine*. The irony lies in the fact that the original meaning of the word suggested the *breaking* or *opening* of something – and it does indeed require courage to 'break' something in our life that is not working – such as a self-defeating routine.

We are generally fiercely protective of our routines or very defensive if challenged about them. Few things in life drive us crazier than someone pushing us out of our comfort zone or suggesting that there is something wrong with our comfort zone ('Why aren't you different from the way you are?'). The reason we get so defensive is not just because we don't like criticism, but because we are afraid of the unknown. We have it hardwired in us to equate the unknown with death. For the ancients, to venture off into the night would mean a good chance of not returning. Human physical senses are not particularly strong (compared to many other animals) and on a dark night we are as good as blind. Our instincts tell us that the unknown is hazardous for our survival.

It is for this reason that comparatively few venture beyond the boundaries of mediocrity. It is also for this reason that even fewer embrace an authentic spiritual life, one given to a daily remembrance of truth, and to a daily effort to shine the light of attention *inward*, upon our being. That is because to do so is to encounter the unknown in the form of our own naked self – and in particular, in the form of our actual thought processes.

Where Do Thoughts Come From?

There is a fascinating experiment we can try: to sit quietly, and simply observe our own thoughts. For one who has never tried this, it can seem very difficult, owing to the natural tendency to become distracted by things around us, or even more commonly to get lost in thoughts ('daydreaming'). But if we keep trying, we eventually have an interesting experience: we actually *witness* a thought arising in our consciousness. We then realize that there is the thought, and there is 'me' witnessing it. There is an actual distinction between 'me' as observer, as witness, and the thought that is arising for me to observe. (Deeper realizations later reveal this to not be the whole picture, but for now this is how we are apt to understand it.)

If we are able to see this apparent distinction between 'me' as observer and 'my thoughts' (and it does not take too much effort to do so), we are then able to see something even more interesting. We are able to see that we have *no control* over the thought that is arising. It seems to appear of its own accord, 'popping' into existence seemingly out of nowhere. Try as hard as we might, we cannot find any 'thought-generator' in the background that is choosing what thought to have when. One moment the thought is not there, the next moment it is.

An even simpler way to recognize this is by paying attention to our dreams at night. It is the very essence of a dream to be comprised of one unpredictable scene unfolding after the next. We simply have no control. This is true even if we have a 'lucid dream' – a term commonly used to describe a dream where we know to some degree that we are dreaming – we still have no ultimate control over the dreamscape. We can control it to *some* extent, perhaps even a great deal if we are practiced, but sooner or later something always shows up in the dream that is a complete surprise to us.

From all this it soon becomes clear that every moment we exist in – whether in dreams at night, or during our waking daylight hours – carries with it the reality of the unknown. To quote Hamlet, we do not know 'what dreams may come'. We do not even know the 'conscious thought' that is coming next. To be conscious is to be in a perpetual state of facing the unknown.

None of this is truly hard to see. And yet remarkably we have the ability to fool ourselves into believing that we can actually control our lives; or even worse, believing that we can control others, or the world around us. The illusion of control results in us acquiring a false view of reality. The entire edifice of our life is constructed upon this basic delusion: that we are, somehow, in *control*. (And even if we believe the opposite about our life – that we are a helpless victim with no control at all and are simply being controlled by others – that too is a type of control. It is the belief that we *can* be controlled. More precisely, it is the belief that *others* have control. Either way, it is a belief in control.)

Knocking on the Door

Once sufficiently convinced of the illusion of control and of the need to embrace the unknown, we stand at the threshold of a great journey. We are, effectively, knocking on the door of truth for the first time.

The reason we are knocking on this door is because we are admitting just how little wisdom we actually have. We may be in possession of all kinds of facts and knowledge; we may even have considerable life experience. We may no longer be young. But all our facts, all our experience, all of what has passed for knowledge for us, is seen to have been inherited, borrowed, copied from other sources, parroted, mimicked, repeated. When we honestly take stock of ourselves we see that we have been buffeted by the winds of cause and effect, pushed along by a tide of momentum that is itself the product of the actions of our ancestors, and of the surrounding world, of all the factors that have influenced and shaped us into the person we seem to have become.

It is at this point that we need be on our guard against succumbing to a despair that may arise in us. We may think that our whole life has been a waste, 'a tale of sound and fury signifying nothing'. This is a crucial point on our journey. Christ makes reference to it when he says, 'He that loveth his life shall lose it; and he that hateth his life in this world shall keep it unto life eternal.' (John 12:25, KJV)

He is referring to the crossroads of choosing between defending the life we have known – with all its illusions – and *letting it go* in order to enter the unknown. To defend our life is to 'loveth it', but because it has been based on illusion, we can only sooner or later 'lose it'. To 'hateth our life' means, in this context, to recognize the illusion of control and decide that we are finally ready to face Reality in the truest sense of that word.

What is Reality? It is that which reveals itself to us when the dust from our 'inner eye' has been cleaned, when we can begin to see clearly through the windows of our soul – both outwardly at the infinity that surrounds us, and inwardly at the infinity within. We begin to glimpse that this Reality has one essential feature – it is infinitely greater than our personality. We are immersed in it, like a fish in a fathomless sea. It is not 'within us'; rather, *we* are within *it*. At times it may appear that we must turn within to sense this Reality, to taste it; that we need to pray, meditate, contemplate, and spend time in solitude. And there is certainly truth to this. However, this Reality is not only to be found via silent withdrawal. It is also all around us, in the very immediacy of this moment. Truth is not truly *within*; it is the infinity that includes both the apparent inner and the outer, and in which we abide.

We Cannot Truly Be Alone

We do not achieve anything in life on our own, for to be 'on our own' is yet another illusion. We are always in relationship with existence. So to avoid relationship in its many faces is not the solution – even *if* it becomes clear that we must abandon certain particular relationships to proceed. This is a paradox. We must often let go of some relationships in order to brighten inwardly, and yet we must not avoid relationships either. Running from our issues does not solve them. What we must let go of is the deadening routine of relating that does nothing but sustain our slumber. That might mean changing the inner dynamics of our relationships rather than releasing them. But whatever way we proceed, we must leave behind whatever we have made into an excuse for avoiding our greater potential. We must abandon our lesser gods.

Reality is to be found both in silent solitude and in the noisy marketplace. It is to be found in the vast terrain of consciousness, whether focused inward in spiritual discipline, or shone outward in moment-by-moment relating to the world around us. The main point is to see that we are immersed in something and that this something is a perpetual *surprise*. As a good experiment we can sit on a bench in a park or stroll down a busy street in a city, or sit at a sidewalk café, and simply pay attention to the constant surprises of each and every moment. The miraculous unfolding of this moment is such that nothing is repeated in the same details, ever. It is only in our private delusions, powered by dreams of control and fear, that things can possibly appear predictable or commonplace.

To be 'boring' is to be predictable. The word originally was taken from the term 'bore', which referred to a 'boring tool' moving forward through the earth in a predictable fashion. However, if we pay attention to our thoughts, it soon becomes clear that boredom arises from a failure to properly perceive Reality. We see instead only the dull, predictable movement of our own thoughts, of our own static perceptions, beliefs, and opinions. It is our own mind that causes us to see a 'boring' existence around us. In short, whenever we think we are bored, it is because *we ourselves* have become boring; and more, in our very fear of the unknown, we have always been boring, even if we have been practiced in convincing ourselves (and others) otherwise.

To embrace the unknown is to die to boredom once and for all; to shed the illusion that we can control Reality, or that Reality is somehow beholden to us, obligated to entertain us by sending us charismatic people to keep us endlessly off balance, or to flatter us so as to help us forget our insecurities or self-loathing. To shed boredom is to begin to grow up, truly, and to enter an adult life where we begin to see our utter lack of status in the world. By 'lack of status' is not meant inability to contribute; on the contrary, each of us has a powerful and unique contribution to make to the blossoming of the human race. Each of us is a particular color in an infinite spectrum of color shining through the prism of the universe. 'Lack of status' means rather that we come to face the stark reality that we may be unique, but we carry no specialness. We have no 'distinct society' status within; we are not more important, or less important, than our brother or sister.

It is at this point that something new begins to arise within us. As we sincerely make these most sacred of twin decisions to abandon the false and embrace the unknown, we begin to enter a kind of love affair with truth. We become passionate about Reality. This passion is the fuel that fires our journey past the more difficult – and treacherous – obstacles thrown up by the ego-mind that await us in the path up the mountain. In doing so, we begin to catch glimpses of the top of the mountain, however distant. We begin to taste awakening.

Summary

1. We control because we are afraid of the unknown.

2. We cannot truly grow in life without entering the unknown.

3. Where our thoughts are coming from is a mystery. As a famous Zen master once said, 'Not even a sage can utter a word about that Realm from which thoughts issue – not even a Buddha.' Therefore, even the place where our thoughts arise from is unknown.

4. We are ready to truly grow only when we can admit how little we really know – that is, how much of our 'knowledge' is in fact borrowed.

5. We do not really achieve anything in life on our own. We cannot be truly alone, no matter how much we may try.

6. To truly embrace the unknown is to become passionate about truth.

Chapter 24

Awakening: Passion for Truth

As touched on earlier, we remain somewhere, or in something, only because that is where we truly want to be. In finding something interesting, compelling, attractive, we are involved in giving it our attention. This in turn 'charges it with energy'; that is, our attention makes real what we direct it on, just like a searchlight illuminates something shrouded in darkness. Prior to turning our light on it, it did not exist in our direct field of experience. By giving it attention it leaps into appearance. By giving it prolonged and sustained attention it becomes so real that it is part of our life, and can even become the *center* of our life. Worse, it can come to control us.

The problem is that what we direct our attention to are things, objects – whether they be a person, a car, a house, money, sex, status, accomplishments, and so on. Once we begin to see that none of these things can provide us with higher truth, there is the real possibility of directing our attention – and more to the point, our passion – toward truth. We begin, in a very real sense, a love affair with truth.

To be 'in love' with something is to be fascinated by it, discovering its endlessly interesting quality. To make such a love enduring, we have only to allow ourselves to enter it. Much like going into an infinite ocean, we begin by getting our feet wet, and then gradually wading in, eventually becoming comfortable in its depths but never losing our fascination with its essence.

The essence of higher truth is that it yields both courage and deep peace. That may seem like an unlikely combination but in fact each makes the other possible. The 'peace' arises from the powerful conviction that we are on the path toward Home, regardless of how far the path may appear to stretch out before us, and so gives rise to the courage to continue *no matter what.* The courage arises from the certainty that we have finally turned our back on the 'lesser gods' of our previous journey, and so recognize a deep peace that accompanies such a realization, something like a war-weary soldier feeling relieved about the fact that his war is *finally over.*

That does not mean, of course, that battles do not remain. On the contrary, our old habits put up a fierce struggle to retain control and will generally test us every step of the way. But as we begin to see, first in peeks and glimpses and then in longer views, the magnificence of the Reality that we are in fact immersed in every moment, the seductive power of our old habits begins to fade. We acquire a *taste for higher truth*, and our life becomes oriented toward that. It is here, very often, where our first genuine 'spiritual awakening event' may occur, because we have prepared the ground for an entirely new understanding to arise.

The Awakening Experience

Technically it is true that enlightenment, the realization of our true nature, is not an 'experience', simply because an 'experience' requires a separate ego-self to confirm and evaluate the experience. If a self remains that is confirming and evaluating, then clearly we are still in the realm of duality – me here, and 'enlightenment' over there (as an object). *Ultimate* Reality is not an experience because it reveals the underlying non-duality of existence, in which no separate self can abide.

However, prior to being established in such a condition, a separate self seems to remain, and thus it is true (in the vast majority of cases) that initial awakenings are indeed classifiable as experiences. This experience, if profound enough, is more properly an 'event' in which we glimpse non-duality. After the event, 'returning' to our conventional self and its usual dualistic perspective, we struggle to make sense of the glimpse, and it gets reduced to a memory. That does not mean this memory is invalid, however. On the contrary, it becomes both the key and the inspiration to beckon us on, especially if we return to dim and dark valleys.

The essence of the glimpse of enlightenment – what I'm calling here an 'awakening' – is seeing and understanding that *all is as it is*, that Reality is seamless and already Whole, and that we are in no way separate from that Whole. A good example of the idea of 'all is as it is' can be found in the Zen tradition, where Hakuin (profiled in Chapter 32) had one of his awakenings precipitated by the sudden sound of a bell. This sound, though faint and from a distance, resonated deeply within him, resulting in his 'mind's eye' opening to the radiance and perfection of this moment.

The bell had nothing to do with it. It could have been a bird, or a thunderclap, or perhaps the sound of running water. It might even have been someone farting. The idea is that the sound represented and embodied the intrinsic perfection of things as they are. It is our ego-self that struggles with reality and that is in a perpetual state of resistance to it. Realization is a state of effortless acceptance of what is (which, of course, does not imply passivity – 'effortless acceptance' can also imply activity on our part).

Awakening experiences also commonly involve a deep and direct realization of the inherent 'emptiness' (to use the Buddhist term) of the self, meaning that we see and understand that we have no essential existence as a discretely separate (and isolated) entity, that that is a profound illusion (and ultimately the source of all of our suffering).

Having had a taste of Reality, a glimpse of what is possible, there is the accompanying possibility of learning to discern the difference between desire and passion. This is important, because our awakening, and the insights and energies it releases, needs to be actualized and shared with the world we are part of.

The Difference between Desire and Passion
Desire and passion are two different conditions. Desire is fear-based and always ultimately increases our sense of disconnection from existence and isolation in life. Passion flows directly from higher

truths. When true passion is directly experienced it takes us closer to inner fulfillment.

The difference between desire and passion has to do with what they are reinforcing. Desire ultimately reinforces division within us and separation from the world around us, because its basic message is that we are *lacking something,* and that we must find that something *out there,* somewhere, in order to be completed. Once that something, be it thing or person, is attained, we usually want more of it. Even when we become tired with the object of our desire, it is only a matter of time before we desire something else, which is typically closely related to the previous attainment. We become like the 'hungry ghosts' of Buddhist cosmology, beings who are perpetually famished and can never jam enough food inside of their long, narrow throats to fill up their huge bellies.

Desire is ultimately founded on a mistaken view – the view that we are truly separate from the universe – and that we must *get things* from the universe in order to be fulfilled. The motto of desire is 'Seek but never find.' This motto keeps alive the illusion that we are separate from everything else. The further irony is, that which we desire is that which we believe makes us happy, but every time we attain this 'happiness' we reinforce the mistaken belief that our happiness lies *outside of us.* That necessitates us continuing to seek for a Holy Grail that never truly materializes, like a mirage that recedes the closer we try to get to it.

Desire is directly related to self-rejection and belief systems that we are inherently flawed. The more we are in denial of these belief systems, repressing them so we don't have to feel the pain that goes with them, the more we will be running away from the pain, toward the object we desire – thinking that this object will take away our pain. We become locked into an existence of addictions, endlessly looking for our next fix so as to distract us from our core-level pain, fear, and feelings of inner emptiness. We get hooked on desire – whether for food, stimulants, sex, relationships, material things, status, power, fame, recognition, even 'spiritual growth', and so on

– in the hopes of papering over our negative self-image.

Honest self-assessment and honest expression are critical to the process of bringing about the shift from desire to passion. By honestly facing our inner fears we become more authentic. This authenticity serves to wean us off our dependency on the outer objects of our desires. We begin to take responsibility for our issues and psychological baggage. In doing so we gradually become aware of the infinite potential for excitement – and even freedom – both within us and inherent in life itself. From this excitement and empowerment we tap into our capacity for *passion*.

Passion is the direct link to our highest reason for being. It is what informs us of our greatest calling in life. It is not dependent on others and yet may work happily in cooperation with many, if need be. It can also function without stimulus from others. True passion enables us to be truly alone – or truly with others. Desire, while able to operate blissfully when wedded to its object of attainment (whatever we think we desire), withers and crumbles when alone, or creates endless problems – games of manipulation – when with others who seem not to fulfill our desires.

The ability to be *truly alone* yields the ability to be *truly with others*. It is passion, free of desire, that marks the mature level that enables us to deeply experience others, *without wanting anything from them*. To be with someone, without wanting anything from them – even if only for one moment in time – is the hallmark of both maturity and passion, free of possessive desire. It also gives rise to compassion, the most mature flowering of passion.

Passion and Compassion

To desire someone is to see them as an object to be used. To feel passion for someone is to rejoice inwardly in the sharing of consciousness, of energy, *with* them. If desire objectifies the other, passion renders them a co-creator with us.

An important point needs to be raised here. Desire is not to be regarded as something 'bad', something morally problematic, something to be avoided or feared or denied. No. Avoidance, denial, repression or pious moralizing is not the way. Desire is deeply intertwined with our personality, but our personality is not to be crushed, denied, or feared. It is merely the force of habit. Desires will continue to arise strongly within us, often in the form of desiring to objectify others – to see a woman or man as nothing but a body or a wallet or a source of energy, attention, flattery, or happiness for us – as a means to an end. At times we may want to go with these desires, and may even resent truth-teachings for 'getting in the way', for making us feel guilty. All of this is common and to be expected. The idea is to keep our eyes open as we explore desire. As we develop our passion for higher truth, we will want to increasingly experiment with bringing awareness into our older habits and routines. It's not reasonable to expect our negative habits and desires to evaporate overnight. However, what *is* possible, and what is required, is to use our old habits and desires as a training ground for being awake. We do this by attempting to maintain some level of awareness, of watchfulness, as we engage in these old habits and desires. We practice self-observation as we walk down our old familiar paths. For example, when manifesting negative behavior, our challenge is to pause in the middle of it and bring awareness to our present-time actions. When eating junk food, we do the same. When watching a conventional TV program, we try to maintain a degree of awareness and intelligent inquiry while doing so (not to become righteously judgmental, but simply to become actually present in the midst of what we are watching, perhaps without much attention, or perhaps because we have 'nothing better to do').

We do all this until such point as the paths become old and worn, no longer interesting. At that point we are truly ready to drop our old and useless habits. As we awaken to a passion for truth, as we begin to feel *inspired* – in the literal sense of that word, to 'breathe in spirit' – we begin to be capable of *compassion*. When Christ said, 'Love your enemies', he was pointing toward that highest expression of love – in short, this is love that *does not manipulate*. It is compassion that enables us to purify our character at deeper levels because it allows us to disentangle our relationships – to begin to truly become free from all elements of co-dependency, no matter how subtle.

Compassion is not the same as false piety, although false piety or phony holiness can and often does masquerade as compassion. Our 'compassion' is false if we are in denial of our desires. This is why it is essential to investigate our desires with awareness, because if they are merely repressed, our compassion will be cultivated, practiced – it will be false.

Unconditional love – compassion – is indeed our highest potential in relating with others, but we will be surprised by our inability to exercise true compassion, by how controlling, jealous, insecure, afraid, or just plain coldly indifferent we can be.

As our passion for higher truth begins to grow and mature, the personality – the entire history of our old habits and patterns – begins to put up a fight. It is at this point that it becomes essential for us to develop 'radical honesty'.

Summary

1. As we begin to truly see that which is false in our life, we have the possibility of developing a hunger – and specifically a passion – for higher truth.

2. Passion for higher truth is essential if we are to wake up to, and realize, our highest potential.

3. It is common to have an awakening experience at this time, which usually gets reduced to a memory.

4. There is a crucial difference between desire and passion. Desire is always based on the belief that we lack something, and so need someone, or something, to fill that lack. But this is ultimately an

endless task. Desires can never be truly fulfilled, in the strictest sense. The very mechanism of desire rather needs to be unearthed, and its raw energy converted into passion.

5. True passion leads naturally to the capacity for true *com*passion – the ability to disentangle from messy relationship patterns and to truly grant freedom, both to others and to ourselves.

Chapter 25

Purification I: Radical Honesty

There Is No Shortcut to God

Following our initial awakening (regardless of its depth or duration), we typically enter into a period of purification (which may include further awakenings). This phase can be painful and drawn out, or it can pass with relatively less raw suffering – depending mostly on our willingness to 'be wrong' about our views, to let go of attachments and positions we maintain that are slowly poisoning us. If not – if we remain rigidly righteous even *after* experiencing an opening to higher truth – we are going to get cooked mercilessly by existence (not to mention, we may become a menace to others).

Our journey to higher truth and Reality is not like climbing a mountain from bottom to top along one relatively straight uphill path. No. For most seekers it is more like alternating periods of ascending followed by periods of descending into 'valleys'. It is possible and even common to get hung up in these valleys, lost, distracted, and to forget we were ever trying to get to the top of the mountain in the first place.

In this metaphor the valley is symbolic of the realization that we have been bypassing certain keys areas within us – that we have been trying to *find a shortcut to God* – and so we have to go back down into the valley in order to keep ourselves properly balanced. After a period of time in the valley we are ready again to resume our ascent up the mountain. What enables us to recognize the need to visit the 'valley', and eventually to leave it and continue climbing again, is *radical honesty*.

The word 'radical', although now usually implying 'unconventional', has gone through several changes in meaning over the centuries. The word stems from the Latin *radix*, meaning 'root'. It originated in a word referring to the essence or core of something. To be radically honest is, in this sense, to apply honesty as a sharp, uncompromising light directly upon ourselves. It is to leave no stone unturned in our journey up the mountain.

The reason we have to make occasional 'descents into valleys' is because, in applying radical honesty in looking at ourselves, we become aware that we need to handle matters, to clean up unfinished business. If we fail to cultivate radical honesty we become prone to bypassing key areas on our journey that we need to visit. Put another way, our spiritual development begins to outpace our psychological maturity. We may begin to get very real glimpses of the peak of the mountain, while other parts of our life lag behind. We may be out of integrity on certain issues. We may have unfinished business in some of our relationships. We may have turned too many blind eyes to 'mere other matters' in our pursuit of the lofty mountaintop.

Radical honesty arises as a function of our passion for higher truth. Although the truth we seek is in fact *ultimate* truth, it does not ignore the 'lesser' truths, such as those that are part of our need for personal accountability. Committing ourselves to the journey to the highest peak does not mean that we get free bailouts for the parts of our journey that we have chosen to ignore.

This does not mean that our life needs to be in perfect order for us to proceed on the path to enlightenment. The Buddha famously left his wife and child (without warning) to go wandering in the forest for six years before his great awakening. There are even rare stories of prison inmates attaining deep levels of spiritual awakening while serving out their terms. We do not need to be squeaky clean examples of integrity in order to cultivate a deep interest in ultimate truth.

That said, our life does need to be 'together' to a degree in order to truly make the journey (as opposed to going through the motions). To what degree this must be so falls to each individual to determine, but a general rule of thumb is that if an issue is bothering us, weighing on our mind, feeling like a weight that we are dragging around, then it is good to address it and clean it up as best we can before trying to proceed further on the path. It is difficult to climb a mountain if we are carrying too much weight. To 'shed weight' is to take a side trip into a valley, until such time as the matter is handled, whereupon we continue our ascent – lighter and less distracted. Further, we begin to see that this 'side trip' into the valley to deal with the 'uncooked business' was not a mere pit stop; it was itself an essential part of our overall maturation. The mountain path is not complete without its valleys. In fact, the very issue we are avoiding often *is* our mountain path.

Facing the Guardian: Fear and Guilt

By 'Guardian' in this sense is meant a barrier that appears to block us on our journey. In the earlier stages this roadblock may appear troublesome or annoying, but is generally manageable. Further along the path, as we seem to really be making progress, this Guardian can appear fierce and be quite intimidating. The Guardian has a job to do, and that is to *test* us. By appearing as an obstacle it requires us to show our quality. This enables us to more clearly assess ourselves, to judge how far we have truly come, and how ready we really are to progress further. It is not uncommon to be 'defeated' by the Guardian. Such a setback may result in us retreating until we feel ready to resume our journey and challenge the Guardian again.

What is the actual nature of the Guardian? Although it takes the very convincing form of difficult circumstances – a relationship that falls apart, a business arrangement gone sour, a health problem, an unforeseen 'dark night of the soul' – it is ultimately nothing other than a projection of the deeper, darker, still disowned elements of our own mind. *The Tibetan Book of the Dead* describes a process that a dead person undergoes in the *bardo* ('afterlife') in which they commonly encounter all sorts of energies, patterns, and apparent entities. These entities, the book explains, are in fact projected elements of their own mind that they have not previously been able to recognize. In the afterlife, stripped of their physical body and their identification with it, the contents of the mind are opened and become unavoidable. Minus the distractions of physical reality, we face the totality of what we really believe we are, warts and all.

Whether we view the *bardo* as a metaphor or as actual, such projections need not appear only after death, however. They also show up when we commit ourselves to realizing ultimate truth. These projections can take many different forms but usually they boil down to two essential states of mind: fear and guilt. Fear and guilt are the primary negative mind-states and may be said to form the bedrock of the ego. Both have their function and purpose in this world (it is a good idea to fear standing in the path of a train, and it is natural to feel guilt if we have acted wrongfully). Fear in its positive sense is simply an element of the survival instinct. Guilt in its positive sense is simply an element of conscience. However, as we proceed along our path we encounter more rarefied air, in which negative mind-states serve us less and less. Fear may have had its purpose on our journey, but increasingly we see that it gets in the way as we try to move further along. The same is true for guilt. Both become barriers to deeper awakening.

This does not mean, of course, that we lose our common-sense discernment or our conscience. We still get out of the way of a train. We still remain responsible citizens. It is rather that we begin to face deeper elements of fear and guilt, and begin to understand what they really mean on the spiritual level. Guilt, in this deeper sense, is not to do with having acted 'wrongfully', but rather with a deep-seated sense of *being* wrong. It is not 'I *made* a mistake', but rather, 'I *am* a living, breathing, walking mistake. There is something wrong with who I am.' That is the mental level. The physical, energetic expression of such core-level guilt becomes *fear*. The fear we speak of here is the deep-seated fear of life, fear of love, fear of being controlled, fear of death, fear of the infinite (God, the Void, etc.), and ultimately fear of our highest potential, and of its vastness.

Why do we have core-level guilt? Why do we have a deep-seated sense of feeling somehow flawed? It is because we know, in a vaguely intuitive way, that we are disconnected from our highest potential and from the totality of existence. As to how or why this condition came about, there have been many explanations – everything from 'the Fall' of the Old Testament, to the delusional self of Buddhism, to the work of the 'false god' of Gnosticism, to the idea from *A Course in Miracles* that 'the Fall' never truly happened, that we only dreamt that it did. Ultimately, however, all that matters is that we cultivate the powerful willingness to encounter our core guilt and fear head-on, not shying away from the fierce manifestations they will often take when confronting us in outer form as the 'Guardian' blocking our path – in the form of challenging personal circumstances.

These circumstances, the forms that the Guardian will take, often show up in our relationships. For centuries, mystics, monks, and nuns have fled from traditional family or intimate relationships, to mountaintops, caves, forests, monasteries, ashrams. At times this move to solitude, or shared space with other celibates, has been based on genuine passion for higher truth (when not simply mandated, as when parents send their children to the monastery, as occurs in some cultures). In other cases, especially in more modern cultures, it has been based in part on a desire to avoid intimate relationship. And there is good reason for this movement away from relationship: everyone knows, or sooner or later finds out, that our most difficult characteristics, our deepest core-level guilt and fear, are sooner or later provoked in relationship.

That does not mean that we have to be in sustained intimate relationship with one person in order to face these core-level issues. But it does imply that running from our relationship-issues simply means that we will have to confront them in a different form, sooner or later. And what we will be confronting is always the same thing: our self-image.

The self-image lies at the root of all of our issues, forming the very essence of the 'Guardian', this intimidating periodic roadblock – sometimes appearing as an outright monster – that we confront on our journey. The Guardian is nothing other than our self-image projected outwardly. But this 'self-image' is not the common view we have of ourselves, the 'who I think I am'. It is something much deeper than this. It is the entire content of our unconscious mind, including all the forces that have shaped the self that we have come to see as 'me'. This is the self that emerges in dreams at night, in moments when we are pushed to the wall in life, when challenged by others, during periods of stress or illness, in relationship difficulties and breakups, during periods when we are presented with a fork in the road. It is the 'me' that is hardest to see unless provoked.

Our main ally in the battle of dealing with the Guardian is radical honesty. We must be willing to be uncompromisingly honest, unflinchingly truthful with ourselves, if there is to be any hope of moving beyond the Guardian. Otherwise we will be defeated, and we will beat a retreat back down the path to the comfort of one of the valleys – sometimes to rest, but sometimes to forget altogether about the path to truth.

The Dark Night of the Soul

It is here where we may (though not all do) enter the classic 'dark night of the soul'. During this phase all our spiritual practices (meditation, prayer, etc.) seem to be producing no results. Everything seems to fall flat and dry, and many of our relationships go sour. All this seems very bad when in it, but in fact our spirit is being matured by the ordeal. Our spirituality is beginning to grow up. We are starting to understand that awakening is not about having blissful experiences, it is about serving a much higher and more profound cause – the collective growth of the human race, something we as individuals can never be separate from.

As we learn to deepen our passion for ultimate truth via applying radical honesty toward ourselves, we begin to understand the true lessons that the Guardian is trying to teach us: the lesson of joining opposites, of becoming whole, so as to become truly responsible. This hastens our journey; and if we have fallen into the dark night of the soul, our passage through that.

Summary

1. We cannot 'quantum leap' to God. There is no shortcut to self-realization.

2. Occasionally we need to retreat off the path up the mountain, making pit stops in valleys, where we integrate what we've been learning.

3. What directs us to make a pit stop is radical honesty. This is a deep honesty we apply to ourselves that prevents our spiritual development from outstripping our psychological maturity, and our need to handle practical matters responsibly.

4. Sooner or later we encounter the 'Guardian' on our path. This is our fear and guilt manifesting outwardly in our life as difficult circumstances (relationship breakdown, ill health, financial struggle, etc.). This Guardian, correctly understood, is a teacher. It is our projected self-image, and what it is showing us is what must be done: the need to join opposites within us, to become a unified person, and to become more responsible in the deeper sense of that word – *able to truly respond* to the movement of existence.

5. If we insist on fighting against this lesson, we may enter into a very painful 'dark night of the soul', although the end result will likely ultimately be a deeper maturity.

Chapter 26

Purification II: Joining Opposites

Some of the ideas of this chapter may at first glance appear difficult, but they are of crucial importance to grasp, as in some respects they mark the key step on our journey. Many fail at this point, abandoning the path, settling for the more familiar matters.

As we develop the willingness to honestly confront the deeper and darker elements of ourselves – our capacity for anger, hate, jealousy, manipulativeness, dishonesty, greed, and so on – we begin to notice something, at first tentatively, but over time with increasing clarity. It is this: the secret to understanding and working with these darker elements, and a key secret to wisdom itself, is *joining opposites*.

The reason why a clear understanding of the dance of opposites is so important is because spiritual enlightenment, at its core, is about non-duality – seeing and sensing the profound interrelatedness, interconnectivity, and ultimate Oneness, of everything. However, we cannot properly see this Oneness without first seeing the dance of separate parts within it all. And we cannot understand this interdependent 'dance' without learning the art of joining opposites. In capsule form, it looks like this:

1. Recognizing opposites within us: spirit–sex; good–bad; love–hate; kind–mean; rough–gentle; generous–greedy; selfless–selfish; light–dark, patient compassion–intolerant condemnation, active–passive, and so on.

2. Learning how to bridge these opposites within ourselves, by first recognizing that we *have* all these capacities and qualities within us, even if only in potential form. That is, I see and am honest about my capacity for all spectrums of thought, feeling, and action.

3. Recognizing the interplay of these opposing forces, how they generate relationships, life, and reality as we experience it. For example, to appreciate warmth, we must have had some experience of cold. To feel the impact of cold, we must have known warmth. To suffer the pain of separation, we must have known the pleasures of intimacy. To appreciate peace and quiet, we must have experienced noise and chaos, and so on. Our failure to come to terms with opposites – to experience balance – is one of the prime causes behind suffering in all of its facets.

4. Recognizing the underlying unity behind the dance of opposites – how both sides of a given set of opposites are reflections of each other, and in fact are not separate. This takes us to the core of the matter of enlightenment, which is realizing that the division between subject ('me') and object ('you', or 'that') is something that we have learned – in the strictest sense, 'made up'. We are thus capable of 'unmaking it', seeing beyond it into a glimpse of non-duality, where 'I and That', or 'I and Thou' no longer exists.

Thus far on our journey, we have learned some essential things. We have learned of the need to let go of what no longer works for us, to abandon useless habits and life circumstances. We have learned from this the importance of embracing the unknown, of developing the courage to face deeper truths by recognizing the need to let go of excessive control. We have also learned of the crucial importance of cultivating a passion for higher truth, and along with it, applying a radically deep honesty toward ourselves.

Equipped with this essential knowledge, we begin to tackle the deeper face of our resistance to our highest potential. We begin to see that this deeper face of resistance – a loud 'NO!' within us largely hidden from view until now – is the foundation of our experience of duality, divisiveness, and separation itself. This 'NO!', this fear of letting go, is what keeps us stuck in limitation, remaining small and terrified of our greater potential.

The key to understanding our resistance lies in understanding opposites, and in particular, the realm of opposites within us. This is essential because if we don't, our spirituality will not only become bogus, but we also run the risk of misguiding others. We may become a 'false prophet', one who does not truly live what they teach.

Opposites Embraced Reveal our Inner Face

The opposites that show up around us are, of course, much easier to see. For example, as we pay attention to our relationship patterns, we begin to notice that what often attracts us in others are qualities they appear to have that seem to be lacking in ourselves. Quite literally, 'opposites attract'. A good metaphor for this can be found in what we call a 'full moon' night. The moon appears 'full' to us when it is on the opposite side of Earth relative to the sun (in astronomy and astrology this is called an 'opposition'). When, relative to our position on Earth, the sun and moon are opposite to each other, we perceive the moon as 'full' because its entire visible face is reflecting the light of the sun. That is, moonshine is brightest in opposition.

Similarly with us, we 'shine brightest' when confronted with qualities that appear to be opposite to our own. In this analogy 'shining brightest' does not necessarily mean showing our best quality; indeed, it might mean revealing our *worst* traits. The point is that the oppositional factor brings out what is within us, be that attractive and noble, or hideous and ignoble. Either way, opposition helps to *reveal*. This is why being 'challenged' in life is usually the best way to see parts of ourselves more clearly. We literally cannot see these hidden parts within us until confronted by something that appears to be very different, or even opposite. For example, we cannot see our capacity for compassion until we have been confronted with coldness or indifference or great suffering. We cannot see our capacity for fear until confronted with great love, or our capacity for gentleness until confronted by harshness, and so on.

When we are attracted to a person – whether they be of the

'opposite sex' (even our language hints at the power of opposition) or simply of opposite character or circumstances – what we are effectively expressing is that we want to learn about that part of ourselves that the other person represents. It will appear as if the other person 'completes' or 'fulfills' us, but in fact what is going on is that their presence is stirring within us an awareness of what they appear to embody. That is, if they are courageous, they make us aware of our own capacity to be courageous – as well as our capacity to be fearful.

As we move deeper into relationships, if we remain curious and sensitive, we begin to notice that these factors in others that attract us, these qualities that seem in some way different from who we are, are only *appearances*. Even the more outwardly obvious ones – a woman's softness to a man's hardness – are dependent on many interpretations, perspectives generated by sensory input (visual, sounds, smell, touch) and outer displays of behavior. As we look a bit deeper, we see, for example, that men are also capable of great softness, and women of great hardness. We begin to see beyond the conventional ways of viewing the 'other'. We start to see beyond perceived opposites.

The aging process itself is a natural way of helping us to see through the illusory nature of appearances. An opposition such as 'young–old' begins to mean much less as we ourselves begin to physically age. Our appearance in the mirror at 70 is very different from what it was at 20, yet the person gazing into the mirror retains the same name and general sense of 'I am' awareness that they had fifty years before. They are a different person, yet also the same. They are *both* young, and old. In looking honestly and openly into opposites, we start to move beyond opposites.

Beyond the Relationship Dance

As we begin to notice the changing nature of appearances, we begin to move beyond the relationship dance. That does not necessarily mean that we forsake intimate partnership, including intimate sexual relationships. It rather means that we begin to let go of the fantasy, the pictures in our mind that make up the more immature elements of relationship. We begin to drop the quest for the Holy Grail of fulfillment – the 'perfect partner' – noticing that after years of seeking it, it remains on the horizon, mirage-like, never truly having come any closer. We have been chasing a phantom.

Such restless seeking is not limited to those who have had multiple partners, or who have spent large periods of their life avoiding sustained intimacy. It also applies to those who have been with one person for a long time. It's entirely possible, and relatively common, to be married for decades to one person and still, even into old age, persist in trying to change them, in trying to control them, to shape them in some way that we think gives us something that we believe we lack within us. Our challenge is to let go of this manipulative quality. We must even let go of our attachment to 'harmony', realizing that it is not up to us to manage or control our relationships, because control itself is increasingly understood to be an illusion, arising from a false sense of self.

Until we begin to go beyond the relationship dance, we are usually using people. This is a hard thing to see, and we are going to have to apply to it all of our radical honesty and passion for truth because it is one of the most unattractive human traits. There is an effective scene in the 1999 movie *The Matrix*, where Agent Smith is angrily lamenting to the character Morpheus how humans are 'like a virus', simply spreading from one part of the planet to the other, consuming and consuming, and then moving elsewhere when resources run out. It's a bleak view, but painfully familiar, because deep down we all recognize our capacity to use *everything* as a means to an end – not just material objects, but more to the point, the relationships in our life.

The reason we use others is because we have not yet taken responsibility for the entire spectrum of human qualities and capacities within us. We are still living in the fantasy-world of believing that we lack the capacity for certain qualities – either that we are two-dimensional angels, incapable of darker thoughts or behavior, or that we are two-dimensional devils, incapable of goodness or contributing to human civilization. When we limit ourselves inwardly, we outwardly hold others hostage to our limiting beliefs about ourselves. We make them responsible for giving us what we believe we do not have.

The deeper purpose of relationship is always to teach us something about ourselves, something that is particularly difficult to see. Other people are ultimately there to remind us about who we are, about the fact that we are not two-dimensional beings. In fact we are multidimensional and virtually limitless in possible range of experience. This is vitally important to see, because until we do, we remain incomplete. And only a complete, fully fleshed-out human being is capable of moving into deeper stages of spiritual awakening.

Maturing on the Spiritual Path

In the beginning we may embrace a spiritual path – therapy, meditation, yoga, esoteric practice, philosophical introspection, wide reading, association with gurus, teachers, therapists, and so forth – with enthusiasm and with sincere practice and study. It is common, however, to eventually recognize that we have been using the spiritual path as well, just like we use everything else. The way we 'use' the spiritual path, in the egocentric sense, is by using it as an escape route, a means by which to avoid responsibility, commitment, and the need to truly face our core-level guilt and fear and resulting contraction and recoil from Truth. The spiritual path becomes yet another thing to pursue, a new star to follow, simply replacing the older 'gods' of money, true love, fame, status, power, and so on. But the job of this new god is the same: to distract us from facing *fully into* who we are, and being responsible for that.

This may seem ironic, as the spiritual path is supposed to be about 'facing who we are', but our minds are very clever and inventive. We are capable of using anything for egocentric purposes, *even the spiritual path.* We are even capable of believing that we are superior to others because now we are 'more spiritually advanced' than they are.

What marks our maturation on the path up the mountain is when we stop *fleeing* from relationships because we fear what they show us about ourselves; and when we stop *clinging* to relationships, manipulating others into giving us what we believe we do not have or did not receive from others in the past. In short, we begin to grow up when we stop using the world, and others, as a toy to comfort us, to console us, and to entertain us – all because we fear ourselves.

When we begin to recognize that the opposite qualities in others that fascinate us so much – 'I am serious, he is funny'; or 'I am so hard, she is so soft' – are in fact within us as well, even if only in potential form, we are weaning ourselves off of dependency. We are becoming a true individual. This is a crucial step because only a well-defined individual can move *into* individuality, and then *beyond* individuality – into a glimpse of the Oneness of existence. Until we learn to stop using others as a means to an end, our individuality remains vague, stunted; we have not yet truly emerged as an individual, let alone become 'conscious' or 'spiritual'.

When we begin to take responsibility for our multidimensional nature – when we begin to see and understand both the angel and the devil within us, and endless other tendencies and qualities, from sexual capacity to artistic and intellectual potential, from sadism to masochism, from gentleness and tenderness to roughness and brutality, from heart to heartlessness, from selflessness to selfishness, from love to hate – only then do we begin to manifest our human fullness. It is only at that point, *fully* human, that we are capable of becoming something more than 'merely' human. The key to this transition point is the art of living with *totality of experience.*

Summary

1. We cannot purify further and progress further on the path of awakening without understanding what it means to reconcile opposites.

2. To reconcile opposites means to bring together all parts of our personality, so that we become consistent and authentic – truly balanced, and above all, *responsible*. This is essential because only a balanced and responsible person can progress into deeper, genuine spiritual awakening

.

3. It is only through encountering opposites, both within us and around us, that we begin to become fully aware of who we are – just as the 'full moon' in 'opposition' to the sun shines fullest and brightest.

4. If we do not take responsibility for the entire spectrum of potential within us, we will inevitably use other people. If we pursue spiritual practices quite far, yet remain divided inwardly – for example, rejecting our darker qualities – we run the risk of becoming a 'false prophet', a teacher who (usually unknowingly) misguides others.

Chapter 27

Enlightenment: Totality of Experience

Presence

There is a natural by-product of our willingness to see and take responsibility for the capacity for polar-opposite qualities that exist within us. It is an increased ability to be truly *present* in our life on a moment-to-moment basis. In short, it is the enhanced ability to live our lives with fullness and totality.

In the early 1970s Ram Dass wrote a book about the importance of present-time awareness (among other things) called *Be Here Now*. About twenty-five years after that book, Eckhart Tolle's *The Power of Now* appeared, which essentially dealt with the same theme – the importance of present-time awareness. Both books were highly popular, because most people recognize, even if only vaguely, how the key to life is all about attentiveness to the present moment. However, it is equally true that most people have a hard time truly employing the deceptively simple ideas in books like Ram Dass's and Tolle's. This is because the ability to live present to the moment is not actually something acquired at the beginning of the journey. It only comes about (in all except the rarest of cases) after we have passed through some of the key steps outlined in the previous five chapters. Prior to that it's mostly just an appealing idea, especially during these times of information excess and corresponding attention deficit that afflicts so many (and not just in the clinical sense). Tolle's work has been popular because the whole idea seems so simple. Just be here, now, in the 'power of the now', and everything will be good. Alas, it rarely works that way.

We cannot be truly present to reality if we are carrying too much burdensome baggage (Chapter 22); or if we have not cultivated a willingness to embrace the unknown (Chapter 23); or if we have not yet birthed a passion for truth (Chapter 24); or if we have not yet developed sincere self-honesty and the willingness to apply it (Chapter 25); or if we have not yet matured psychologically by learning how to recognize and resolve opposites in life and within ourselves (Chapter 26). Until these steps have been faced to a sufficient degree, any experience we have of present-time awareness, of 'being here now' and of the 'power of now', will tend to be fleeting, a glimpse or taste of something, which will rapidly fade. Most commonly, such experiences are reduced to mere memories, 'highlights' of our 'spiritual' life to be filed away in the 'photo albums' of our memory, tales to be told of legendary times when we glimpsed the top of the mountain.

Much as we may wish, we cannot bypass preliminary steps on our journey, any more than we can write quality literature without first mastering the alphabet and proper grammar. However, as we deal with these preliminary stages we find our capacity for living present to reality, to the vastness of each moment, deepening naturally.

As we honestly recognize and take 'ownership' of our shadow tendencies and capacities, our courage to face ourselves, and life, grows. Our deepening honesty and growing passion for truth renders all so-called undesirable human traits much less fearsome, and therefore much easier to recognize within us. As our ability to assume responsibility for our shadow side increases, an interesting paradox begins to unfold. We begin to understand, tentatively at first, but with growing conviction and confidence, that we are *not* these negative states of mind. They are simply manifestations of 'inner weather', and much like the weather of our outer landscapes, are changing all the time, appearing and disappearing into nothingness. These dualities, these patterns of opposition – love and hate, trust and doubt, attraction and repulsion, gentleness and violence, acceptance and judgmentalism – arise within us, and fall away again, just as Monday can be warm and sunny, Tuesday cold and rainy, and Wednesday like neither. As we begin to understand the key point, that even though we embody and experience these

polar-opposite states, they are not who we truly are, then it become possible to glimpse and taste what it is like to be free of identification with *all* states of mind, and open more fully to Reality.

Presence and Memory

One of the traps we have to guard against, in particular as we age, is the increasing richness of our memory bank. Our life experience can be likened to a library; the more life experience we have, the larger our inner library. For one who has lived forty, fifty, sixty, or more years, and who has accumulated a fair and varied number of life experiences, the library of their memory is large (regardless if parts of their memory function less keenly, as when younger – where a younger person is something like a library with an efficient librarian but not many books). A large inner library can be a problem on the spiritual path because it can make our mind overly active with useless, repetitive thoughts and memories; brooding over the past, weighing all the facts we 'know' about, assuming that we've 'seen it all before', and so on.

Presence is generally thought to be easier for the young; one has only to recall, however dimly, one's early life years, when all reference points were so unknown as to render them incomprehensibly vast and awesome. A simple object like a flower, or a stuffed toy, or a color, was infinitely fascinating and something our attention could be completely caught and absorbed by. Each day crawled slowly by, a summer stretched out forever – because all was new, and our inner library was relatively empty, full of possibilities and sheer hope.

The pristine presence of the infant or young child is not wisdom, however; nor is it enlightenment, because it lacks understanding. It is like an open field of rich soil that has nothing yet growing in it; a vast field of pure potential energy, uncluttered by ego, in which nothing has yet arisen.

Time seems to move faster as we age because the reference points of life are becoming more and more familiar; we've been down so many alleys and seen it all before. As our memory banks expand, it becomes easier to disconnect from the present moment. Even if our memory slowly begins to falter, as it commonly does by middle age, there is still the underlying sense that very few new lands remain to be discovered.

Yet the sense that we've 'been there before' need not be an obstacle for one wishing to enter the purity of Reality that is always only anchored *here*. In fact, life experience joined with present-moment attentiveness is grounds for the flowering of true wisdom. The point at which we embark on our journey to Reality is ultimately not important – what matters is setting out. That said, there are unquestionable advantages to beginning at a younger age, prior to accumulating too much heavy baggage – financial debt, relationship scars, health issues, and so on. The older we get, the more effort we have to put into being present. Meditation practice is best for this.

The Japanese word *Zen* and the Chinese word *Cha'an* (from Buddhism) derive from the Sanskrit word *dhyana*. The word translates inadequately into English as 'meditation'. In fact it carries complex meaning, denoting various levels of progressive deepening of meditation, but the essence of the meaning of the word is to 'join with the flow' of each moment. This is a key insight because in the realm of experience, there actually *is* no 'now', because all is in perpetual flux, perpetual change, like a moving river. The only thing that is static is consciousness itself. To meditate, in the true sense of the word, is to move beyond the constant change of existence, into the immutable and crystal-clear nature of pure awareness.

Preparing for the Abyss

As our passion for higher truth, aided by our developing ability to be truly present, becomes the foundation of our life, and as we maturely come to terms with the capacity for polar-opposite qualities in our personality, then our ability to experience life fully, totally, deepens. As we live more and more with totality – as we learn to love fully, to laugh fully, to think, read, work, create, meditate, or eat with full attentiveness, to truly give our attention to what is in front of us

– we begin to accumulate less and less baggage. We learn to allow each moment to simply move on without grasping at it, without clinging to the past – or without anxiously 'forcing' the future to arrive faster.

It is at this point that we are *truly* ready to begin regarding every moment of life, and every experience we undergo, as 'sacred'. Each moment, the universe is reflecting back to us the truth of Reality and the truth of who we are. We are now becoming sensitive enough to understand this. We are now truly ready to see that we are constantly being taught, and known, by that formless essence of intelligence that animates existence. We begin to sense the Light that is without luminosity, the Light that we cannot see, the invisible aliveness of presence and Reality.

This 'Light', however, remains something separate from us. It seems from our present vantage point to be something beyond us, higher than us. We may regard it in mystical terms, or rather as a pure potential, a symbol for the highest. Either way, there seems to be some sort of gulf that separates us from it. This 'gulf' is real enough, from where we stand. It can be likened to an Abyss (as some traditions call it). It is an Abyss that we all must journey through on our way. Not only must we all pass through it, we must all pass through it *alone*. No one makes this passage in the company of other personalities.

We have a final choice at this point, whether to turn back to the world of objects and desires and to the bittersweet dreams of the personality. Or to make the jump. The only prerequisite for making this jump is that we must be prepared to leave everything behind, or to have everything taken away from us. *Everything.*

Entering the Abyss

The journey through the Abyss is the end of the dream. It is not the end of the journey, but it is the death of our identification with illusions and with the quest for the Grail of fulfillment. It is not the death of the adventurer, of the explorer, or even of the teacher or the student. But it is the death of the seeker. This is so because what is destroyed in the passage through the Abyss is the neurotic basis of the ego-personality itself, the essential belief that 'I am disconnected from the Totality of existence, an island unto myself'.

This death is not easy, and indeed can be very painful. Famous legends of history have hinted at it in the crucifixion of Jesus, in the struggles of Buddha in the forest for six years, in the terrible ordeals of the Tibetan mystic Milarepa prior to his final awakening, in the 'Zen sickness' of the Japanese master Hakuin. It is not an 'easy death' because we do not fully grasp just how deeply attached we are to this world, to our personality, to our subjective, separate existence, with all its dreams, ambitions, and desire for recognition and love. This attachment is so powerful that it may even persist after the death of the physical body, creating dream-worlds in the subtle realms of existence in which these desires get played out, possibly even re-organizing and re-identifying as another physically embodied human life.

The Abyss takes the dream away from us, stripping us naked to the core, allowing no attachments to accompany us in the passage through its realm. Because of the sheer challenge of this passage, many who enter it turn back, frightened by what they see. Those who turn back deal with new difficulties, the most troublesome of these being the belief, based on faulty understanding, that Self-realization is itself a dream, an illusion.

It is not good to approach the Abyss prematurely (that is, to try to 'force' the death of the separate self). It is better to live honestly, honorably, and enjoyably (as best we can) as a conventional person, as a personality in the world of personalities, rather than attempting to jump into the Abyss before we are truly ready. Our jump will be premature if it is based on any desires to escape this world. We cannot run away from our human lessons. We are rather taken naturally to the edge of the Abyss when we live our life fully, totally, with integrity, and come to an organic sense of completion with it.

When we do step into the Abyss, and if we do successfully

navigate it, we emerge on the 'other side' as both human and something more. We are now carrying within us an undying light that illuminates all things. We see ourselves in the eyes of all whom we look at – that is, we realize directly that there is, and always has been, only One Person. We truly know that we 'need do nothing' to be established in the perpetual remembrance of Reality, of who we really are. The illusion of being an isolated entity in an ocean of isolated entities has been broken. We rest in this Understanding.

This Understanding is simple and direct, and reveals one essential truth: the *separate self does not exist*. Accordingly, free will does not truly exist either. And further, *no-thing* has any substantial existence. All is radiant, empty, luminous, and is *as it is*.

Summary

1. The by-product of 'joining opposites' – of taking responsibility for our potential for negative thoughts, feelings, and actions – is an increased ability to penetrate the present moment, and glimpse Reality, beyond the 'reality-tunnels' of our conceptual constructions and beliefs.

2. As we progress in our passion and search for truth, we eventually confront an 'Abyss'. At this point, we reach a crossroads. To proceed through the Abyss, we must be willing to be stripped of everything. Our entire self-image is to be destroyed.

3. It is better not to approach the Abyss prematurely. If we sense that we're not quite ready for that final leap, better to backtrack and live responsibly and 'normally', until ready to take the leap.

Chapter 28

Illumination: Beyond Experience

Leaving the Abyss

In a sense, there is little to be said at this point (and little point in talking about it). The Zen tradition has an effective metaphor to describe the last stage: they liken it to a seeker (now 'finder') leaving a cave in which they have realized their true nature, and then re-entering the marketplace. In some versions of this parable they are depicted entering the marketplace with a gourd for wine. That is, they simply resume their ordinary life – as in the expression 'before enlightenment, chop wood, carry water from the well; after enlightenment, chop wood, carry water from the well' – albeit, with a different consciousness.

The entire notion of what it is to be a distinct personality has been turned inside out at this point. Much, indeed almost all, of what was previously assumed to be real is now seen and understood to be unreal, ghosts created by the mind in its previously deluded state. Shorn clean of illusions and standing naked in Reality, there is only one remaining desire, and that is to share what is now understood with others. The remaining 'ambition' is to help others to grow toward truth and Reality.

For most of us, full enlightenment, full illumination, is a remote matter, and may seem far off, like an impossibly high mountain peak shrouded in cloud. I am not going to console the reader by suggesting this is not really true. In fact, it is; full and true enlightenment is extremely rare, for the simple reason that we are enjoying this 'degraded game' that we play as phantom selves in a universe of phantom separate objects. We are too attached to our world to let it go.

Be that as it may, the rarity of enlightenment, like a remote precious gem, should not stop us from making the journey. On the contrary, it is precisely what makes the journey so exquisitely precious.

Summary

Full enlightenment is very, very rare. Most likely we will not successfully make the whole journey to the end in our life. But we must *try*, because nothing else is of equal value in this entire universe of infinite possible experiences.

Part V

Case Studies: Seven Radically Awakened Sages

Gate gate pāragate pārasamgate bodhi svāhā.
(Gone gone, gone beyond, gone altogether beyond! Awakened! So be it!)
From the Heart Sutra

Note to the Reader

What follows are the stories and teachings connected to seven radically awakened mystics. Most of these, with the likely exception of Yaeko Iwasaki, will be well known to sincere truth-seekers. Some of their life stories are largely legendary (especially in the cases of Socrates, Jesus and Milarepa); some are well documented, as in the case of recent sages like Ramana and Nisargadatta. But in all cases what these seven sages hold in common is that they represent a wisdom that involves a radical discontinuity with the conventional and mass-consensus mindset. By all appearances, and as demonstrated by the piercing wisdom of their words, these are sages who truly broke free and embodied both a purity of understanding and an originality of expression.

There have certainly been more than seven such mystics in recorded history. This book is intended to be reasonably compact, however, and so seven – the 'virgin number' of Pythagorean mysticism – seems a good 'un-round' figure to stop at. More to the point, however, these seven people represent the key theme of this book, which is that authentic awakening is truly an 'all or nothing' matter. Reading through the stories of these sages, one is left with a distinct sense of the overwhelming passion for truth that consumed all of them. They were all worthy ambassadors for 'rude awakening' in the best sense of that term, jolting seekers out of their deep slumber, and inevitably disturbing the dreams of those who were not seeking truth (to the extent that two of them, Socrates and Jesus, paid for it with their lives). Yaeko Iwasaki's case may not seem to apply to this last point, as she died young, shortly after her awakening. And yet the passion she evinced for ultimate truth, even in the face of the jaws of looming death, showed the best face of the courage needed to truly awaken.

Chapter 29

Socrates: The First Zen Master

Socrates is a legendary figure in Western philosophy and, as with most ancient sages, not a clearly defined historical character. Some facts about him are known.[1] He was born in Athens in 469 BCE and died there seventy years later in 399 BCE. He was the quintessential seeker of truth, and his life was dedicated to the discovery of the essence of who we are. His timeless maxim, 'The unexamined life is not worth living', is testament to the powerful resolve that echoes the creed of awakened sages everywhere, which is that none of the 'treasures' of the world offer anything of ultimate worth, and that only the absolute truths of Reality, and of our essential nature, are worth pursuing. More to the point, these priceless truths can only be discovered via the hard work of self-examination. With this one insight alone, Socrates sets the stage for the modern paths of work on self for the purposes of uncovering our greatest potential – and how such potential does not have a real hope of manifesting if we do not make it the main priority of our life.

Socrates lived during the fertile explosion of wisdom that occurred, especially in Greece, India, and China, between approximately 600 and 300 BCE. During that time there came the Buddha and Mahavira in India, Lao Tzu and Chuang Tzu in China, and Heraclitus, Socrates, Diogenes, Plato and Aristotle in Greece. (Some purists of transcendent wisdom would question the inclusion of Plato and Aristotle on that list, particularly the latter, who was not a mystic; but their sheer influence on Western philosophy, esotericism, and science warrants mention.)

Socrates wrote nothing. What we know of him is via others, mostly his famed student Plato. But what most people recognize first about Socrates, if they recognize anything at all, is the dramatic manner of his death. Although arguments have been advanced by more recent historians that the causes behind this death may be more complex than is usually supposed, what is known is that he was condemned to death for 'corrupting the youth of Athens' via his relentless philosophical inquiry, and in specific, his constant questioning of authorities. This, along with the quality of his wisdom, makes him the awakened and courageous sage *par excellence.*

Throughout history, radically awakened sages – in the rare times during which they've emerged – have usually met with difficulties, particularly if they have been influential. This is because their message generally runs counter to the political and religious zeitgeist of their times. Deeply realized sages are rarely good diplomats. This is so because the values of the world are centered on survival, above all else – whether that survival be connected to the urge of a ruling secular regime to perpetuate itself, or of an ideology or religious dogma to maintain control over the masses. Put simply, those who hold traditional religious or secular power almost never willingly yield control, even if they have become manifestly corrupt. Awakened sages bring a message that, more than anything, has to do with the inner freedom of the individual – his or her empowerment as a liberated and awakened person. Political or religious organizations are, generally speaking, not interested in that sort of person and in fact tend to automatically seek to control them because of their potential to be subversive; in particular, to disturb the young and turn them away from serving the ruling state or church.

Courage is an essential quality of deep awakening, because it can be daunting to peer into the face of the ego. However, in seeing the truth we gradually become more fearless in the face of illusion. When a dreamer recognizes that they are dreaming, therefore becoming awake in so doing, they naturally lose much of the fear of the dream they inhabit. That does not mean they become reckless or immature in their actions. It simply means that they become free of the terrible fears gripping one who is attached to their dreams and who is controlled by illusions.

Socrates was the embodiment of intellectual and spiritual courage, much like Jesus, another sage who was executed for his refusal to compromise his views. In modern times in the West we take for granted things like 'freedom of speech', but for much of the history of civilization there was no such thing (as there is no such thing for substantial parts of the human race even now). It has always been easy to be killed for speaking out, or for refusing to recant one's words. This was true even in the Athens of Socrates' time, which in many ways was a relatively advanced culture.

Socrates was the archetypal shit-disturber. His whole approach was based on relentlessly questioning dogma, so-called 'certainties', and the lazy thinking that is based on taking on the views of others without ever bothering to truly look closely at them. But he wasn't doing this merely for the sake of disturbing apple-carts. He had a specific purpose, what Gurdjieff called an 'aim', and that was to instill in others the understanding that the ultimate purpose of reason, and self-examination, was to discover what is pure, good, and sacred within us – our supreme potential. He called this *agathon*, or 'absolute Good'. The modern term, as borrowed from our great Eastern wisdom traditions, is 'enlightenment'. For Socrates, the true purpose of human life is to attain this.

There are not a lot of facts about Socrates' life, and most of what he taught, as conveyed by Plato, was colored by Plato's additions and insights. But this is a secondary issue; what matters are the insights themselves. There were other philosophers who wrote about Socrates – Xenophon, Aristophanes, and Aristotle being three – but Plato's writings, which have survived the tempest of time, are considered by most to accurately reflect the master's teachings.

As recorded in Plato's *Apology*, Socrates during his trial (that resulted in his being condemned to death) proclaimed: 'For I spend all my time going about trying to persuade you, young and old, to make your first and chief concern not to care for your persons or your property more than for the perfection of your souls.'

That level of commitment is typically common to radical sages – insisting on the 'all or nothing' approach. We find this theme time and again among the wisest. They fearlessly prioritize the search for wisdom and truth above all else, even if this requires trenchant criticism of the mediocre values of mainstream life and even if this means being criticized or condemned in the eyes of the public.

Socrates was renowned for dialectics (especially in its simple form of questioning and answering), and in particular, something called 'Socratic method'. This is basically a type of cross-examining, via constant questioning, of anyone who holds a strong belief about something, so that they can deepen their understanding of the issue they hold beliefs about – or until they are shown the inevitable contradictions held in their views.

Socrates is renowned for once having been declared, by the Delphi Oracle, the 'wisest man in Athens'. He famously objected to this, believing that he had no real wisdom at all. To prove his point he then set about questioning several so-called wise people in Athens, to find out if they indeed knew more than he. What he found in each case, however, was that the people he was questioning actually believed that they were wise when he could see that they were not. In the end, Socrates concluded that the Delphi Oracle had been right all along, and that, in fact, he was the wisest person in Athens – but only for the reason that he alone realized that he was not truly wise at all. That is, he had the wisdom of recognizing his own ignorance. In other words, he was not *pretending* to be anything – which is arguably the greatest fault of 'truth-seekers' and 'spiritual people' (see Chapter 1).

The 'ignorance' Socrates refers to is not the ignorance of being ill-educated but rather the profounder ignorance born out of the realization that conventional knowledge cannot truly penetrate to the heart of matters. For example, we can ask ourselves the simple question 'What is the color green?' Even with modern knowledge of wavelengths and reflected light and so on, we are still left with the realization that all of our knowledge amounts to labels we put on the thing we call 'green'. They do not truly capture the thing in itself, for the simple reason that conventional thinking separates us from what it is observing. This basic separation allows us to make detailed observations about the *appearance* of the thing, but not to truly know it *directly*. Worse, it sustains the illusion that there really *are* 'things out there' that are truly isolated and disconnected from the totality of all that is, and from our own consciousness. In short, Socrates declares his ignorance not to denounce knowledge, but to point the way to a newer, deeper form of knowledge. This is consistent with what all awakened sages teach: in order to realize the true, we must first recognize and relinquish the false.

The wisdom of 'not-knowing' is a theme commonly echoed in the Zen tradition in particular. In many ways Socrates was the first Zen master (the traditionally accepted first Zen master, Bodhidharma, lived a thousand years after Socrates). Socrates, consistent with the Zen tradition, was a vocal critic of pretentiousness in all its guises, and perhaps never more so than in the realm of *spiritual* pretentiousness. He was merciless in exposing falsehood, and this of course made him enemies, as it typically will do for a sage who is both wise and influential. In particular he was critical of the 'sophists' of his time, philosophers whom he saw as posing as wise (and at times earning money for it), but who in fact lacked real wisdom – similar to how Jesus was to be vociferously critical of some of the priesthoods of his time.

A main target for Socrates in his criticism of sophists was the language games he saw them engaging in. This was somewhat ironic because Socrates himself was reputed to be a master of language – capable, as one commentator put it, of arguing any point of view and making it seem good. However, he used his skill with language to make those who hid behind words aware of their weaknesses. Like all realized sages, he saw through the thicket of language and penetrated beyond the dull thinking that categorizes so many who are merely parroting what they've been told is true. In short, Socrates' overwhelming aim was to enable people to truly think for themselves.

Some of Socrates' contemporaries reported that as a young man the philosopher had some interest in natural science – in the things of the world – but that this faded as he realized the overriding importance of discovering the truth and nature of consciousness, of our own being. One modern historian, in referring to Socrates, suggested that at some point he must have voiced St. Augustine's famous line, 'I no longer dream of the stars.'

This is a deceptively simple point, but crucially important for one who seeks truth. The 'things of the world' – be they ugly, or the wonders and beauties of Nature – are all enormously seductive, and all have a similar effect, that being the tendency to pull us out of ourselves. To 'dream' is to forget ourselves, to become lost in the dream and its terrors and wonders. There comes a time when we tire of this, much as we can tire of watching a fireworks display. We begin to crave the vaster and deeper truths of *being* – the being that we are.

Socrates' teaching boils down to the famous maxim on Apollo's temple at Delphi: Know Thyself. This is the time-honored creed of awakening. It is, of course, a teaching that can be wildly abused, as the endless examples of self-absorption disguised as 'self-knowledge' in modern times attest to. 'Know thyself' properly understood is not narcissism, nor does it invite it. In spirit it is closer to the Zen maxim, 'To know yourself is to forget yourself. To forget yourself is to be enlightened by all things.' What this means is that in examining, with deep honesty, our own mind and personality, we enter into a process of deconstruction in which cherished illusions are taken apart, or fall away (depending on how well we cooperate with the process). As these illusions dissolve we literally begin to 'forget' our past delusions and neuroses. We lose the annoying self-consciousness that arises from thinking ourselves special – in either the superior or inferior forms. We become comfortable with who we are, which in turn prepares us for deeper awakenings.

There is an interesting paradox inherent in Socrates, as there is in all radically awakened adepts, and it is this: while seemingly darkly pessimistic, he is in fact a supreme optimist. By critiquing so much about human life, and by being stubbornly adversarial and judgmental of conventional values and mediocre thinking – to the point where such stubbornness earned him a death sentence – he is actually a true optimist, because he holds that ultimate truth (which, naturally, he claimed existed) is also ultimate good; and that moreover, this state of being is truly attainable.

A famous element of the legend of Socrates was the manner of his death. Condemned in a dubious trial for 'not acknowledging the gods' ('impiety' or 'irreligiosity' were the terms) and 'corrupting the youth of Athens', he was sentenced to be poisoned by drinking hemlock. He had the opportunity to flee the city afterward, but declined, and voluntarily drank the hemlock, dying with both awareness and dignity.

He has been called the 'first martyr of free speech', but in fact he was something much more. He was a pointer to both what is possible for a human being, and what is ill in the human world – the sickness of the soul – that has been at the root of human suffering for recorded history and doubtless beyond. Great sages characteristically make others aware of this illness by drawing a stark contrast between the values of higher truth, and the intolerances and agendas of both worldly authorities and the mass man.

Chapter 30

Jesus: Rebel Lion

The figure of Jesus is of course of towering significance in Western civilization (an extraordinary fact alone, given that his ministry lasted, according to at least three of the gospels, for only around three years and that he died a young man, in his mid-thirties). A tremendous edifice of myth and legend has been built around him. Despite the sheer confusing bulk of this history, and its frequently clumsy (and ugly) interfacing with politics, it is possible to break the matter down and see Jesus in three main lights: the 'historical Jesus', the 'dogmatic Christ', and the 'awakened sage'.[2]

The 'historical Jesus' is exactly that, the Jesus of history. However, this matter has represented a real problem for historians, because outside of the New Testament there is very little corroborating evidence for the existence of a Jewish messiah-sage who was convicted by Pontius Pilate and crucified around 30 CE. Nevertheless, the material in the New Testament and related apocryphal gospels is considered substantial enough for scholars to attempt to tease out a reasonably clear picture of what this man was about. The historical Jesus is frequently at odds with the Jesus of organized Christian religion, and so there is, naturally, a great deal of controversy in all of this.

The details of the research into the historical Jesus, and how the results up to now have contrasted (and often clashed loudly) with the Christ of faith – the 'dogmatic Christ' – are fascinating but fall outside of the scope of this book. Suffice to say, a few brief conclusions generally reached by scholars and historians can be mentioned here in passing. One of the themes (and purposes) of this book is to make us aware of our conditioning (which often involves getting our buttons pushed); looking into the research around the historical Jesus can aid in making us more aware of our religious conditioning by close examination of our reactions as we read. This is important because the simple fact is that Christianity claims more adherents than any other faith on Earth – approximately one-third of the human race, or, as of this writing in 2010, over two billion people. Moreover, Christianity (or more accurately, Judeo-Christianity) is deeply intertwined with the cultural history of Western civilization. Even those postmodern souls who claim indifferent agnosticism or 'liberated' intellectual atheism have been influenced by Judeo-Christian ideals, values, and limitations more than they are usually aware of.

Critical scholarship applied to the life of Jesus – the attempt to separate the man from the enormous cloud of myth, superstition, and legend – had its roots in the 18th and 19th centuries via the work of some brave German scholars, but really began to hit its stride in the mid-1980s with the founding of the 'Jesus Seminar' by Bible scholars Robert Funk, John Dominic Crossan, Marcus Borg, and others, under the sponsorship of the Westar Institute. This group, aided by up to two hundred (mostly liberal) scholars, eventually produced a work that gave a cautious estimation of what exactly Jesus probably did and did not say, based on the words traditionally ascribed to him. The Jesus Seminar concluded that 82% of the words that he is supposed to have said, according to the four traditional gospels, were 'not actually spoken by him'. This, predictably, unleashed a firestorm of controversy from conservative Christians, who then attempted to attack the findings of the Jesus Seminar from many angles; one result from the backlash was that some Seminar Fellows ended up having to resign their teaching posts.

Dogma, especially when tied to many vested interests, never dies easily. Equally so, our own 'personal dogma' – that is, the conditioning that we've been programmed with and have come to believe is 'mine' – does not die easily either. Every truth-seeker sooner or later faces their conditioning, and it can be surprising how stubborn this conditioning can be, and how much clarity and determination it can take to shake it off.

Many things emerged from the critical analysis of these hard-working scholars concerning the gospels and other associated writings, and many of their conclusions were published in the early 1990s, a heyday for a wider public outreach by scholars of the historical Jesus. Amongst these have been: no evidence that Herod 'murdered babies' en masse in the infamous 'slaughter of the innocents' in an attempt to eliminate Jesus as a possible rival king; that Jesus was likely born in Nazareth, not Bethlehem; that he never claimed to be the Messiah, or the 'Son of God'; that he was not born of a 'virgin birth'; and that the resurrection story, as literally told, is almost certainly a fairy tale.

The number of internal contradictions in the gospels concerning the history of Jesus, his genealogy, the manner and place of his birth, and so forth, are so many that it soon becomes clear to the unbiased reader that the New Testament is not a true historical document, but rather a document of faith. Even most Christian faithful would not ultimately deny that, despite the fact that the Bible does contain plenty of actual history. As the German historian and Bible scholar Rudolf Bultmann pointed out, 'Only the crucifixion matters'; that is, for an actual inner or mystical connection with Christ, or faith in what he represents, the more outlandish New Testament legends and myths are not necessary.

What has become increasingly clear is that the historical Jesus of Nazareth is really not reconcilable with the Jesus of faith – the Incarnation (and Son) of God. In a span of around three hundred years Jesus of Nazareth became the Christ of the Nicene Creed as ratified by Emperor Constantine and a few hundred bishops in Nicaea in 325 CE. He went from being a wandering Jewish sage, perhaps similar in some respects to a youthful version of Siddhartha Gautama (the historical Buddha), to God Himself, the Logos, the Infinite One, both the Son of the Father and the Father Himself, forever distinct from mere humanity and human beings. He became the Christ of dogma.

However, what is of real interest to us here is the 'awakened sage' Jesus, for it is clear that such a man existed, regardless of what he was called, what he looked like, where he lived, whether or not he bedded Mary Magdalene and left behind a mysterious bloodline, whether or not he was the Son of God, and other related matters. It's even possible that the 'Jesus' of scripture was a composite character of sorts, possibly how Lao Tzu (author of the famed *Tao Te Ching*) is occasionally speculated to have been, owing to the scant amount of historical data on him.

The point is that it doesn't matter who Jesus was. What matters are the teachings ascribed to him – at least those that appear to be clearly wise – and even more to the point, how we can apply them to our own awakening process. Below, some of those teachings are considered. For the record – not that we need their blessing to continue – but the 'Jesus Seminar' scholars concluded that most of the teachings we're about to look at were part of the small percentage of words ascribed to Jesus that he very probably did say. (Although it is perhaps not coincidental that the words I select below to comment on are also manifestly wise.)

Teachings
A particular quality of Jesus that emerges from the gospels (once purged of fanciful legend, thundering prophecies, miraculous powers, threats of gnashing and wailing and hellfire, and related crudities) is that of a rebellious and ruthless lion. His more recognizable teachings are sharp and uncompromising (a quality that probably contributed toward his eventual persecution). He was similar to other radical sages and 'dangerous masters' in that he specialized in cutting against the grain of convention – in short, he was the quintessential alarm clock, come to disturb sleepers and rouse them from their sleep – even if such an approach ultimately cost him his life. What follows are some of Jesus' more profound insights.

Perhaps the clearest example of Jesus as radically awakened

sage is this statement: 'But seek ye first the kingdom of God, and his righteousness; and all these things shall be added unto you.' (Matthew 6:33, KJV)

That is the time-honored rallying cry of one awake to their true nature (and, admittedly, an easy one to twist to serve a political agenda). The mystical text *A Course in Miracles* phrases it as 'Be vigilant only for God and His kingdom.' The classic text of Renaissance high magic, *The Sacred Magic of Abramelin the Mage*, refers to it in its teaching that the mystic must first contact his 'holy guardian angel' (his direct link to God), prior to doing anything else.

The central idea that runs through all legitimate transformational work is that prioritization in life is crucial. Our life tends to reflect how we prioritize things. If our chief 'God' is money, or relationships, or sex, or status, or power, or any host of more negative ideals, that will be mirrored in our life. For one desiring to be awake to their highest potential, they must cultivate passion for *that* and put it as number one on the list. Our life needs to be oriented around the intention to be awake. That doesn't mean we become obsessed with it. Our task is to live a balanced life, but one that has a central aim, that being, as Gurdjieff put it, to 'remember yourself, always and everywhere'.

Most people, especially in these current eBay and Walmart times, tend to be dabblers and samplers, trying out something before rushing off to try out the next thing. Perhaps no better metaphor for this sheer superficiality can be found in the modern online social networking phenomenon, where on such sites as Facebook individuals have lists of hundreds (or even thousands) of 'friends', the vast majority of whom they have no direct communication with (or do not even know), and who can scarcely be recognized as a friend in the actual meaning of the word. We live during a time of vast breadth but little depth. Everything is spread wide and very thin, owing largely to the advances in communication technology. Naturally there are some benefits from this, but there are serious drawbacks, one of which is a diminished effect on attention spans, restlessness and cynicism, and a knowledge-diet of 'sound bites', snippets, YouTube mini-movies and endless related mundane downloads of trivia.

All this largely works completely counter to the spiritual impulse, which requires focus, a single-minded passion for depth, and a willingness to develop a capacity for sustained attention via meditation practice and close study of the words of awakened sages. In that regard, sages like Jesus are a good antidote for these times, provided we actually hear what they are saying.

'Blessed are the poor in spirit: for theirs is the kingdom of heaven.' (Matthew 5:3, KJV)

'Poor in spirit' does not imply a false piety brought about by cultivated poverty, either of personality or material belongings. It rather refers to the opposite of pride. By 'pride' I specifically mean the *need to be right* about things. There is perhaps no greater barrier to our inner awakening. To grow consciously means to develop a deep *willingness to be wrong* about anything that is in the way of our deeper realization of the nature of our being, and of Reality.

The old Zen parable of the Zen master serving a cup of tea to a young, intellectually arrogant student holds here. In the parable the master keeps pouring the tea, even as it overflows and spills on the floor. The student eventually asks him what he is doing – can he not see that this cup is already full? 'So too,' responds the master, 'is your mind. It is too full of knowledge, and you are too full of yourself. There is no room in you to learn anything new.'

To be proud is not, in this sense, to be confident or to have 'good self-esteem', or anything like that. It is rather to be too full of ourselves owing to a great need to always be right about matters. Needless to say, when we have a strong attachment to being right about things, we stand very little chance of truly waking up. Our self-control (and control of others) is suffocating us and making legitimate growth impossible. We need to be right about things either because we have been badly hurt in past relationships (and we now equate 'being wrong' with getting hurt), or because the idea of losing control brings up too much anxiety for us. The anxiety and general fear of being shamed, or of losing control, commonly underlies excessive pride.

'Blessed are they which do hunger and thirst after righteousness: for they shall be filled.' (Matthew 5:6, KJV)

The word 'righteousness' is often seen in a dubious light, especially during these politically sensitive times, along with an acute awareness of the wreckage caused by righteousness in general, especially of the religious or political sort. Modern psycho-spiritual language also reflects this, with terms like 'self-righteous' often used to denote a stubborn-mindedness that erodes relationships (the 'pride' mentioned above).

The word 'righteous' does, however, have an original positive meaning, that being 'genuine' or 'excellent'; it derives from the old English term 'rightwise', which was itself a combination of 'right' (meaning, originally, 'straight') and 'wise'. So to be rightwise, or righteous, was to be both trustworthy and wise. The biblical English translation was rendered with that original meaning of righteousness in mind, so the saying can be read as 'Those who hunger and thirst after true wisdom are blessed.'

To 'hunger and thirst' means, in this context, *to desire above all else.* Here again we see the radical, uncompromising nature of Jesus' message, consistent with all deeply awakened sages. Desire for the highest truth must be the guiding light of our life.

'Blessed are the merciful: for they shall obtain mercy.' (Matthew 5:7, KJV)

To be shown 'mercy' is to be forgiven for our offenses, whatever they have been (or however others have perceived them). The key issue here is not that of the standard pious forgiveness, which is usually spurious ('In order to make an outward display of my character I'll forgive you, but privately I'll continue to think you're an asshole and I'll never trust you again'). True forgiveness is something different. It is directly a function of being awake. When awake to the interconnectedness of life, we begin to understand the foolishness of lazily condemning others when we have not really looked in the mirror. (There is certainly room for accurate assessment of others, or appropriate use of judgment, but this is another matter. For now, we can recognize that the vast majority of judgment arises from personal agendas and the need to blame others for our problems in life.)

By 'giving mercy' – releasing others from the tight mental boxes we've put them in, and being willing to see their deeper underlying connection with us (just as everything is connected) – we let them go, so to speak, and in doing so, we are in turn 'freed'. To truly forgive someone is not just to free *them*, but more importantly, it is to free ourselves from our attachment to them. To hate someone is to remain attached to them. The more 'enemies' we have, the less free we are.

'Blessed are the pure in heart: for they shall see God.' (Matthew 5:8, KJV)

This line is often given as an example of Christ's moral teachings – be a good saint who doesn't fornicate or do other 'bad' things, etc. However, it must be seen in a deeper light. 'Pure' originally simply meant 'unmixed'. If something is unmixed, it is not diluted, and thus is both strong and original. To be 'pure in heart' is, from that perspective, to be untainted by the ideas, agendas, and conditioning put upon us by others.

Of course the simple truth is that none of us escapes being conditioned by the ideas and agendas of others. The task is to begin bravely recognizing this conditioning, and moving beyond it. We have to recognize just what is truly ours, and what we have merely borrowed, inherited, or otherwise uncritically bought into. To begin to let go of our borrowed ideas is to begin to become truly 'pure in heart'. This type of freer heart is capable of recognizing deep truth. Meditation and all forms of legitimate transformational work ultimately amount to a type of deconditioning – or as one psychotherapist once put it, 'de-hypnosis'. We have to un-learn much, in order to create the space inwardly, so to speak, to allow fresh, clear, and natural wisdom to arise. To 'see God' is to open the inner eye, to become sensitive to the immensity of being and existence. 'Purity of heart' can be understood more as becoming 'inwardly uncluttered' rather than attaining to some forced moral standard.

'Blessed are the peacemakers: for they shall be called the children of God.' (Matthew 5:9, KJV)

To be a 'child of God' means, in this context, to be awake to our true nature. To be a 'peacemaker' is to be one who contributes to the awakening of the human race, one who serves Truth. It is again a variation of a consistent theme of Jesus' teaching, which is that passion for Truth must be our guiding light, and all our energies committed to that purpose. This is not, of course, the same thing as becoming a fanatic, or a proselytizer. To have passion for awakening is not to be in the business of converting others (as if there is any 'thing' to convert them to). It addresses rather the issue of balance. That is, to commit ourselves to awakening is to have an inner practice of some sort, but *not* to become insulated from the world. Our 'outer practice' is how we serve, and that can be done in endless ways, but it always involves some sort of participation in the matter of sharing energy and consciousness with others. The word 'peacemakers' does appear very specific, but rather than conventional social activism it can be seen as referring to those outer actions that support the activity of inner work in the world, what in the East is sometimes called *karma yoga*, or what the contemporary mystic Andrew Harvey has called an element of 'sacred' activism. A simple example might be helping a teacher one is inspired by, or assisting a wise person in helping to make their work become more accessible to others, and so on.

'Blessed are they which are persecuted for righteousness' sake: for theirs is the kingdom of heaven.' (Matthew 5:10, KJV)

'Blessed are ye, when men shall revile you, and persecute you.' (Matthew 5:11, KJV)

These two statements emit a sharp light that will be difficult to look at for some. What they are basically saying is that one who aspires to be awake is not going to experience their life path being reinforced by the world, by the mass man, or even (as is most likely) by one's family. As Goethe once wrote, 'Tell a wise man, or else keep silent; for the mass man will mock it right away.' It was true in Jesus' time, and it remains true today. To be awake in a sleeping world is to be seen as eccentric (or worse). The conventional way of putting it is that a 'prophet is never recognized in his own country', or a 'genius is never recognized while they live'. However, a more direct way of saying it is 'The awake person is homeless, nationless, and unknown.' That is not grounds, of course, for resigning ourselves to a victim-position and giving up on the whole matter. But it is important to remember that our intention to be awake will usually not be recognized by most people; or worse, may even be actively opposed or undermined by them. None of that need be a real problem, however, and in fact we can simply use it to sharpen our practice and inner work, something like how a weightlifter is strengthened by pushing against weights. And therein lies the real point. Being awake is not contingent on what others think of us, or how they see us – regardless of who they are. To get beyond that fear is one of the most significant barriers to surmount for one who aspires to realization.

'Thou hypocrite, first cast out the beam out of thine own eye; and then shalt thou see clearly to cast out the mote out of thy brother's eye.' (Matthew 7:5, KJV

With this expression, Jesus reveals his psychological clarity, anticipating Freud's views on 'projection' nineteen centuries later. The statement needs little comment. We have to practice what we preach, to walk our talk, if our search for truth is to be authentic, and more than mere show.

'For whosoever will save his life shall lose it; and whosoever will lose his life for my sake shall find it. For what is a man profited, if he shall gain the whole world, and lose his own soul?' (Matthew16:25–

26, KJV)

The main delusion of the sleeping person (or, in psycho-spiritual language, 'the ego') is the belief that our salvation comes from the things of the world. To commit to awakening is, in a sense, to lose our life – not our real life, but the life of dreams and illusions, the life that we have been conditioned with, and taught to believe in, by the world.

'If any man come to me, and hate not his father, and mother, and wife, and children, and brethren and sisters, yea, and his own life also, he cannot be my disciple.' (Luke 14:26, KJV)

A very powerful saying, full of the uncompromising edge and fire that is so indicative of radically awakened sages like Socrates, Hakuin, or Jesus. What he is really saying there is, again, the supreme importance of prioritizing the search for truth. 'Hating' father, mother, etc., is a metaphor for placing everything beneath the intention to be awake. It may sound supremely selfish, but it is actually the reverse; in fact being spiritually asleep is synonymous with selfishness and utter inability to truly help anyone.

> 'Ye hath heard that it hath been said, Thou shalt love thy neighbor, and hate thine enemy. But I say unto you, Love your enemies, bless them that curse you, do good to them that hate you, and pray for them which despitefully use you, and persecute you; That ye may be the children of your Father which is in heaven; for he maketh his sun to rise on the evil and on the good, and sendeth rain on the just and on the unjust. For if ye love them which love you, what reward have ye? do not even the publicans the same? And if ye salute your brethren only, what do ye more than others? do not even the publicans so? Be ye therefore perfect, even as your Father which is in heaven is perfect.'
> (Matthew 5:43–48, KJV)

What does it mean to love our enemies? It is more than a clever psycho-social device to disarm those who are opposed to us. The injunction is not to be taken superficially, as some false piety, some phony holiness. It rather is reflective of some of the deepest wisdom of mystical tradition, perhaps nowhere echoed more clearly than in these lines from the *Tao Te Ching*:

> See the world as yourself.
> Have faith in the way things are.
> Love the world as yourself;
> then you can care for all things.
> (verse 13)

The key is to see the world *as us*. That is one of the central teachings at the core of most wisdom traditions, but the way Jesus tackles it is unique, and so starkly unconventional that it immediately grabs our attention. Jesus here represents our capacity to forgive in a profound and radical way, to 'be grand and mature' in the truest sense of those words. When we react petulantly, vengefully, we diminish our spirit in some way, if only by reinforcing our attachments. Not that passionate expression is to be denied – it is rather that our passion is to be redirected back toward a love of Truth. The surest way to do this is to stop wasting our passion, our life-force, on hating, on righteously condemning others, on 'maintaining enemies'.

The passage quoted above from Matthew referring to God 'making his sun to rise on the evil and the good, and sending rain on the just and the unjust', gives a glimpse into the profound non-dualism found in the teachings of all deeply realized sages. Ultimate truth transcends human conventions of good and evil, of just and unjust, and embraces a much vaster totality in which nothing is disconnected from anything else.

The Crucifixion

Jesus, like Socrates, paid a heavy price for his brazen teachings.

His crucifixion – and, as Christians believe, his resurrection – are of crucial importance to Christian faith. However, I think there is a teaching connected to the crucifixion that can be seen as a straightforward shedding of light on the 'crucifier' within each of us. Jesus was killed for what he claimed to represent – truth. Accordingly, we can understand his execution, from the esoteric perspective, as 'killing truth'. And in fact, there is an element within all of us (at least, practically all of us – perhaps a few rare souls are free of this) that is in the business of killing off truth. *A Course in Miracles* makes reference to the 'murderous' nature of the ego, in a section of its teachings called 'It can be but myself I crucify'. It is the part of our being that is so profoundly threatened by truth that it must silence it no matter what:

> There is an instant in which terror seems to grip your mind so wholly that escape appears quite hopeless. When you realize, once and for all, that it is you you fear, the mind perceives itself as split. And this had been concealed while you believed attack could be directed outward, and returned from outside to within. It seemed to be an enemy from outside you had to fear. And thus a god outside yourself became your mortal enemy; the source of fear. Now, for an instant, is a murderer perceived within you, eager for your death, intent on plotting punishment for you until the time when it can kill at last.
> (ACIM Workbook, #196)[3]

The 'murderer within' is vivid symbolism for all guilt and self-loathing, and all fear of relinquishing control – the control of our own identity, and the fear of being dominated, controlled, killed, by something bigger, and thus the fear of light and truth and life – the 'Way' represented by Jesus. There is a part of us that fears being 'killed' by truth, and so seeks to kill it first.

Truth is a fire and it does, in a very real sense, 'kill' us – the part of us that is false, illusory, what the Buddha referred to as our attachments, and the entire constructed edifice of the personal self that seeks to wall itself off from the true reality of the infinite. In that sense, the 'murderous' and traitorous face of the mind represents what in us fears Truth, and in particular, the consequences it will entail if we decide to commit our lives to that.

Ultimately, we are all cowards in the face of radical, uncompromising spiritual truth, and if we are not busy with running from it, we are involved in undermining it. That does not mean, however, that we need crucify ourselves for this fact. Such a punishment has already been done; we need not repeat it. Our task is, rather, to 'love our enemies' – to look deeply into the face of our fear, to summon compassion for it, and to penetrate beyond it with fearless passion for truth.

Chapter 31

Milarepa: Reformed Sorcerer

Story

Jetsun Milarepa, the famous yogi-saint of Tibet, lived from approximately 1052 to 1135 CE.[4] His name in Tibetan literally means 'Mila who Wears Cotton', referring to the extreme asceticism of his later years, and the one piece of garment he owned during that time. Milarepa's life story is of the archetypal spiritual hero. Much as with other ancient sages like Pythagoras, Lao Tzu, Socrates, and Jesus, little is known for sure about the kind of person he was and what exactly his 'life script' truly involved. However, as with all myths and legends it is what the stories *represent* that, above all, carries weight and meaning. This is very much the case from the perspective of ultimate spiritual truths, because from the deepest perspective *all* stories, regardless of whether they happened in physical reality or only in some scribe's imagination, are equally 'legendary' in the sense that they do not point to the unchangeable existence of any discrete, separate entity we may know as a 'person' to whom these stories have supposedly occurred. They rather point to the timeless *message*, which is always of a deeper substance than the messenger, whether this messenger be fictive or factual. Milarepa, regardless of how purely mythic his legend may be, is no less or no more real than you and I in this moment. Our very personalities are, ultimately, largely a collection of stories. These stories can, however, point toward ultimate truths, and this is especially so in the case of legends that surround awakened sages.

The legend of Milarepa's life tells of exceptional qualities. He started out as an innocent boy, became a destructive sorcerer, went through a profound remorse of conscience, followed that up with a purifying ordeal at the hands of a powerful taskmaster, and later attained to full enlightenment. There was an unusual degree of suffering in his ordeal, not just for himself, of course, but for those whom he'd harmed in his earlier years. It is rare in the lore of sages and mystics that criminals – let alone murderers – become awakened masters, and this is in large part what makes Milarepa's story as compelling as it is.

As for the source of the story, this appears to come from the written records of a Tibetan scribe who lived about four hundred years after Milarepa. He reports that Milarepa was born in western Tibet, near the sacred Mount Kailas. At the age of 7 his father died. His father's property was then confiscated by a greedy uncle and aunt. Milarepa's mother, angry and wanting revenge, eventually sent the young boy off to study with a *Bon* (shamanic) sorcerer, who proceeded to train him in harmful forms of magic, which included the alleged ability to alter weather patterns by harnessing certain destructive elemental forces.

Shamanism had been present in Tibet long before the arrival of Buddhism around the 7th century CE. Tibetan (as well as Mongolian and Siberian) shamans were widely known and on occasion feared for their unusual powers. In pre-industrial, pre-scientific times, magicians and shamans and sorcerers were, in most respects, the only 'wonder-workers'; the fact that many of these 'wonders' occurred only in the perception or imagination of others, did not diminish the power and esteem that these people were mostly held in. Tibet in particular has a history of rich lore on the topic of fantastic shamanic powers, to an extent that the wonders credited to Jesus in the New Testament are very ordinary compared to the stories of Tibetan magic. [A good example of these accounts can be found in Keith Dowman, *Sky Dancer* (Snow Lion Publications, 1996).] Perhaps the rarefied and pristine Tibetan landscape, high on the 'rooftop' of the world, contributed to a particularly vivid imagination. However, it is just as likely that many of these alleged powers – what Indian yogis call *siddhis* – were in fact real on a physical level, perhaps made possible by the almost total lack of distractions in such a vast and barren landscape to interfere with the concentrative practices needed to develop such abilities. Tibetan monks have been called the 'psychonauts' of the inner world, as their environment was ideal for inner exploration and a significant percentage of their population became monks or nuns. It is likely that the ancient shamanic traditions also attained to equally pronounced accomplishments for similar reasons.

According to the records Milarepa was a good student and learned the Black Arts well. When he had grown older he returned to the scene of the crime, carrying the dangerous mix of magical skill and ill intent. He sought out the greedy relatives and then manipulated certain 'elemental keys' (the essence of 'low magic'), which caused his uncle's house to collapse during a wedding celebration. Thirty-five people, all of whom were allies of the uncle and aunt who had betrayed Milarepa's mother, were crushed to death. According to the legend some demons visited Milarepa and asked him if they should kill the uncle and aunt also, to which Milarepa replied, 'No. Let them live to know my vengeance.' Milarepa the sorcerer was not done, however. He later conjured a huge hailstorm that destroyed a vast swath of crops that belonged to a village whose people had also been allied with Milarepa's uncle and aunt.

At this point Milarepa had, naturally, made many enemies. A number of them had put curses on him, and so he was being met by an oppositional psychic force that would begin to push him in the other direction, away from his dark path. More importantly, however, Milarepa carried the seeds of something great and noble within him. Consequently he experienced something that most criminals don't – that being a burning remorse for his actions. Feeling a desire for atonement growing stronger and stronger, he decided to seek out a teacher who could guide him through the requisite purification that he would need were he to have any chance to avoid (as he believed) rebirth into the remedial hell realms, or as a lower life-form (consistent with Buddhist theology).

He first went back to his original teacher who had taught him low magic, but this man recognized that he was not the one to perform the difficult task, and thus sent him on to a *lama* ('teacher') named Rongton Lhaga. This teacher was a renowned master of *Dzogchen*, one of the highest teachings within Tibetan Buddhism, reputed to be one of the 'direct' paths to enlightenment. After Milarepa found Rongton Lhaga, the *lama* gave him some instructions, but soon realized that he was not the right teacher either for this 'terrible sinner' (the words used by Milarepa when he had presented himself). He then told Milarepa to seek out a powerful master named Marpa the Translator who lived in the Lhobrak valley in southern Tibet. The *lama* added that Marpa and Milarepa had 'karmic links from the past' that made Marpa the appropriate teacher for him. When Milarepa heard the name Marpa the Translator he felt inexplicable joy, and knew that this would be his root guru who would be able to guide him to full awakening. (The deep passion that arose in him is reminiscent of the passion felt by a young Ramana Maharshi upon first hearing the name of the holy Mount Arunachala that he was destined to spend his life at.)

Marpa Lotsawa (1012–1097) was a Tibetan Buddhist master (and farmer) who had a reputation for being tough and disciplined. He had learned Sanskrit at a young age, and had subsequently traveled several times to India where he made lengthy stays, studying under his guru, the famed Indian master Naropa. (The first Buddhist university in America, founded in 1974 in Boulder, Colorado, was named after Naropa.) Marpa brought back many Buddhist texts from India, translating them into Tibetan. He is usually credited with being the main transmitter of some of the most advanced teachings now found in Tibetan Buddhism, such as Mahamudra.

Marpa lived up to his reputation as a tough taskmaster, and proceeded to subject Milarepa to an extended period of harsh and, at times, openly cruel disciplines. Milarepa, convinced of the terrible karmic debt that he needed to repay, surrendered to the treatment. One of the main devices Marpa used was to instruct Milarepa to build a large stone tower. At the point of his nearing completion of this back-breaking job, Marpa would assess the work, and inform Milarepa that the tower was in the wrong place, and would need to be torn down and built again. He had him do this several times – tearing down the stone tower and building it elsewhere – in addition to other physical deprivations. At other times Marpa would be drunk or pretending to be drunk, and at times he would disclaim having given certain instructions to Milarepa the day before. He also gave continuous false promises to give the teachings to Milarepa and would constantly break those promises. In this way he put Milarepa through not just great physical hardships but mental trials as well, especially designed to test his faith. On top of all that, Marpa was physically abusive, frequently beating Milarepa. During the years of harsh labor and abuse Milarepa was not given any teachings but functioned only as a servant. At one point, unable to bear Marpa's treatment any longer, he resolved to leave. Marpa's wife, who took great pity on him, forged a letter of introduction from Marpa to another *lama* not far away, who could teach Milarepa. He went to this *lama*, but after practicing his teachings for some time with no results, he admitted that the introductory letter had been forged. The *lama* then sent him back to Marpa, explaining that the practices were not working because Marpa had not blessed Milarepa's presence with the *lama*. It seemed there was no way to escape Marpa, and so Milarepa returned to him. But still Marpa would not teach him. When Milarepa was finally driven to the point of deciding to commit suicide, Marpa relented and began to instruct him.

As Marpa explained, because Milarepa's earlier crimes had been so extreme he needed to go over the edge in order to be deemed worthy of the gift he was seeking. The last of Milarepa's powerful karmic residues had been destroyed, and he was now an 'empty cup', ready to receive the higher knowledge that would lead to his liberation. As might be expected, he excelled as a student, progressing very quickly. After a while Milarepa retreated to the mountains where he lived in seclusion, absorbed in deep meditation practice for nine years. He dwelt in a frigid cave, but was given the psychic technique of *tummo* (heat creation) which enabled him to withstand the cold. He was said to have attained to the highest enlightenment. Many seekers of truth were drawn to him, a number of whom became his disciples. One of these disciples, the physician Gampopa, in turn became the teacher of Dusum Kenpa, who was to be recognized as the first Karmapa, or 'Black Hat Lama'. This is the office of the continuously reincarnating master of the Karma Kargyu lineage, the seventeenth incarnation of whom is alive today (in fact there are currently two recognized seventeenth Karmapas in an unusual and somewhat bizarre controversy that has been ongoing since the 1980s). The Karmapa is an older lineage than that of the Dalai Lama (of whom the current one, Tenzin Gyatso (b. 1935) is the fourteenth).

Teachings

Milarepa also became a poet, and spontaneously composed over 100,000 lyric songs, the manuscript of which exists today as *The Hundred Thousand Songs of Milarepa*. Here is one of them, illustrating the classic Buddhist realization of *shunyata* ('emptiness'):

> In the realm of Absolute Truth, Buddha Himself does not exist.
> There are no practices nor practitioners, no path, no realization,
> and no stages, no Buddha's bodies and no Wisdom.
> There is then no Nirvana, for these are merely names and thoughts.
>
> Matter and beings in the universe are non-existent from the start; they have never come to be.
> There is no Truth, no Innate-Born Wisdom, no Karma, and no effect therefrom;

The World even has no name,
such is Absolute Truth.

This is a very deep realization, possible only for one who has 'gone beyond'. It is reminiscent of the 7th century Chinese Cha'an (Zen) master Hui-neng, who, seeing a few lines written by an advanced monk – 'The body is the tree of salvation / The mind is a clear mirror / Incessantly wipe and polish it / Let no dust fall on it' – famously countered with 'Salvation is nothing like a tree / Nor a clear mirror / Essentially, not a 'thing' exists / What is there, then, for the dust to fall on?'

All fully awakened sages ultimately recognized the pure 'emptiness' of existence. 'Emptiness' in this context needs to be understood. It simply means that all things lack inherent and discrete existence – that is, all things are interdependent and in a state of flux, and thus the idea that a 'thing' can exist in and of itself (which naturally includes the ego) is ultimately an illusion. This is not the same as the Western idea of nihilism (although the two can be easily confused with each other). Nihilism involves a view that implies that existence has a lack of objective meaning, value, and overall purpose (the word comes from the Latin *nihil*, meaning 'nothing'). Nihilism has become more relevant in current times, with our global population spike and advanced communication technologies, making information in general more accessible. That in turn has many side-effects, some of which are increased doubt, cynicism and a general loss of a sense of the sacred.

Seeing into the illusoriness of the existence of discrete objects (and the personal self) does not negate meaning or value, but is rather a pointer toward something of such profundity that our conventionally conditioned minds need to be deconditioned in order to begin to recognize it. Nihilism is all too often used as a disguise for fear of life, or unwillingness to be responsible for oneself. The insight of Milarepa or Hui-neng is much deeper than mere nihilism and only comes after years of committed practice and relentless willingness to deconstruct the false self and see deeply into the nature of Reality.

In the passage quoted above, Milarepa is not actually saying that nothing *per se* exists, he is pointing to the understanding that prior to full awakening, we see everything through the filter of deluded concepts. We do not see Reality, but only our *ideas* of it (including 'spiritual' ideas, which can prove to be some of the most stubborn illusions). When we remove the filters of ego-based projection – that is, the delusion of duality – the world is revealed to be something far beyond the world we've constructed with our minds. In fact, Milarepa, despite his deep insight into Reality and his ascetic nature (living in caves for many years) had a great love for the play of existence, and the vividly beautiful landscape he dwelt in. He once expressed it thusly:

Beneath the bright light in the sky, stand snow mountains to the North.
Near these are the holy pasture lands, and fertile Medicine Valley.
Like a golden divan is the narrow basin, round it winds the river, Earth's great blessing ...
When one approaches closer, one sees a great rock towering above a meadow.
As prophesied by Buddha in past ages, it is the Black Hill, the rock of Bije Mountain Range.
It is the central place, north of the woodlands on the border between Tibet and India,
where tigers roam freely.
The medicine trees, Tsandam and Zundru, are found here growing wild.
The rock looks like a heap of glistening jewels...

One can see that those are not the words of a 'nihilist'. Like some of the Japanese Zen haiku poets (such as Basho), Milarepa combined a radical insight into Being with the realization that the universe of form was one and the same as formlessness. As the famous Buddhist Heart Sutra expresses it, 'Form is Emptiness, and Emptiness is Form.' Milarepa wrote,

Thunder, lightning, and the clouds,
Arising as they do out of the sky,
Vanish and recede back into it.

The rainbow, fog, and mist,
Arising as they do from the firmament,
Vanish and recede back into it.

Honey, fruit, and crops grow out of the earth;
All vanish and recede back into it …

Self-awareness, self-illumination, and self-liberation,
Arising as they do from the Mind-Essence,
All vanish and dissolve back into the mind…

He who realizes the nature of the mind,
Sees the great Illumination without coming and going,
Observing the nature of all outer forms,
He realizes that they are but illusory visions of the mind.

He sees also the identity of the Void and the Form
…
Discrimination of 'the two' is the source of all wrong views.
From the ultimate viewpoint there is no view whatsoever.

Mahamudra is the name of the teaching that Milarepa transmitted, from his guru Marpa, to some of his own students (such as Gampopa). The word means 'Great Seal', but has a deeper meaning, denoting the experience of Reality – vividly, and beyond all mental distortions – as had by one who has mastered it. What Mahamudra points toward is both profound and simple, the essential paradox that all deeply realized sages embody and teach. It is profound because our minds are deeply mired in the illusion of duality (the experience of separation and disconnection), and so a teaching pointing toward non-duality seems impossible to fully realize. And it is simple because nothing, in the final analysis, could possibly be more simple than non-duality.

The basis of the realization of Mahamudra is in recognizing the 'gap' of non-dual wisdom that is naturally present between all thoughts. Normally we remain unaware of this 'gap', because we are too identified with our thoughts, and in particular, with the 'self' we take ourselves to be, who is apparently having these thoughts. Between the sense of ourselves as a particular 'me' – with all my attendant dramas and stories and dreams and fears, and so on – and the endless display of the thoughts themselves, it's no small wonder that we simply fail to notice the vast and pure 'background' or 'space' within which all our mental activity is arising.

Milarepa compared the endless display of the mind, and the experiences it produces, to a 'morning mist', and said that trying to hold onto the mist is pointless. Our task is always to return our bare attention to the reality of space – that is, the space between thoughts, which is in fact the vastness of pure potential energy. To even call this 'space' is inadequate as no concept can capture it or adequately define it. Even to refer to it as 'it' – a necessary utility of language – still misses the point, because this 'it' is in fact our own real nature.

According to the legends, Milarepa spent a number of years wandering the lands after his enlightenment, teaching whenever the occasion presented itself. During parts of that time he was said to subsist on an extreme ascetic diet that consisted largely of stinging-nettle tea, which caused his skin to take on a green tinge. This is why many of the Tibetan *tangka* (religious painting) renderings of him show him with a greenish skin. However one takes a legend like that – and it probably is at least partly true, as Tibetan and Indian wandering mystics have long been famed for extreme ascetic practices – it is a fitting metaphor for what a figure like Milarepa embodies: fierce and unrelenting commitment. Milarepa is the classic example of totality of action. Whatever he did, he went all out at (a common trait of one destined to become a great sage). Marpa had nicknamed him 'Great Magician' because of his (deadly) proficiency in that area. When serving as Marpa's slave for several years, he gave that his all. And in studying and practicing the dharma, he again was full-on, with the result being that he was said to attain to the highest realizations in the shortest time ever known in his particular tradition.

A sage like Milarepa teaches us the supreme value of cultivating passion for awakening above all else; and that in doing so, it becomes possible to reverse even the darkest of fortunes.

Chapter 32

Hakuin: Zen Executioner

Hakuin Ekaku (1686–1768) is generally recognized as the most important Japanese Zen master of recent centuries.[5] He was born Nagasawa Iwajiro (in Japan, the family name precedes the first name) on January 19, 1686, near Mount Fuji, the youngest of five children. From an early age his inclination toward the spiritual life was clear. He was ordained a Zen monk at just 15 years old. The seeds of his desire for awakening originated, in part, from a natural sensitivity and a type of psychological trauma he passed through at age 11. He had been listening to a Buddhist priest of his mother's faith (the Nichiren Buddhist tradition) give a lecture on the 'hell realms' of the afterlife, when he became caught in the throes of a deep and overwhelming fear. Determined to overcome this fear (note the striking similarity with Ramana Maharshi's story, below), he decided to totally commit himself to the Buddhist path, and began even at that young age to practice some basic spiritual austerities (such as waking early, reciting prayers, performing prostrations, reading scriptures, and so forth). These practices had limited effect, and so Iwajiro decided his only hope to conquer his deep fear of a hellish afterlife was to become a Buddhist priest.

When he was 14, his parents, realizing their young son could not be dissuaded from his chosen path, took him to a local temple, which in turn sent him right away to the Daisho-ji temple in a nearby town. He spent the next few years at this temple undertaking novice duties, serving as attendant to the resident priest and being schooled in the classical Chinese language (necessary for any serious Japanese Buddhist, as Buddhism had been transmitted to Japan from China around the 12th century CE, and many important texts were in Chinese).

At this early age Iwajiro had become acquainted with the famous Buddhist scripture known as the Lotus Sutra, but he did not have a high opinion of it. Years later he would return to that particular scripture during the episode of his 'final awakening' in which its teachings became crystal clear to him. He had originally dismissed the Lotus Sutra for its seeming simplicity, but it was this same simplicity that he would later understand as profound wisdom. The association between 'seeming simplicity' and deep wisdom is a common one in the enlightenment tradition. 'Seeming simplicity' in this case means a clear, straightforward view of reality – what typically is obscured by the workings of the mind in its commonly deluded state. Meditation and radical insight are the practices of clearing away the clouds of delusion and illusion, revealing the pristine nature of reality.

At 18 Iwajiro transferred to a different temple, where he was to begin his formal training as a monk. At this temple he underwent a phase of alienation from Zen Buddhism brought on by two main issues: first, his disappointment that the training at the temple appeared to be more academic than experiential (the monks were mainly involved in studying Chinese Zen poetry); and second, his learning about a famous Zen master who had been killed by bandits, and seemed to die in a manner that lacked the dignity of an awakened being. Iwajiro concluded that if a great Zen master could die in such a manner, then he himself would have little hope of conquering his fear of the hell-realms that he still carried within. Rejecting Zen practice for now, he decided to give himself over to the study of literature and the arts (including calligraphy, which he would become an accomplished master of). The next year he transferred to another temple, one that had a large library. Here he haphazardly discovered a particular book that made mention of an ancient Chinese master who emphasized the need for great effort in order to break free of the mind's laziness and delusions. As it happened, this Chinese master had revived a particular lineage, the Lin-chi, that Iwajiro himself would later revive in Japan (a tradition now known as Rinzai, one of the two main lines of Japanese Zen).

Shortly after, Iwajiro embarked on an extended pilgrimage for several years, during which he wandered over many parts of Japan. The main criticism he had developed by then of the existing Zen tradition was that it was dominated by too much passivity – the word he used is sometimes translated in English as 'quietist' – an approach that he believed tended to ruin the drive, focus, and tenacity he had determined by then was necessary for deep awakening. He himself, by his own admission, had not yet passed through the profounder awakenings, so at this point his views were speculative and intuitive.

By 23 years of age, Iwajiro had grown increasingly skeptical of the various Zen teachers and authorities of his time, and had decided to give himself over to intensive sitting meditation practice (*zazen*), focusing mostly on a particular ancient *koan*. (A *koan* is a rationally insoluble problem – such as 'What is the sound of one hand clapping?' – that is designed to quiet the part of the mind that tries to figure things out in a superficial way. The result, if achieved, is a breakthrough in insight that goes beyond the standard rational approach to problems. A *koan* successfully 'solved' leads to mystical realization; that is, a sense of deeper connectedness between self and universe. The depth of this realization can vary greatly, but generally speaking it is a temporary affair that does not significantly transform more entrenched elements of character. Deeper follow-up work and practice is almost always required.)

After considerable effort he experienced a breakthrough in realization (typically called *kensho* or *satori* in Zen – with the latter denoting a somewhat more prolonged or profound awakening), something he felt quite ecstatic about. Because he was working without guidance, however, coarser elements of his ego had not yet been worn down. He had already been given to some intellectual arrogance before (common with the exceptionally bright), and the *satori* (as it will often do) simply highlighted that part of his character more clearly. He later wrote of this period that he was 'puffed up with soaring pride, bursting with arrogance'.

The arrogance was soon to be busted by a fierce and eccentric old Zen master named Shoju, whom Iwajiro spent the better part of the next year with. There are stories from this period that mark some of the more notorious images of Zen that typically come to mind for one who reads up on the tradition: the rough old master who treats his disciple with seemingly little mercy and less gentleness (Shoju, in addition to berating his young charge verbally, once physically tossed Iwajiro off his veranda – compare the stories of Marpa physically and psychologically manhandling Milarepa), and the inevitable assigning to the student difficult *koans* to solve. Shoju also pointed out that Iwajiro's original motivation for dedicating his life to the spiritual path – his fear of the 'afterlife hell-realms' – in fact revealed his self-absorption, another character trait that would have to be honestly faced.

The key element of training that Iwajiro absorbed from his time with Shoju was what he called 'post-*satori*' training; that is, continuing to practice deeply and with great commitment, *after* one's initial awakenings. This is an essential point that cannot be emphasized enough. Many teachers and would-be gurus go astray precisely because they stop practicing after their early realizations. If they acquire followers, it then becomes doubly difficult for them to realize that they need to continue working on themselves, deepening their realizations and purifying their character. Shoju was a strong master precisely because he did not let his students get away with thinking that their initial awakening conferred any profound wisdom or special status on them. He did not let them rest on any self-conferred laurels.

At the completion of his practice under Shoju, the old master asked him to remain and become his successor, but Iwajiro declined, choosing to continue his wandering. Biographers at this point sometimes note that an apparent oddity of Iwajiro's life is that he never returned to Shoju, despite the fact that he praised him as his most important teacher – and the only true Zen master of his time – and that Shoju lived on for another thirteen years. The most common explanation given for this is that Iwajiro didn't come to realize Shoju's importance until after the latter died, but it's equally possible that the student needed to keep his distance from the master in order to prevent any sort of dependence from prevailing (a common theme between strong masters and equally strong students – and quite similar to how a son needs to break away from a strong-willed father to come into his own, even if his father is a very good father and an honorable man).

After leaving Shoju (around the year 1710 when he was 24 years old), Iwajiro realized that his awakening was not complete. He'd had profound realizations and understood much of the scriptures, but something was lacking. In particular, he noted that he could not maintain clarity and equanimity in the marketplace as much as he could in the monastery. That might seem completely natural, but the fact that this bothered Iwajiro was testament to his quality (and his maturity at a young age). There are far too many 'awakened sages' who are awake only in the comfortable confines of the monk's meditation hall or private cell. Iwajiro was determined to integrate the worlds of 'spirit' and 'flesh', the time-honored challenge of all who seek authentic awakening.

He then spent the next six years wandering from temple to temple, occasionally visiting a Zen master here or there, but for the most part staying on his own. It was during this period that he contracted his famous 'Zen sickness', some sort of physical or psychological illness (never specified, at least by modern labels – although inner disturbances of many varieties are often reported by those who persist in deep meditation over many years). At age 30 he settled down in a forest hut to undertake an intensive solitary retreat, which he pursued with great zeal. This retreat was broken after a year or so, when he was called back to his hometown on account of his father's illness.

A year after his return to his hometown, in 1718 at age 32, he was installed as head priest at the local temple. At this time he took a new spiritual name – Ekaku Hakuin – and the latter name, Hakuin, is how he has been known to posterity. The name means 'Concealed in White', a reference to the temple that he was now abbot of. He was to retain that position for the last fifty years of his life.

For the next decade or so Hakuin lived a simple life (with meager means, as the temple was poor), meditating many hours every day, studying Buddhist writings by the old masters, and occasionally instructing a few students. He was not well known at this point and so had limited teaching responsibilities. In 1727 at age 41, he underwent his final *satori*, triggered by a combination of reading the Lotus Sutra and listening to the sounds of a nearby cricket. He described this last awakening as profound and total, leaving him with perfect clarity and boundless energy. He then directed this clarity and energy into teaching, which he did with great force of commitment for the remaining four decades of his life. By the time he passed away he had singlehandedly reformed the entire Zen tradition in Japan, and personally instructed thousands of monks and seekers.

During the latter half of his life he received numerous invitations to lecture and teach at various temples around the country; in some of these lectures, several hundred monks would be in the audience at a time. Hakuin became renowned for his outspoken and fearless criticisms of the elements of Buddhism in Japan that he saw as having fallen into a moribund decline over the centuries. Like many great sages he was involved not just with teaching, but with establishing a whole new transmission, or 'current' as the term is known in some esoteric traditions. Any teacher who undertakes such work must be very courageous because of reactionary forces he or she almost always encounters (with Jesus' life story being the most vivid example).

Hakuin's fame peaked in the early 1740s when in his mid-50s – he on occasion lectured for up to four hundred monks and seekers at a time. It was around then that he became established as the greatest Zen master in Japan. He began to write more in his late 50s and into his old age, producing a vast body of prose and poetry, all dedicated to conveying his grasp of enlightenment. In addition, he was a prolific artist and calligrapher. His many renderings of the famed Indian monk Bodhidharma are easily recognized by many around the world (though many probably know little about the artist).

Hakuin is reported to have died peacefully, lying on his right side, in 1768 at age 82.

Teachings

There seems little question that Hakuin's depth and quality of understanding was very great. His story is rare for several reasons, two prime ones being that he possessed an exceptional determination and stamina, enough to break through the barriers of his mind and penetrate deep into the essence of reality; and in addition, he went to the trouble to write his life story down in a book he called *Wild Ivy* (very few gurus or masters write autobiographies).

Most important of all, however, is that Hakuin had the clarity to recognize what needed to be changed in the Zen scene, and the courage to set about creating that change. He shook up the whole sleepy state of affairs of Zen of his time, taking aim in particular at what he saw as the 'quietist' or passive approach to realization that he believed was destroying the true tradition. Hakuin was, above all, an ambassador for the 'radical awakening' model, asserting that any real understanding was impossible without *kensho* or *satori*. He wrote: 'Anyone who would call himself a member of the Zen family must first of all achieve kensho ... if a person who has not achieved kensho says he is a follower of Zen, he is an outrageous fraud. A swindler pure and simple.'[6]

He was the quintessential 'rude master', fearless in speaking his mind. Here, reminiscent of other sharp-tongued sages like Socrates, Jesus, U.G. Krishnamurti and Osho, he takes aim at what he saw in much of the clergy of his time and tradition:

In recent times Zen schools have been engaging in

the practice of 'silent illumination', doing nothing but sitting lifelessly like wooden blocks. What, aside from that, do you suppose they consider their most urgent concern? They twitter on about being 'men of nobility' who have 'nothing at all to do'. They proceed to live up to that self-proclaimed role. Consuming lots of good rice. Passing day after day in a state of seated sleep ... the cotton robe they wear as Buddhist priests is no more than a disguise.[7]

Much like Jesus blasting the Pharisees of his time, Hakuin spoke out eloquently and forcefully against elements of the Zen priesthood, accusing many of them of living off the hard work of the laypeople. He maintained that the job of the priesthood was to provide genuine inspiration to laypeople, but that the clergy of his time were not capable of this because of the degenerate level of their own practice and understanding. Most particularly, it was his view that too few Zen priests had experienced *kensho* of any sort, and so they amounted to nothing more than lazy, ineffectual intellectuals – 'wooden blocks' – supported by society. He went so far as to call the priesthood 'thieves' for living off of donations, and he saw them as 'worse than the vilest things'.

It's not easy to appreciate just how uncommon this sort of sharp criticism is, especially from a traditional Eastern Zen master. The matter of 'losing face' is big in Asia, and the Japanese culture in particular, despite giving rise to a seemingly 'earthy' tradition like Zen, has always been very concerned with formality of communication and certain rigid behavior protocols (not unlike the English prior to the 1960s). While unusual, it's not that rare to find outspoken or controversial sages or philosophers in the history of the West, owing to the greater Western emphasis on individualism and rebelliousness (Greek history, for example – the intellectual and cultural roots of the West – is full of legends of heroic or rebellious gods, heroes, and anti-heroes). But in the Orient this is much more uncommon. It is therefore a testament to the respect that Hakuin had earned that he could speak in such a manner with minimal negative consequences. This is doubtless due in part to the fact that Hakuin's outspokenness appears to have come about more in his later years. It's interesting to contrast him with Jesus, with whom he shares a number of parallels, and note what happened to Jesus for speaking out so early in his ministry – three of the four gospels have Jesus being executed after only one year of public teaching. Hakuin taught for around five decades, about as long as the Buddha. Obviously the prevailing 18th century culture of Japan, in contrast to 1st century Judea, also had something to do with the response Hakuin met. But none of that diminishes the clarity and courageousness of his message.

Hakuin's main dispute was with the meditation practice used mostly by the Soto Zen sect along with a related practice (Bankei's 'Unborn' teachings, which was actually a sub-sect within his own Rinzai lineage). The main feature of these practices was what he called 'silent illumination', the passive practice of resting in 'no-mind', the term given to represent a state of mental quietude in which the movement of thought is greatly slowed down, or stopped altogether. While Hakuin understood that 'inner silence' is indeed an aspect of an awakened mind, he was pointing out that it is an idea that is greatly susceptible to being misused – or in more modern Western language, 'appropriated by the ego'. He saw that far too many who were practicing such an approach were simply deadening their minds, dulling the edge of their insight, with the result being that they ended up little better than passive clones, living in a poor approximation of what is possible from sustained meditation practice.

For Hakuin, the importance of pursuing *kensho* was that it acted as a crucial counterweight to the trickery of the ego, which in its fear of facing inward, sought a passive practice that allowed it to go through the motions of inquiry into truth, when in fact it was in a state of mind that was closer to dreaming that one is awake – what

Hakuin called 'seated sleep'.

We have a parallel for this in our modern forms of 'spiritual work', and it relates to several of the issues highlighted in the first part of this book. As Gurdjieff pointed out, it is not only possible to *imagine* that we are awake, it is actually very common. Awakening gets easily confused with the idea of 'feeling better' and so forth, and accordingly we set out to take the path of least resistance. Hakuin's main underlying point is that there is no easy route to realization, for the main reason that we have taken a very difficult route to become as confused and deluded as we are – therefore, to get out of such a place, an equally difficult challenge awaits us.

Hakuin's critique of the Zen priesthood of his time was based on the simple observation that an unclear teacher can only guide students in an unclear fashion. There is again a modern-day parallel: in current times, 'spiritual teachers' and 'healers' of all possible stripes are commonplace. It can be safely said that the vast majority are of mediocre or low quality, because the vast majority have not made serious headway in breaking through their own inner barriers. Why? Because the vast majority had teachers of similar mediocre quality. Hakuin's caution against shallow inner work is the time-honored cry of the deeply awakened sage. It just so happens that in modern times, with our population spike and the sheer availability of information concerning personal transformation, superficiality has become a problem. Diminished attention spans, brought on in part by sophisticated advances in communication and entertainment technology, certainly don't help.

The Koan

It's impossible to understand Hakuin's teachings without looking at *koan* practice. A *koan*, as mentioned above, is a type of problem or seeming riddle that has no real logical answer. Examples of well-known ones from the Zen tradition are: 'Show me your face before your parents were born', 'Why did Bodhidharma go to China?', 'Does a dog have Buddha-nature?', and so on. Perhaps the most well-known *koan*, 'Who am I?', was the method used and taught by the famous Advaitin sage Ramana Maharshi (see Chapter 33).

The idea when working with a *koan* is to concentrate on it deeply, inquiring profoundly into it. This inquiring, however, is not the typical inquiring, as when we set out to solve a problem. The difference with *koan* practice is that we are inquiring into the nature of the *one who knows* – the 'questioner', if you will, rather than the question itself; the knower, rather than that which is known. It is a type of reversal of thought. Attention is kept with the subject, rather than shone outwardly onto the object (be that object a thought, or a thing).

This is persisted with until a type of breakthrough in understanding is achieved. The ultimate essence of this breakthrough is a deeper grasp of the unity of all things – what is sometimes called 'One Mind', or 'Big Mind' – which is essentially consciousness free of confused conceptual obstructions, free of the lazy, deluded thinking that we typically engage in. Once such confused and deluded thinking is arrested, our 'inner eye' opens and certain truths become obvious. These truths usually involve some of the following:

1. Direct understanding of cause and effect, and more precisely, of the seamless interrelatedness of all things.

2. A strong sense of the 'natural perfection' of this moment, here and now.

3. A deeper sense of effortlessness, and a falling away of self-loathing or self-defeating thought patterns.

4. Renewed energy, and an increased sense of compassion for all things.

5. Direct insight into the 'emptiness' of the self – or, put another way, how the self is not discrete or separate, but is fundamentally connected to all things. Deeper insight reveals that there *is* no true separate self, and that there are no discrete 'things' in any absolute sense, and that all appearance of duality – 'I and you', or 'this and that' – is an elaborate illusion generated by the mind.

And so forth. The breakthrough experienced – *kensho* – can vary widely in quality, from a relatively shallow glimpse, to a profound and sustained awakening (the latter usually called *satori*). Deeper awakenings are usually life-altering events, serving to clarify one's overall life path and as is most often the case, leading to an interest in helping others (teaching) or more often, serving a *sangha* (spiritual community) in some fashion.

It should also be stressed that *koan* work is not easy, and does not always produce enjoyable effects. For example, it is possible, and somewhat common, to experience a disturbing state of mind when focusing deeply on a *koan*, because the very effort we make can have the effect of opening the mind – or what in Western psychology would be called opening the unconscious mind – resulting in the release of repressed material from the psyche. If this repressed material is of a particularly painful sort (say, as the result of past trauma) then the effects endured during its release can be unpleasant. It is for this reason that *koan* work is best undertaken with experienced guidance from a qualified Zen teacher.

Hakuin was not fixated on the breakthroughs resulting from *koan* practice, however. He also emphasized the necessity of continuing to practice *zazen* (meditation) even after the experience of *kensho*. He once remarked that meditation amid intense activity was much more valuable than meditation in a silent, still environment. That was something Gurdjieff was to echo two centuries later in his 'Fourth Way' (way of the householder) teachings that emphasize the practice of being awake in the marketplace as opposed to the monastery. Although Hakuin himself spent many years in solitary meditation, he did not generally advocate this lifestyle, all the more so as he had many lay students, most of whom were busy with the matters of domesticity and work, just as people are now. Accordingly he advised people not to avoid worldly life, but rather to practice in the midst of it. He used the analogy of a man who drops some pieces of gold in a crowded public square swarming with people. He will not simply give up and leave; rather, he will do whatever is necessary (including pushing people away) to retrieve his gold pieces. Hakuin said that this intensity of determination needs to be our attitude toward practicing meditation in the midst of our busy life. We must be determined to 'find the truth' in the midst of our busy-ness, just as the man would be determined to get back the gold he'd dropped in the midst of chaos.

222222

Chapter 33

Ramana Maharshi: Solid as a Mountain

Ramana Maharshi was one of the rarest lights of wisdom of the 20th century, one of the few high-profile gurus of recent times who was not just scandal-free, but who escaped any noticeable criticism as well (and most notably, from his peers). His rarity lay partly in his purity and in his utter simplicity. Following a profound and radical awakening at age 16, he subsequently spent fifty-four years around one particular small mountain. He was a living, breathing demonstration of one who had clearly gone beyond all personal agenda or egocentric desire. Although born into the Hindu tradition, and essentially teaching Advaita Vedanta (generally recognized as the cream of the Hindu wisdom teachings), he was in many ways the quintessential Buddha, manifesting to a high degree of perfection such Buddhist ideals as penetrating wisdom, utter non-attachment, desirelessness, and compassionate action (via his tireless teaching).

He was born Venkataraman Ayyar on December 30, 1879, in a small village in Tamil Nadu, the southernmost state of India, the second of what would become a family of four children.[8] At this point most biographers of his life tend to remark that Venkataraman was apparently a rather ordinary boy growing up, athletically inclined, and somewhat lazy in his studies, but that he did have one notable feature and that was an exceptional memory. (He would use this memory to get by in his studies without putting in too much effort.) However, if one reads the stories of his youth closely enough it becomes clear that he was not quite 'ordinary'. He did have some strong qualities, in addition to his outstanding memory. In particular he was given to a type of remarkable steadfastness (or stubbornness) that showed in several ways. For one, he was an unusually deep sleeper. In his later years he would tell comical tales of how his childhood mates, fascinated with how difficult it was to wake him, used to carry his body around, slap him this way and that, and then put his body back in bed, all the while the boy never waking and not knowing anything of what had happened. This apparent ability to be inwardly immoveable like a mountain – a fascinating foreshadowing of his later deep affinity for one famed mountain and his decision to spend his whole life living by it – would serve him well in two keys ways. The first was when he underwent his great awakening (by dint of sheer focus and determination), and the second when he refused to allow himself to be controlled by his uncle and elder brother after his awakening (see below).

In addition, Ramana's biographer David Godman reported that the young Venkataraman was known to be very lucky; for example, whatever sports team he would play for, that team would invariably win. As a result he was called *Tangakai* ('Golden Hand'). What we typically dismiss as 'good luck' can also be associated with an ability to be present with what one is doing. The old expression in sports is 'A good player creates good luck.' A 'good player' is, at heart, one who can truly focus, who can truly be present with what it is he or she is doing (the best athletes tend to be the most committed, just as the 'best' in most activities in life tend to be).

Venkataraman's father passed away when he was 12 years old, at which point the boy and his siblings went to live with his uncle. As he entered his adolescence there were no signs of what was going to happen to him in a few short years. His first spiritual glimmerings began to be awakened in 1895, shortly before he turned 16. These consisted of his hearing someone speak the name of the south Indian holy mountain 'Arunachala'; Venkataraman was struck by the sound and quality of the name. Shortly after, he read a book about some south Indian saints and a spark was ignited. His is not the story of an adult who stumbled onto the path of illumination, or who was 'forced' to it by difficult circumstances – much like Hakuin, he had the innate disposition of the truth-seeker *par excellence*, and so responded naturally and enthusiastically, even at that tender age, to the writings and stories of wise sages.

It was in mid-1896, at age 16, when his famous awakening occurred. It was precipitated by an intense fear of death that suddenly overtook and overwhelmed him. Arguably it was similar to a sudden psychotic break, because the fear arose out of nowhere and immobilized him. As he described it, the shock drove his mind inward with what must have been an extraordinary degree of force. He then lay down on the ground and, feeling his body frozen, began to examine his mental processes carefully with minute attention. He truly believed he was dying, and so this permitted him a measure of detachment from his body. In a remarkable display of natural spiritual maturity, he conquered the fear and his panic subsided. He then intentionally dramatized the process of death, holding his breath and enacting a *rigor mortis*. What soon emerged was the sudden realization that his true nature was not the body, or the earthly identity-personality known as Venkataraman. His real nature was pure Consciousness, or what he would later call 'the Self'. He further observed that he now became fully absorbed in the Self, and experienced a steady and passionate fascination with this timeless Presence that he tacitly realized was his own actual nature. This soon led to the realization that 'he' was not 'absorbed into' the Self. He *was* the Self.

And basically, that was it. What is so remarkable about this story is that awakenings of this nature are not altogether uncommon (even if not of this depth), especially among devoted and committed mystics or meditators. However, in almost all cases such an awakening is temporary, and even more commonly, is but a glimpse. Typically a truth-seeker, upon having such a glimpse, or even an awakening that lasts for several days, soon returns to the usual identification with the personality and body. But in Venkataraman's case the break between 'sleep' and 'awakening' was both profound and final. There would be no going back after this event, no retreating into a conventional life. As it turned out, his powerful premonition of death that preceded the awakening was, essentially, correct – it was just that identification with the ego-mind died, not his physical body. (That is not to say that Ramana's inner process was over – he subsequently spent many years adapting his body-mind to his awakening to the Self – but the essential insight into his true nature was, in his case, both total and irreversible.)

His awakening event – and 'event' is the correct word, not 'experience' – apparently unfolded in the course of a mere thirty minutes. Arthur Osborne, one of Ramana's chief chroniclers, reported that Ramana had completed in half an hour what most seekers 'take an entire lifetime, or several lifetimes, to achieve'. He further points out that there was nothing 'effortless' about this attainment. The young boy had, in fact, employed a combination of enormous intensity, determination, and passion in one half-hour burst to break through the barriers of the mind that stand in the way of full realization of the Self.

Following his awakening Venkataraman opted to tell no one what had happened, and continued to attend school. However, he found himself disconnected from most of what was around him. He went through the motions with his school work, began to lose interest in relations with other people, and even lost interest in the taste of food (he reported that he continued to eat as before, but didn't care whether what he was eating tasted good or not). He also reported that his behavior with others became indifferent, even submissive at times, because he had lost all egocentric tendencies to retaliate, to compete, to prove himself, and so on.

All that might sound perilously close to some sort of mental illness – in particular, 'depersonalization syndrome' as psychoanalysis terms it – but in fact the boy was not emotionally disconnected and had not lost the ability to feel alive or passionate. It was rather that his passion had been redirected toward a much loftier view. Even as he lost all interest in what his schoolmates were up to – the usual thing 16-year-olds everywhere are up to – Venkataraman was in fact paying nightly visits to a particular temple where, full of passion and deep emotion, he would stand for hours in front of certain icons, such as those of Shiva or Nataraj, sometimes with tears streaming down his face.

About two months after his great awakening, in late August of 1896, matters came to a head. Venkataraman's uncle and older brother did not approve of his constant absorption in meditation and his neglect of his school studies, and made no bones about it. One day, while performing some routine school homework, the boy was suddenly seized with an overwhelming realization that he could no longer go through the motions of being a normal schoolboy. He put aside his homework and sank into meditation. His older brother rebuked him, suggesting that Venkataraman was unworthy of the comfortable home life that he was being provided with. Realizing that in some ways his brother was correct, Venkataraman seized the moment and determined to leave home for good. He resolved to travel south, to the sacred mountain of Arunachala.

Many adolescent boys (or girls) dream about running away from home, but few do it, and even fewer make it permanent if they do. And those who do are usually doing so on the basis of some sort of resentment toward their family or their caretakers. Venkataraman's case was all the more unusual because he left not out of any resentment, but simply because he had become completely disconnected with conventional life. Not because he 'rejected' such a life, but rather because a profound passion for spiritual truth had been awakened in him to such an extent that nothing else mattered anymore. He simply wanted to be left alone to enjoy, and reside in, his absorption in the Self, *as* the Self.

He was given a small amount of money by his aunt, which turned out to be enough (along with later selling his Brahman-caste earrings) to travel south by train, and then foot, until he reached Mount Arunachala. He arrived on September 1, 1896, and would not leave the mountain's side until he passed away on April 14, 1950. In many ways his 'story' ends here, although he would spend more than half a century teaching, and radiating the Presence of his true nature.

The Sage of Arunachala

After initially arriving at the sacred mountain, Venkataraman found a nearby temple, which was wide open and empty when he arrived. He entered and sat in blissful meditation. The next day he strolled through the town and proceeded to shave his head and throw away his remaining pocket change. In short, he was committing to the life of the renunciate. It's very easy to misuse such a path, for example by using it as a disguise to hide from the world or from worldly responsibilities, but in Venkataraman's case it was clear that his renunciation was the natural outer expression of the depth of his inner awakening. All true awakening involves a radical break or discontinuity with something – not necessarily with one's hair or one's clothes or money – but it always involves a profound demonstration that is possible only because of the certainty – the 'true' faith, essentially – aroused by the awakening.

Venkataraman spent a number of weeks in seclusion, meditating in the temple. Some local boys, intrigued by a lad around their age sitting motionless day after day, began to taunt him and throw stones at him. Accordingly Venkataraman decided to retreat further into the temple, into one of its subterranean vaults. This act alone was highly courageous and yet another demonstration of the boy's depth of trust in his awakening, because the vault was old, neglected, dark, and had nothing in it but vermin and bugs. The boys who had been taunting him were too afraid to enter the vault so contented themselves with throwing objects at the entrance to the vault. They were eventually chased off by a passerby who, directed by a local mystic who had been fruitlessly trying to protect Venkataraman from his tormentors, descended into the vault. The passerby was astonished by what he saw: a motionless adolescent boy absorbed utterly in profound trance, with his legs covered in wounds from the bites of vermin and bugs. His inner absorption was so pronounced that he apparently was unaware (or didn't care) that he was being bitten. He went into such deep trances that he neglected to care for even the most basic needs of his body, such as food and water. The benevolent passerby, concerned, conferred with a local swami, and they and some others had the boy carried out of the vault. Venkataraman remained largely unresponsive for another couple of months (he was practically force-fed in order to keep him alive). It's a testament to the spiritual maturity of Indian culture (at least at that time and place) that the boy was, in fact, cared for. In most other cultures such a person would likely have met with a worse fate, or at least would have been treated in an unsupportive manner, with the intent of invalidating his experience.

According to most teachings on the matter of enlightenment, Venkataraman's state at that time was characteristic of an earlier stage of realization, what is sometimes called *Nirvikalpa Samadhi*. In this state the mind is absorbed inwardly, in a form of trance, even to the point of the body being practically immobilized. A younger contemporary of Ramana, the Indian sage Meher Baba (1894–1969), devoted part of his life work to helping certain mystics who were absorbed in such a state. Meher Baba referred to them by the Sufi term *mast* (literally, 'intoxicated with God') and mentioned how easily it was for them to be mistaken for insane people.

At this time Venkataraman began to be known as the 'Brahmana Swami'. He was initially cared for by a mystic named Mouni Swami (*mouni* being the Sanskrit word for 'silence'), who in addition to protecting him also arranged for the minimum necessary daily nourishment for the young sage's body. The boy soon found a nearby tree that he spent weeks sitting under, deep in *samadhi*. It was around this time that some passing pilgrims began to gaze upon the luminous young sage and some even prostrated before him. A wandering seeker named Uddandi, who had spent years studying and meditating but felt frustrated by his lack of progress, noticed the youthful Brahmana Swami and became his first disciple, even though there was no verbal teaching. The boy merely continued to sit in silence, yet his demeanor and the quality of presence around him suggested to Uddandi that he was self-realized, and that to merely sit in his company would be direct spiritual instruction itself.

The 'silent transmission' approach would always be Ramana's main teaching method.

Soon after, more pilgrims found the young sage, including a seeker named Palaniswami, who immediately recognized Brahmana Swami as his master and spent the next two decades serving him as his main attendant. The sage was soon moved by caring attendants to a nearby orchard grove, and it was here that he began to engage his intellect again by reading various scriptures in Tamil or Sanskrit so as to answer questions brought to him by Palaniswami. In this way the young Brahmana Swami was prepared for more intellectual seekers who would attach themselves to him as disciples in future years.

All this time the young sage's family, especially his mother, had been distressed by his disappearance and had sent out small search parties to try to find him. Through various connections they eventually tracked him down in late 1898, about two years after he had left home. One of his uncles implored the swami to return to his family, assuring him that they would not interfere with his chosen ascetic path, and that there was even a nearby temple where he could stay and be cared for. Brahmana Swami was entirely unresponsive. He simply refused to allow for any attachments to be reinforced by providing false hope. Several months later his mother and older brother visited the young sage, with his mother trying, day after day, sometimes tearfully and sometimes angrily, to get him to return home. (The fact that the young swami's body was largely uncared for – like a typical Indian *sadhu* he had grown thin, rarely washed and his hair had grown long and matted – doubtless added to his mother's upset.) Matters came to a head when one day his mother became very demonstrative and the young sage not only totally ignored her, he stood up (a rare enough thing in itself) and walked away. His mother gave up and left. (She would return, eighteen years later, along with Ramana's older brother, and become his disciple. At her death in 1922 Ramana declared her 'liberated'.)

As Arthur Osborne pointed out, this whole sequence is reminiscent of the scene in the New Testament where Jesus is reputed to have not recognized his mother, implying that he had gone beyond the 'small family' to become a full member of the 'cosmic family' of the totality of all. Only one who is radically awakened can make such a claim, indicating that they have broken all familiar attachments, and in particular, the attachment to form (essentially, the gross body and its gene pool; i.e., the nuclear family). Here again the fine line between radical awakening and mental illness is seen (a fascinating study in itself, and one tackled to some extent by the brave Scottish psychiatrist R.D. Laing in the early 20th century). Many mentally ill people have 'disconnected' from family for endless possible reasons and remained 'unresponsive' in the face of family members attempting to re-establish connection or human intimacy. Brahmana Swami's state was not illness, however. He still had certain lessons to learn around caring for his body, if only so that he could adequately guide others, but his state was one of bliss and deep peace (something even tangibly felt by others merely by sitting in his presence). That is not the state of a mentally ill person, but rather one who has transcended egocentric contraction and pain.

In 1899 Brahmana Swami, now 20 years old, abandoned the nearby temples and began living in various caves found in Mount Arunachala. (Though called 'Mount', it is really only a broad, flattened hill, not even 3,000 feet high, though it has a large ground circumference of some eight miles, used traditionally by pilgrims to make circumambulations.) He would remain in these caves for some twenty-three years; although not, strictly speaking, in seclusion, as he always had attendants and disciples around him. In 1907, an accomplished Vedic scholar named Sri Ganapati Sastri visited Brahmana Swami and joined his slowly growing group of disciples, while at the same time bestowing on the 28-year-old sage the name Bhagwan Sri Ramana Maharshi. 'Bhagwan' is an honorific meaning, roughly, 'Lord'; 'Maharshi' means 'Great Sage'. 'Ramana' was a shortened version of his birth name Venkata*raman*. Ramana accepted the name and was known mostly as 'Bhagwan',

'Sri Ramana', or 'the Maharshi' for the rest of his life.

In 1922, aged 43, Ramana left the caves and relocated at the foot of the mountain. An ashram was gradually built around him. He remained there for the last twenty-seven years of his life, teaching a steady stream of visitors from far and wide, sometimes with pithy verbal discourse or question and answer sessions, but more often through his powerfully illumined silent presence.

Teachings

Although relatively long books have been written about Ramana's teachings, in fact what he taught is supremely simple. He taught that our true nature is the transcendent, impersonal and universal Self, and that we merely suffer from a type of ignorance or mental confusion that prevents us from seeing this. His prime method for uncovering this true nature was via Self-enquiry, the relentless posing of the essential question 'Who am I?' This is a Zen *koan* (and in fact, there are striking similarities between Zen master Hakuin and Ramana, although their outer dispositions appear to have been very different – Hakuin aggressive and confrontational, Ramana outwardly gentle and largely passive, although he did, on occasion, challenge seekers).

Attaining to Self-realization via usage of Self-enquiry needs to be understood. As Ramana taught, the primal thought, the 'I', is to be penetrated entirely. Initially when we look within, we will find this 'I'-thought readily enough. It is the standard sense of 'I am-ness' that most people are aware of, even if only vaguely. However, Self-enquiry is not about resting in this I am-ness, because that is really just the conventional self – the ego – observing itself. We need to go further, beyond the conventional sense of I am-ness, and see what is 'behind' that; or more accurately, *prior* to that. What is prior to that is the 'true I', or 'I-I' as it is sometimes referred to.

Ramana taught that the main cause of our ignorance of the true Self is our identification with the physical body, and with being a separate entity in general. The true Self is not identified with the body, and is not, strictly speaking, located within time or space. Because it is timeless, it is therefore unborn and deathless. Nor can it be truly known via thought. Obviously, we can *think* about the true Self, and we can even *imagine* it, but what we are thinking about and what we are imagining is only a thought or imagination; it is *not* the true Self. This is essentially identical in meaning to the famous line from the *Tao Te Ching*:

> The Tao that can be told is not the eternal Tao;
> the name that can be named is not the eternal Name.

We can allow the translators of the *Tao Te Ching* some liberty, but strictly speaking, the Tao (the true Self) is not 'eternal', as that implies a state within time; rather it is time*less*. Ramana taught that this 'timelessness' is not some special state existing outside of the 'real universe' or any such thing. It is rather that the timeless *is* the Real. It is only because of our confused and deluded state, brought about mostly by our identification with the body, that we conceive of time as objectively real, when in fact it is a mental construct, something we have, in essence, 'made up'.

Ramana further taught that it is not only 'time' that we have made up. We have made up everything, including our bodies – the gross (physical or 'waking'), the subtle (higher energy frequency, or 'dream body') and the causal (highest frequency, or 'deep sleep'). To awaken fully to the true Self is to 'dissolve' our identification with all three bodies; that is, to be liberated into the formless.

The method of Self-enquiry is not a process of intellectual investigation. It rather involves keeping the attention on the 'I' with great determination and consistency. However, Ramana *did* teach an alternative approach, that of surrender to the Divine (*bhakti yoga*). This approach could be said to be more appropriate for those emotionally inclined, or those who find the direct approach of Self-enquiry not appropriate for them. Ramana did teach that both approaches ultimately lead to the same thing, realization of the true Self.

Ramana's highest teaching was via silent transmission. The question of whether or not a guru can actually 'transmit' wisdom or realization has long been debated, but the whole issue was perhaps best summed up when a young U.G. Krishnamurti (not to be confused with his more famous namesake J. Krishnamurti) visited Ramana in 1939 and asked him if he could transmit his wisdom. 'I can,' replied Ramana. 'But can you receive it?' It's the perfect reply, because although wisdom cannot be 'sent' to another person like a piece of mail, it can be radiated in that person's presence. It is then simply a question of whether or not the seeker can allow his or her own innate wisdom to *respond* to that radiance, that presence which is manifestly embodied by a deeply awakened teacher.

Perhaps a perfect example of Ramana's teaching style was given when a seeker once asked him, 'How does one control the mind?' to which Ramana replied, 'What is the mind? Whose is the mind?' When the seeker countered with 'I cannot control my mind', Ramana responded with 'It is the nature of the mind to wander. *You* are not the mind ... never mind the mind. If its source is sought, it will vanish, leaving the Self unaffected.' The seeker tried a different angle, asking 'So one need not seek to control the mind?' Ramana, with laser-like precision, answered, 'There *is* no mind to control if you realize the Self.'

He also taught that the world we typically perceive arises only with the mind. For example, every night we go to sleep. In deep dreamless sleep, there is (in our experience) no body and no world. It is only when we wake up in the morning and the mind resumes its activity that the world we perceive springs back into existence for us. Our perception of this world is such an enormous distraction that it effectively blocks us from awareness of the Self. To penetrate the illusion of the false self – the conventional 'I' (ego) that upholds the perception of the world – is to awaken to the Self, and finally to understand that the world we experience is not separate from the Self. That is, nothing truly exists but the Self, or pure Consciousness.

It may be noted by the attentive reader that these teachings sound suspiciously similar to some of the problems touched on in Chapter 2 (Eastern Fundamentalism), such as the facile (and easily misused) view that 'only Truth (the Self) is real', or put another way, that 'you are already enlightened'. But the crucial difference with a master of Ramana's caliber is that he himself has truly realized this state, and thus what he says is not empty doctrine or dogma. He himself is a living scripture, and speaks only from his direct experience. And so to be with Ramana was to undergo *darshan* in the truest meaning of that word – 'to be in the light of the master' – which, for the seeker, is the same thing as a plant being nurtured by the rays of the sun. Ramana was not just passing on doctrinal truths; he *was* the doctrinal truth.

The same applied to Ramana's teachings on the matter of free will. Asked once if a person had free will, he pointed out that the question is only relevant for one who still believes that he or she is a separate person. From the point of view of absolute truth, there *is* no separate person, and therefore questions about whether or not 'the person' has free will automatically drop.

That entire idea, if taught by one who has not directly realized that the discrete separate ego-identity is ultimately unreal, will simply be dogma, and if taken on by one who has not realized their greater nature, can easily be corrupted into excuses to not be responsible, and so forth. ('Free will is an illusion, so why bother doing anything?') Again, the matter depends on who is teaching it. Ramana could teach such principles of ultimate truth effectively, because he himself was the living answer.

Ramana taught tirelessly into his late 60s until his health began to fail due to cancer that appeared in one of his arms. Despite several operations, the cancer kept reappearing. Doctors advised that the arm be amputated, but Ramana refused. He passed away as he had lived – with great serenity, and surrounded by hundreds of deeply devoted disciples – on April 14, 1950, at 70 years of age.

His legacy lives on, and as with many great sages has become more pervasive over time. By the early 1990s in particular, Ramana's life and teachings, already respected worldwide by sincere seekers, grew in stature and fame, especially in Europe and North America. This was largely due to the work of H.W.L. Poonja (1910–1997), an Advaitin master living in Lucknow (in north central India), who had spent a few years with Ramana in the 1940s and underwent a deep awakening in the sage's presence. Poonja subsequently lived and taught quietly to a small circle of students until the American seeker Andrew Cohen discovered him in the mid-1980s. Although Cohen later broke with Poonja, he had energetically promoted Poonja's name in the West. Hundreds of seekers then made their way to Poonja, and thousands more subsequently become aware of Poonja's guru, Ramana, via the work of a whole new generation of Western satsang teachers endorsed by Poonja and a plethora of newly published books on Ramana, Poonja, and Advaita. Many leading-edge thinkers in the field of human transformation regard Advaita as a major potential light leading forward into a more awakened future in general, in large part because of the remarkable simplicity of Advaita and the universality of its principles – and in no small part because of the impeccable example set for it by its greatest modern exponent, the sage of Arunachala.

That said, it would be remiss to not point out that Ramana himself never actually claimed to be a guru and never claimed to be part of, let alone start, any 'lineage'. The fact that a number of modern satsang teachers (most of them students of Poonja) have claimed Ramana as part of their lineage must be seen as their own doing, and not reflecting anything initiated by Ramana. Unlike Jesus, Ramana did not go seeking disciples to make them 'fishers of men' – he simply sat there and people eventually gathered around him. His whole life and work remained an uncompromising testament to an exquisite solitude that was yet openly available to others – much like his beloved mountain.

Chapter 34

Nisargadatta Maharaj: Passionate Tiger

Nisargadatta Maharaj makes for an interesting contrast with the previous great sage discussed, Ramana Maharshi. This is because although they taught essentially the same thing – the very highest truths of the great wisdom tradition known as Advaita – they were remarkably different expressions of that truth. In some ways Nisargadatta and Ramana were opposites, something hinted at even in the many photos of them. As gentle, reticent, and quietly powerful as Ramana was, Nisargadatta was fierce and vocal. As rural as Ramana was (living by a mountain), Nisargadatta was urban, teaching out of a small home in a huge metropolis (Bombay, now known as Mumbai) among millions of people. As detached and unworldly as Ramana was, Nisargadatta was engaged and 'ordinary', marrying, raising a family, and working for many years to support them via running a simple retail trade (selling household goods; mainly Indian cigarettes). As much as Ramana's entire life was devoted to living and teaching from the Self-realized state (he had awoken at just 16), Nisargadatta did not begin seeking until age 36, and had his awakening a few years later. And as much as Ramana had no human teacher, Nisargadatta did (the guru Siddharameshwar Maharaj, 1888–1936), and would later credit his awakening as due to simply following his guru's instructions. (Although Nisargadatta did not talk about it much, in his later years he did state that he was part of a teaching lineage, via his guru, known as the Navnath Sampradaya, a semi-mythological lineage of Hindu mystics).

According to Nisargadatta's well-known disciple Ramesh Balsekar, Nisargadatta was scornful of biographical information about his life. He once remarked to Ramesh with his characteristic bluntness, 'Instead of wasting your time on such useless pursuits, why don't you go to the root of the matter and enquire into the nature of time itself?' It is perhaps for that reason that not much is known about his earlier years. As with many Indian sages the name he came to be known by was not his birth name. He was born Maruti Shivrampant Kambli, on April 17, 1897, in Bombay, one of six children born to a pious Hindu couple.[9] Maruti was raised in the country, in a small village. When he was 18 his father, a farmer, died; Maruti then moved to Bombay, following his elder brother, so as to work and help support his family.

Growing up, Maruti had worked assisting his father on the farm, and had not received a traditional education. Despite that, he was bright and inquisitive. His first spiritual influence was a friend of his father's, a pious Brahmin who would often engage the young Maruti in discussion about philosophical and religious matters. This seed, planted in his boyhood, would later bloom into his passionate dedication to the highest truths of life. In the meantime his responsibilities lay elsewhere. After arriving in Bombay he worked as a junior clerk, but apparently hated the job and quit after a few months. It's possible that he had a headstrong nature and needed to be his own boss. This seems likely as he soon started his own business, selling children's clothing and Indian cigarettes (usually called 'beedies' – which accounted for the later informal name sometimes heard to describe him: 'Beedie Baba').

Maruti's business prospered and he was eventually able to open a few more shops. The relative financial stability brought by this allowed him to settle down. At age 27 he married a woman named Sumatibai, and went on to have four children (three daughters and a son) with her. His life up until his mid-30s was routine and very typical for a hard-working family man in the city. However, he did have one friend who was unusual, a dedicated spiritual seeker who happened to be a disciple of a somewhat obscure Hindu guru named Siddharameshwar Maharaj. (One has always to bear in mind that 'gurus' are very common in India; practically every village has its local sage, and major cities have many religious priests, spiritual teachers, and wandering mystics of all conceivable levels of quality. Few, however, could be said to be deeply realized.)

On a fateful day in 1933 Maruti went with his friend to see the guru, and was strongly impacted. One might wonder if this was due to the quality of the guru, or to the fact that Maruti had been unconsciously seeking something and was primed to break out of his routine psychological rut, into a higher consciousness. Probably both are true. Regardless of Maruti's level of readiness, he was sufficiently impressed by Siddharameshwar to dutifully follow the guru's spiritual instructions, which consisted of a mantra and a guidance to seek his true Self. This took the form of a constant remembrance of the thought-feeling 'I am'. (In essence, very similar to the 'self-remembering' taught by the famed Greek-Armenian sage G.I. Gurdjieff in the early 20th century.)

The guru had said to Maruti, 'You are not what you take yourself to be.' That is the ultimate pointer toward higher truth, and the time-honored rallying cry of genuine mystics and Self-realized sages everywhere. It is what shakes a seeker, or a potential seeker, out of the conventional slumber of typical life, where we (remarkably) come to take for granted mediocrity, that we should somehow be satisfied with what has been put in front of us. Truth-seekers throughout history have had to work against the grain of convention, and frequently against an unspoken taboo not to challenge these conventions, foremost of which seems to be the consensual agreement that you *are* what you take yourself to be. It may be confidently said that no movement toward Reality can occur until we first begin to challenge that assumption. *I am not what I take myself to be* is the beginning of awakening, the first glimmer of light upon a murky inner landscape.

To receive quality guidance or specific instructions from a reasonably worthy spiritual teacher is not uncommon. What *is* uncommon, however, is to set about following those instructions with great determination and faith in the teacher's guidance. And that is exactly what Maruti did. It is here where he shows his latent quality, in a way that immediately marks him apart from the vast majority of truth-seekers everywhere. For even though Maruti had work and family responsibilities, he still set aside time every evening to retire to a special loft he had constructed in his home to practice his guru's instructions with great commitment.

Maruti did not have long with his guru, only about thirty months. Siddharameshwar died in 1936, leaving his determined student on his own to complete his realization. Maruti resolutely stayed with the practice of remaining focused on the 'I am' awareness, and this began to yield clear results. He awoke deeply to his true nature as the Self, and then decided to take a spiritual name – Nisargadatta – which means 'one who dwells in the natural state'. The second name, Maharaj, is an honorific meaning 'Great King' and would be affectionately bestowed on him in later years by his disciples. For most of his later teaching career he was referred to as 'Maharaj'.

It is interesting to note that not long after his awakening, Nisargadatta temporarily left his family and work, deciding to wander as a mendicant throughout India. He did this for about a year, at age 40, before coming to the realization that the life of a homeless mystical *sadhu* was not for him. He then returned to Bombay and his family, and resumed his work as a shopkeeper. He would remain there for the final forty-four years of his life.

Nisargadatta's wife passed away in 1942, and he spent the following decade working and completing the duties of raising his children. He did not begin formally teaching and taking disciples until age 54. The fact that he spent fifteen years as a realized sage, but did not take students, is testament to his humility. Far too many teachers (especially in the West in modern times) assume a teaching function with minimal time to mature their spirit after an initial awakening (or even without one). It is never hard to find students or followers for a sufficiently charismatic (and hopefully awakened) person. It is far more uncommon to find an awakened individual spending many years living quietly and responsibly, slowly honing their understanding, before assuming a teaching role.

His children now adults and on their own, Nisargadatta began his formal teaching work in 1951 (which was the year after Ramana had died – as one great teacher departed, another one appeared). He did this out of a small room on the upper floor of his Bombay home, where he taught for some thirty years. For his first fifteen years of teaching he continued to run his retail shops. He retired from work in his late 60s, but continued to teach until his death from cancer on September 8, 1981, aged 84.

Teachings

Nisargadatta did not teach the lazy man's way to enlightenment. He was a fierce teacher who had much more in common with the old Chinese and Japanese Rinzai Zen masters and the path of 'sudden awakening'. The fact that he himself had attained Self-realization in a relatively short time (under three years of intensive meditation practice) no doubt shaped his teaching style. There are many stories of his passionate approach, his bluntness and ruthlessness, and his seeming lack of patience with lazy students or seekers who were merely 'spiritual tourists' come to see the latest guru. All of this is clear enough in surviving videos of some of his talks and interactions with students. One can see from these videos, mostly recorded when Nisargadatta was already in his 80s, his fiery nature, as well as his obvious passion. His manner was diametrically opposite to Ramana Maharshi's serenity.

Nisargadatta's student Maurice Frydman, a Polish Jew who had once lived at Mahatma Gandhi's ashram, recorded a series of Nisargadatta's talks, translated them from Marathi (Nisargadatta spoke no English), and published them in 1973 as the book *I Am That*. This book went on to achieve classic status, having a strong influence on many young Western seekers during the 1970s and 80s. The main quality of the book is the direct forcefulness of Nisargadatta's presence, and the uncompromising clarity of his answers to questions put to him. A number of seekers over the years would report that they'd had profound openings and even direct awakening experiences merely by reading the book. More than one seeker claimed that the book itself was a legitimate spiritual transmission. (As any writing can be, if coming from an awakened consciousness and read by a receptive and ready reader. And as an amusing side-note, I once was in a bookstore and saw a book credited to Ramana, titled *Who are You?*, paired side by side and appropriately 'answered' by Nisargadatta's *I Am That*.)

On the jacket of *I Am That* is the line, 'The real does not die, the unreal never lived.' We can contrast that with a well-known line from the mystical text *A Course in Miracles*: 'What is real cannot be threatened, what is unreal does not exist.' This is one of the classic refrains of Advaita-based teachings, and it was the central point that Nisargadatta drove home over and over again in thirty years of teaching. When his guru had said to him, 'You are not what you take yourself to be', he was preparing Nisargadatta for that essential realization, which ultimately became his main teaching tool.

Similar to Ramana, Nisargadatta did not exclusively teach Self-remembering or Self-enquiry, both of which are part of the path of *jnana yoga* (realization of the Divine via mental discipline and penetrating insight). If he felt that a seeker's temperament warranted it, he would advise them to follow a path of devotion (*bhakti yoga*). Regardless of the choice made to follow whichever path, Nisargadatta taught (paradoxically) that at the ultimate level there is no such thing as 'free will' or a 'doer'. He said that the mind and body, created as they have been by endless preceding causal factors, are merely mechanical. The mind has the ability to create the illusion of being a 'doer' or a 'chooser', but in fact it is 'doing' and 'choosing' based purely on past causes. The true Self actually does nothing, being merely a silent witness to all that is arising in the field of consciousness.

Accordingly, there is 'doing' but there is no 'doer'. There is walking, but no walker. There is reading, eating, and sleeping, but no reader, eater, or sleeper, and so forth. To see directly into the illusion of the willful doer is the same as seeing into the illusion of the false self, the separate personality. There is always only *functioning* occurring, but no actual 'entity' behind the scenes pulling levers to make things happen. Because there is no actual doer, the questions of 'bondage' and 'liberation' are therefore rendered meaningless. For who is there to be in bondage? And who is there to achieve liberation? The whole idea of enlightenment, or any sort of 'spiritual path', is rendered meaningless once we grasp the essential truth, that there is no discrete entity that is 'me' to attain any such thing – nor is there any discrete entity that is 'me' to suffer miserably. We suffer only because we are caught in a deep illusion in which we appear to exist as distinct entities.

As touched on in the last chapter, all these ideas have become well known among sincere Western seekers in recent years, especially those who have studied some Advaita (or Buddhism). All of them are easy to misunderstand and misuse. The idea of there being 'no doer' is extremely susceptible to a confused interpretation and to being hijacked by the ego. It needs to always be borne in mind that when sages like Ramana or Nisargadatta speak of there being no real personality, or no actual doer, they are speaking from the perspective of one who has put enormous effort into coming to that realization. Ramana may have awakened in one thirty-minute burst of intense focus and longing for truth, but he subsequently spent many years sitting in solitary meditation, sometimes in dark and miserable vaults, almost starving his body, perfecting his clarity and wisdom. Nisargadatta spent nearly three years meditating many hours – 'all my available time' was how he put it – without fail, making stupendous concentrative efforts. And so while these sages ultimately saw into the illusion of the personal self and free will, they only got to that place of clarity by making profound effort – and an effort that was, above all, full of a burning passion for truth.

No less is required of us for the same realization. There is no free pass to awakening. To merely 'know' that there is no separate self, or willful doer, and yet to not attempt to directly realize this – to summon no effort or burning passion to *truly* see and know this – is worse than useless, because we run the risk of dreaming that we are awake, or aborting our own awakening, or worse, misleading others by a cynical 'I've heard those ideas before and they don't work' attitude.

Nisargadatta had some interesting angles on the subject of 'time'. Consistent with most realized sages, he spoke about the essential illusion of time as we typically experience it. However, he added a deeper piece: not only is 'past' and 'future' nothing more than a construct of the mind, but so is 'present'. As he put it, the present is never truly present because it 'never stays still'. He rather pointed to a deeper element found within pure consciousness, which Ramesh Balsekar translated as 'intemporality' (timelessness). Nisargadatta then added that as we normally experience ourselves to be, *we* are time – that is, we exist entirely as illusory separate selves by defining ourselves within the field of illusory time.

This does not require too much thought to see. We normally define ourselves on the basis of our memory, our accumulated life experience. Things like 'maturity' or 'wisdom', in the conventional sense of those words, are based entirely on accumulated memory. Who we know ourselves to be, in the usual sense of that, is all memory-based. And so our basic identity – literally, 'who I am' (in the conventional sense) – is, in essence, nothing more than time itself.

One sign of a deeply awakened sage is that they will often surprise a seeker by phrasing things with great originality, or in unexpected ways. Nisargadatta was famous for this. A good example follows, excerpted from *I Am That*:

> Q: Are awareness and love one and the same?
> Nisargadatta: Of course. Awareness is dynamic, love is being. Awareness is love in action. By itself the mind can actualize any number of possibilities, but unless they are prompted by love they are valueless. Love precedes creation. Without it there is only chaos.

The comment 'Awareness is love in action' may at first glance seem strange; we are not accustomed to associating awareness with 'action'. Predictably the student wonders about this, and gets 'hit' with a Zen stick by Nisargadatta.

> Q: Where is the action in awareness?
> Nisargadatta: You are so incurably operational! Unless there is movement, restlessness, turmoil, you do not call it action. Chaos is movement for movement's sake. True action does not displace; it transforms. A change of place is mere transportation; a change of heart is action. Just remember, nothing perceivable is real. Activity is not action. Action is hidden, unknown, unknowable. You can only know the fruit.

The teaching there is profound and especially relevant for our modern hectic times. The lives of most people are full of empty activity; restless motion that accomplishes little. Nisargadatta is pointing out that 'true activity' arises from within, as a function of consciousness, of presence, of mindfulness.

> Q: Is not God all-doer?
> Nisargadatta: Why do you bring in an outer doer? The world recreates itself out of itself. It is an endless process, the transitory begetting the transitory. It is your ego that makes you think there must be a doer. You create a God in your own image, however dismal the image. Through the film of your mind you project a world and also a God to give it cause and purpose. It is all your imagination – step out of it.[10]

And here Nisargadatta echoes the wisdom of all awakened sages, which is that the entire perceivable universe is both arising in the field of our awareness and is interdependent with it. What we commonly take to be real is in fact a function of our mind and its projections. Our task is to seek out the Real, and this is done by penetrating into the mystery of 'I am'.

Although like most Advaitin sages Nisargadatta taught that our real nature is already whole and complete, he did not teach a passive acceptance of this. He taught that until one realizes one's true nature, one should continue with *sadhana* (spiritual practice) until free of the delusion that one is not already enlightened. This of course is a subtle point, and as pointed out in Chapter 2, is easily misused. Our task as sincere seekers is to respond fully to the wise counsel of a master like Nisargadatta, and continue with our practices without expectation or attachment to outcome.

Chapter 35

Yaeko Iwasaki: Deathbed Awakening

Yaeko Iwasaki (1910–1935) is one of the more obscure and unlikely mystics of history. The story of her radical awakening at a young age while on her deathbed is extraordinary. In the English language her story is recorded, to my knowledge, in only one book. That book just so happens to be one of the two or three most famed books on Zen Buddhism ever written, the American Zen master Roshi Philip Kapleau's *The Three Pillars of Zen* (first published in 1965).[11] Kapleau (1912–2004) had been a court reporter at the Nuremburg War Trials in 1945. From 1953 to 1965 he trained under several Zen masters in Japan, later returning to America where he founded what was to become one of the more influential American Zen schools, in Rochester, New York.

Yaeko was just a girl in most respects, in frail health, who developed a spark of interest in Zen and deep awakening. And yet the 'spark', and in particular how she responded to it, is of great importance and in many ways lies at the heart of the awakening process. The birth of the 'spark' is always a mystery; it is more what is done with it that matters. To experience the spark of enthusiasm for awakening is not entirely uncommon. What *is* extremely uncommon is to tackle it with gusto, all the more so for a young person who is physically unwell.

Yaeko was guided through her awakening by the well-known Zen master Roshi Sogaku Harada (1870–1961). He was one of Roshi Kapleau's main teachers, and had a reputation for being among the fiercest of 20th century Japanese Zen masters. His monastery was renowned for the harsh climate – both the outer weather, and in inner austerity and discipline. Harada, much like his great forebear Hakuin, was a lion, not a polite oriental priest. Although he worked within the structure of an old tradition (and even worked for many years as a university professor as well), he was unrelenting in his dealings with his Zen students, never compromising when it came to the matter of ultimate truth.

This latter quality of Roshi Harada was important, because in guiding Yaeko he had to summon great courage in face of the fact that she was very ill, possibly on death's doorstep (which turned out to be the case). It is more than tempting to 'be gentle' with one who is very sick; indeed it is almost a moral imperative. However, a deeply awakened sage can see beyond moral constraint, recognizing a bigger fish to fry. (That, granted, is a grey area, and more than one guru supposedly 'beyond moral constraint' has is in fact turned out to have exercised poor judgment, but that is an entirely separate study.[12])

Yaeko began practicing *zazen* (Zen meditation) at the age of 20. She continued to practice with great diligence and passion for truth for the next five years. Then, in a dramatic deepening of insight that unfolded in five fascinating days, she reached a very advanced level of realization before her body succumbed to chronic illness a week later at age 25. Concerning her passing, Roshi Kapleau made an interesting observation. He wrote, 'In India she would undoubtedly have been heralded as a saint … in Japan the story of her intrepid life and its crowning achievement is scarcely known outside of Zen circles.'[13]

What is of note about Kapleau's remark is not the relative degree of Yaeko's renown, but the fact that her story was known in *any* circles at all. Here in the West, especially if there had been no Christian basis to her awakening, if her story had been known at all it probably would have been marginalized, or dismissed entirely as a mere 'altered state of consciousness' brought on by her illness and looming death. In other words, her experience probably would have been pathologized.[14]

Yaeko's awakening is documented in a series of remarkable letters written to her master, Roshi Harada, in 1935. Kapleau called these letters 'eloquently revealing of the profoundly enlightened mind' and 'abounding in paradox and overflowing with gratitude, qualities which unfailingly mark off deep spiritual experience from the shallower levels of insight'.[15] What is also remarkable about the letters is that Yaeko is deeply honest, and continually 'busts' herself on her pride as it pops up, unexpectedly, with each deepening of her clarity. In 1936, after her death, Roshi Harada had these letters published in a Buddhist journal, and added the commentaries that he'd jotted down in the margins of the letters when reading them, for the sake of other readers. Yaeko never had the chance to read these comments, but they are extremely useful for any seeker to study, and can be taken as the old master guiding his student through, among other things, the thickets of what Chogyam Trungpa would later call 'spiritual materialism' (the tendency of the ego to hijack spiritual experiences and try to claim them for its own purposes). The exchanges between the Roshi Harada and Yaeko were subsequently published privately in 1937 by the Iwasaki family in a book titled *Yaezakura* ('Double Cherry Blossoms').

Yaeko was no wandering street mystic, nor was she materially underprivileged. In fact she was a 'rich kid', born into the Mitsubishi family dynasty. As a toddler she suffered from a serious life-threatening illness that she survived but which left her with a heart condition. Growing up, she received a scholastic education (in which she excelled) and preparation for marriage and motherhood, consistent with Japanese tradition in the early 20th century. However, at 20 years of age, she fell ill and was diagnosed with tuberculosis. Under doctor's orders she mostly retired to her bed for the next couple of years. Around this time her father was also diagnosed with a serious heart condition. Gripped by fear of his looming mortality, he sought out a Zen master, found Roshi Harada, and apprenticed himself to the old sage. After a year of committed practice he experienced his first *kensho* (awakening). Reinvigorated, he resumed his duties at Mitsubishi, but not for much longer as his heart suddenly gave out and he passed on. Yaeko, deeply attached to her father, was profoundly moved, and opted to devote her own life to the study and practice of Zen, under the same master, Roshi Harada.

Yaeko was not alone in this; remarkably, her mother, as well as her two sisters, also devoted themselves to Zen study and practice under the Roshi. (It is highly unusual for an entire family to engage in serious spiritual discipline; more commonly there is one 'black sheep' who seeks wisdom, often to the consternation of the rest of their family, as in the case of Ramana.) Yaeko was assigned the classic *koan* known as *Mu*. This stems from an old Chinese Cha'an Buddhist *koan*, 'Does a dog have Buddha-nature?' to which the answer is given: '*Mu!*' The word translates approximately as 'No' or 'Not', but this 'No' should not be understood as literal or straightforward negation. All Zen *koans*, when successfully 'solved', involve the transcendence of limited, conventional thinking, and breakthrough into a non-dual perspective – that is, glimpsing the interconnectedness, and primal unity, of existence and all apparent 'things' within it – and in particular, the illusory nature of the split between self and what self is perceiving.

Yaeko not only dove deep into concentrated and sustained *koan* practice, she also studied assiduously, reading the 13th century Zen master Dogen's classic *Shobogenzo* text not once, but seventeen times. (The *Shobogenzo* – the word means 'Treasury of the Eye of the True Dharma' – is a collection of ninety-five essays that cover the gamut of outer spiritual life and inner experience for a Zen practitioner.) After a period of time her tuberculosis went into remission and then passed. Although her body was weakened by the ordeal, she continued to practice and after several years, in December of 1935, she had her first profound awakening. When she died of pneumonia shortly after, she was in a state of deep serenity; so much so, that the attending doctor remarked, 'Never have I seen anyone die so beautifully.'[16]

The letters from Yaeko to her teacher are covered in seventeen brief pages of Kapleau's work. The first letter was dated December

23, 1935; the last is December 28. During these five intense days, she passed through progressively deeper stages of realization. Roshi Harada was not able to guide her in person; he had just left her side on December 22, after visiting her (though he returned a week later, and was with her when she died). What is impressive about her letters is that she very clearly guides herself through the thorns of the spiritualized ego, which attempts to hang on even as realization is deepening.

The Ten Bulls of Zen (or The Ten Ox-herding Pictures)

Throughout Yaeko's awakening, her process unfolded in accordance with the conceptual framework of Zen known as the 'Ten Bulls of Zen' (or alternatively as the 'Ten Ox-herding Pictures'). This is a metaphoric depiction of stages of realization, involving an ox-herder (representing the seeker) and an ox or bull (representing our true, primordial nature). It remains one of the best models for describing the awakening process. It was around from the early days of Cha'an in China, but was developed and completed by the 12th century CE Chinese Cha'an master Kuo-an Shih-yuan (Kakuan Shien). The 'Ten Bulls' defines the stages of deep awakening as follows (with Kakuan's commentary in indented paragraphs. As with many of the old texts there are several different translations into English; what follows is but one version):

1. The Search for the Bull

> In the pasture of this world, I endlessly push aside the tall grasses in search of the bull. Following unnamed rivers, lost upon the interpenetrating paths of distant mountains, my strength failing and my vitality exhausted, I cannot find the bull. I only hear the locusts chirring through the forest at night.

The seeker looks for the bull (symbolic of his or her true nature, the 'Buddha-mind'). This is the beginning of the path. It is usually heralded by a fundamental disappointment with one's life, and a recognition, however dim, that we have been living a life governed by endless distractions leading us down endless 'garden paths' of nonsense. The search for the real meaning of our life begins: we are now seeking, however uncertainly, the bull. In the context of meditation, this can be thought of as marking out initial efforts as we sit.

2. Discovering the Footprints

> Along the riverbank under the trees, I discover footprints! Even under the fragrant grass I see his prints. Deep in remote mountains they are found. These traces no more can be hidden than one's nose, looking heavenward.

The footprints of the bull are spotted. This is the point when the seeker's confidence in the reality of the bull – in the reality of the possibility of awakening – begins to grow. It could be said to represent the intellectual conviction that the possibility of salvation or liberation from the bondage of the mind and its powerful delusions is real. In meditation, it marks the progress that is noted as the mind begins to focus more clearly.

3. First Sight of the Bull

> I hear the song of the nightingale. The sun is warm, the wind is mild, willows are green along the shore, here no bull can hide! What artist can draw that massive head, those majestic horns?

The bull is spotted! The bull appears far away, perhaps even hiding behind a bush, but now there is no doubt that it is real. Visual confirmation has happened. This stage marks the first glimpse of the underlying principle of mysticism, that all that is perceived is ultimately the same as the Source (pure consciousness) that perceives it. This can be likened to an initial mild *satori* (awakening), usually called *kensho* in Zen.

4. Catching the Bull

> I seize him with a terrific struggle. His great will
> and power are inexhaustible. He charges to the
> high plateau far above the cloud-mists, or in an
> impenetrable ravine he stands.

The bull is 'caught', but the seeker's relationship with him is rocky. What this implies is that even after an initial glimpse into our true nature, unruly mental states – in particular, strong feelings and emotions – still arise. The bull is still 'wild'.

5. Taming the Bull

> The whip and rope are necessary, else he might
> stray off down some dusty road. Being well trained,
> he becomes naturally gentle. Then, unfettered, he
> obeys his master.

This stage refers to the important realization that all thoughts arising in the mind are manifestations of our true nature. *All is as it is*, and must be seen that way (as opposed to being 'made wrong' – 'this should not be the way it is').

6. Riding the Bull Home

> Mounting the bull, slowly I return homeward.
> The voice of my flute intones through the evening.

> Measuring with hand-beats the pulsating harmony,
> I direct the endless rhythm. Whoever hears this
> melody will join me.

The sixth stage represents a deepening of understanding, and a corresponding quality of disengaging from struggle – the conventional struggle between oppositional mind-states. Krishna, in the *Bhagavad Gita* (14:24–25) makes reference to this state when he remarks to Arjuna, 'Who dwells in his inner self, and is the same in pleasure and pain; to whom gold or stones or earth are one, and what is pleasing and displeasing leave him in peace; who is beyond both praise and blame, and whose mind is steady and quiet; Who is the same in honor or disgrace, and has the same love for enemies or friends …'

7. The Bull Transcended (Bull Forgotten, Self Alone)

> Astride the bull, I reach home. I am serene. The bull
> too can rest. The dawn has come. In blissful repose,
> within my thatched dwelling I have abandoned the
> whip and rope.

This stage marks the classic definition of enlightenment, when it is finally and directly understood that the seeker (the egoic self) and the bull (the Buddha-mind, our real nature) are not separate, and never have been. Prior to this, awakening has been an 'experience' – requiring a 'me' to experience this 'awakening'. At the seventh stage, the central illusion of this separation is radically realized.

8. Both Bull and Self Transcended (or Forgotten)

> Whip, rope, person, and bull – all merge in No-
> Thing. This heaven is so vast no message can stain
> it. How may a snowflake exist in a raging fire? Here
> are the footprints of the patriarchs.

The eighth stage is a deepening and maturing of the seventh stage; here, all vestiges of what Chogyam Trungpa called 'spiritual materialism', the subtle self-consciousness of 'being awake' – 'I am a Buddha' – is extinguished. Roshi Kapleau, in his commentary on this stage, linked it to an old Chinese parable of a man who became enlightened, and experienced birds 'commemorating' the occasion by showering him with flowers. As his enlightenment deepened, the birds stopped doing this, 'as he no longer gave off any aura, even of devotion or virtue'.[17]

9. Reaching the Source

> Too many steps have been taken returning to the root and the source. Better to have been blind and deaf from the beginning! Dwelling in one's true abode, unconcerned with that without – the river flows tranquilly on and the flowers are red.

This stage marks resting in the full recognition of the Source as 'consciousness without an object'. It can be understood as the complete penetration of Ramana Maharshi's ultimate *koan*, 'Who am I?' It is the return to the center from which all thoughts and all universes arise: pure consciousness itself, self-radiant without cause, unqualified and perfect. *Things are as they are*: the 'river flows tranquilly on and the flowers are red'.

10. In the World (Entering the Marketplace with Helping Hands)

> Barefooted and naked of breast, I mingle with the people of the world. My clothes are ragged and dust-laden, and I am ever blissful. I use no magic to extend my life; now, before me, the dead trees become alive.

In some of the parables of the tenth stage, the seeker (now a finder) re-enters the world with a gourd, traditionally used for holding wine. The wine can be seen as symbolic of the true sage's embrace of the world, and of his willingness to utilize any means to awaken others – even by entering into, and participating in, their 'reality-tunnels' or private dream-worlds. This is sometimes called the way of the 'crazy wisdom master'; however, that term is highly susceptible to being misunderstood or misused. According to Mahayana Buddhist teachings, a true 'crazy wisdom master' is only one who has reached a profound level of awakening and has been purified of character defilements. This enables them to enter into any dimension of reality without concern of becoming tainted and thereby having their clarity, or motives, for helping others compromised.

***

Yaeko's awakening process began with an original 'hazy glimpse', which motivated her to search deeper. She had a breakthrough on December 22, in which she claimed that the 'ox' had suddenly come much closer – 'a hundred miles nearer'. She was seeing something clearly; but at the same time, the spiritualized ego reared its head, and she remarked, 'Even you, my Roshi, no longer count for anything in my eyes', although she hastily followed that up with expressing deep gratitude.

To dismiss one's teacher, in however subtle a fashion, is a fairly common sign of early-stage awakening. It is natural, in the rush of an initial deep understanding, to want to stand forth and proclaim independence. Almost always, however, such a position is entirely premature, because the initial awakening, however impressive, is usually but a glimpse. Even in the case of rare profound and deep sudden awakenings, such as Ramana Maharshi passed through, it is followed up by years of sustained meditation to clarify and deepen the original realization.

Yaeko followed her expression of gratitude by writing about the abundant sense of joy that was arising in her. She then wrote a significant thing:

> Now that my mind's eye has been opened, the vow to save every living being arises within me spontaneously. I am so beholden to you and to all Buddhas. I am ashamed [of my defects], and will make every effort to discipline my character.

Awareness of what remains to be 'cleared up' becomes intensified with early awakenings; this awareness is sometimes called 'remorse of conscience', and can be likened to a 'searing inner pain' based on direct realization that any harmful actions we have done to others is no different from inflicting it on ourselves – because others *are* ourselves.

At this point Roshi Harada comments that although Yaeko has 'seen the Ox clearly' she is still a long way off from grasping it, as her thinking is still obscuring the deeper truth. (It is here that the Roshi marks himself as a skilled master. A lesser teacher would have more of a tendency to immediately sanction any sort of awakening, and even, on occasion, to bless the seeker and encourage them to teach.) Roshi Harada further comments that there are three clear signs that Yaeko's initial awakening is genuine: she feels a desire to help others, she feels a deep sense of inner confidence around her realization, and she is determined to apply strong discipline to her further purification and understanding. Despite that, he concludes that she has a long way to go because she is still entrenched in the subject–object division. As he says, 'As yet there remains a subject who is seeing... she must search more intensely!' That is, she is still very much in the position of a separate self who is 'having a spiritual experience'.

Two days later, on December 25, Yaeko had a deeper breakthrough. She wrote enthusiastically to the Roshi, declaring that she had 'attained great enlightenment' that left her full of joy and ecstasy. (Her progress at this point was compared to 'grasping the Ox', which is stage four in the Ox-herding pictures.) Roshi Harada confirmed that she had indeed had a legitimate realization of the Buddha-mind (true nature). Yaeko wrote that the main realization for her at this point was that there is 'neither Ox nor man', meaning, she had begun to see through the subject–object division. She then added – with a vehemence that reflects earlier, not yet ripened stages of awakening – that 'all *koans* are now like useless furniture to me', that there 'are no sentient beings to save', and that if the Roshi spoke to her in a way that she deemed lacking, she would not hesitate to say so.

The Roshi's comments on this are interesting, and clearly skillful. He voices encouragement and caution at the same time, always a fine balancing act. Too much encouragement can become recklessness, while too much caution can overlook the rarity of what is happening. Roshi Harada exulted at Yaeko's breakthroughs, while the same time stressing that she was in the early stages of awakening.

Yaeko reported that her own consciousness was the same as her master's – 'My mind's eye is absolutely identical with yours.'[18] That is always a key hallmark of awakening, the recognition that there is only One Consciousness, like one infinite ocean running through infinite rivers and tributaries, just as the One Consciousness 'runs' through infinite personalities. That she combines these radical proclamations with statements about her overflowing joy and gratitude for her teacher marks them as powerful and legitimate.

Yaeko at that point was somewhat limited by her view that only the Roshi could possibly understand her. This was likely a reflection of the simple fact that he had been her only teacher, and she had spent most of her time in solitary practice. She wrote, 'You alone can understand my mind,' but immediately followed this with 'yet there is neither you nor me.' At this point, she had a clear view of non-duality, but years of maturing this view lay ahead of her (under normal circumstances). That she in fact only had a few days more to live makes her subsequent realizations poignant and remarkable.

The very next day, on December 26, Yaeko wrote to the Roshi expressing 'remorse and shame' for her previous vehemence. The Roshi counters with a reassuring comment that most early awakenings are accompanied by joyful intensity. Yaeko continues with a self-assessment that sounds remarkably more mature, all the more so given that it comes only a day after her previous outbursts of ecstasy. She writes that now that she has had a taste of awakening, she will continue to persist in her practice 'forever', all the while working to 'perfect' her personality so that she can truly integrate her understanding with embodied life.

The Roshi's comments at this point clearly reflect his affection for the girl, as she single-mindedly strives to open her mind's eye to the deepest levels of Reality. He remarks that he can 'die happily' knowing that he finally found a disciple such as Yaeko, and that he is 'overcome by tears' at the power of her sincerity and earnestness.

Later the same day (December 26), Yaeko writes that she has now attained the 'last level' of realization possible while still a disciple.[19] The hallmark of this new realization is, for her, the understanding that at the ultimate level enlightenment is 'not special', simply because it is intrinsic to our nature. In seeing this, she also understands that heights of joyful ecstasy express a more immature state, one that she has now passed through, reaching a calmer and more stable condition. The Roshi, pleased, comments on her rarity – 'Are there even a handful today who understand all this?'[20] – and acknowledges that she has reached the fifth stage ('Taming the Bull'). He confirms that it indeed marks the completion of work with a teacher; that after this level the seeker is now truly on their own, guided by the light of their own passion and commitment to practice.

The next day, December 27, Yaeko reports that she has now moved deeper, and sees that 'Buddha is none other than Mind'. ('Mind' in this context, refers to Universal Intelligence, or Pure Consciousness, or the Totality of All That Is.) She has now broken fully through the central illusion of 'me' and 'you' (duality). The

Roshi, however, comments that while this is true, her journey is not yet complete, as 'delusive feelings' yet remain to be 'rooted out'. This is a key point, one that arises commonly in intensive spiritual practice. A deep awakening is often accompanied by a profound confidence. This confidence can in turn be used to face further into the unconscious mind (when feelings arise) in order to integrate remaining 'unfinished business'.

Yaeko's entire process at this point was highly compressed; her body would be dead within a few days. She was undergoing in less than a week what the usual seeker might undergo over years, even decades. Later on December 27 she wrote twice more, each time reporting further deepening of insight and understanding, finally ending in a direct and radical realization that her true nature was One with Buddha mind. To this, she added an important aside: '... I have rid myself of the smell of enlightenment.'[21]

Roshi Harada was, however, no pushover of a teacher. In his comments he does not let her off the hook, noting that she was still 'emitting the awful smell' of enlightenment, because she was still expressing 'self-satisfaction' with her state of being. In other words, she had not yet entirely rooted out pride; in particular, the subtle view that her awakened state of mind was something 'special' that made her different. This may sound paradoxical, as the essence of her realization is that she is One with everything, but the ego is very tricky and remarkably adept at surviving even in the face of the most radical awakenings. It is here where skilled guidance from a strong teacher is vitally important.

Yaeko concludes her letters to her master showing yet more ripening of understanding, remarking, 'I am astonished that I am that One' (universal Consciousness). Sadly, she never had the time to integrate her Self-realization with bodily life. The very next day, December 28, she had a strong premonition of her death, and beseeched the Roshi to travel to her bedside. He did, and was with her when she passed away, confirming shortly before that 'her Mind's eye' had indeed 'opened'. He later remarked that she would have needed at least another seven or eight years to fully embody her enlightenment and purify remaining character weaknesses. (This is somewhat standard; interestingly, many wisdom traditions remark on a period of time, often lasting around seven years after an initial deep awakening, needed for purification and integration.)

In his concluding remarks Roshi Harada lamented her passing, commending her spirit as a rare example of a householder, mortally ill and bedridden, who still managed to penetrate deeply into her essential nature. The word 'inspiring' is terribly cliché in the literature of Self-realization, but in Yaeko's case it applies as well as any. She gives off a terrific sense of passion and a deep and powerful yearning to truly *know*. There can be no greater motivating forces. She is a remarkable demonstration of the possibility of profound awakening for anyone, even in the midst of the seemingly forbidding circumstance of a debilitating physical condition. If Yaeko, so handicapped, could achieve such breakthroughs, what holds us back?

Part VI

Eight Guiding Pointers for Awakening

There are an almost endless number of 'transformational methods' available in current times, most easily found in well-stocked metaphysical bookstores, many even on the World Wide Web. Accordingly, I'm only going to outline, in concise fashion, a few such methods here. To that, I add a basic caveat: there is no 'one method' to rule all the others. Some, such as the 'Who am I?' self-enquiry used and taught by Ramana Maharshi, probably approach as close as possible to an 'ultimate technique', if only because of the stark simplicity and straight-to-the-core-of-the-matter relevance of the question. But even Ramana's approach is *still* a method, no matter how effective and no matter how great its recent living exponent.

The point is stressed because the ultimate aim of all transformational work is to directly see and understand that the very 'thing' we think we are seeking is our own *true* nature. That has almost become something of a cliché for any who have spent time with basic teachings from mysticism (in most traditions), but its essential power holds true, and always will.

To be awake in the world – a marketplace mystic in contrast to a monastery mystic – is very challenging. We are trying to come to a deep experiential understanding of what awareness, consciousness, actually is, while at the same time negotiating the endless needs of life in a physical body, in a social context that usually involves living among others who have not the slightest interest in such matters (and not uncommonly, even actively discourage or oppose such interest). I say this simply to reduce expectation to a minimum. This is important because expectation, probably as much as anything, is responsible for disenchantment with spiritual practice.

All that said, let us bravely move forward on this journey, in the safe knowledge that the rarest treasure is at the top of the grand and remote mountaintop.

1. Note, Own, Drop (NOD)

A. To 'note' here means to pay attention to your reactions throughout the course of your day. If angry, note it. If sad, fearful, jealous, bored, and so on, note it. Get into the practice of self-observing. Practice noting the manifestations of your personality as if you were a curious bystander.

B. 'Own' in this sense means to embrace your reactions. *This is my anger (not yours). My sadness, my fear,* etc. Use challenging or difficult relationship issues in life (with whomever) to practice localizing awareness. To 'localize awareness' means to bring it home, into your body, into your emotional and mental states, and away from the other person who seems to be the cause of it. Keep bringing it home, like a fisherman reeling in a fish. This is especially valuable during those times when your buttons have been strongly pushed, and you find yourself very attached to 'being right' about some situation. In particular, be willing to investigate the deeper and darker emotions, like jealousy, and especially fear and hate. Hate in particular can be, paradoxically, a very healing emotion to embrace, because of all emotions it alone has the greatest power to project; that is, to truly believe that the other person is entirely to blame for your conflict with them. As hate is embraced, the pain and deep vulnerability it is protecting opens up; a necessary process if we are to become responsible for our pain and vulnerability.

C. If the first two steps have been truly carried out, the third – dropping, or letting go – becomes possible. Once experiencing a given mental-emotional contraction with fullness of presence – *noting* and *owning* – you will find it much easier to drop this state, to release the contraction, like a closed fist relaxing and opening.

2. Calm Abiding

Practice sitting meditation often (daily is best); at least ten or twenty minutes, longer if possible. To 'calmly abide' means to get into the habit of simply bearing witness to thoughts as they arise within awareness. No thought is special. All are simply thoughts. Note them, witness them, let them move on.

If you find the practice of passively witnessing your mind too difficult, then take a good, hard look at your life, and see what is causing your mental agitation. Invariably you will see that the problem is unresolved issues, or unfinished business. Tend to these matters as best you can. The main purpose of the old moral codes of ancient yoga had very little to do with moral righteousness, and far more to do with the expedience of having a less agitated mind. A life that is more together causes a calmer mind. A calmer mind can penetrate deeper into meditation.

3. Deep Insight

Inquire into your essential nature.

A. From where do thoughts arise? Practice witnessing a thought as it arises into consciousness. See if you can actually do this. Look 'before' the thought, into the Void from which it appears to originate.

B. Who am I? Identity is, in some respects, the ultimate mystery, appearing so convincingly real, and yet is found to be utterly insubstantial when examined closely. Identity may be said to be the great illusion, tethered to the physical body and memory. (Without memory, there is no sense of identity.) Quietly witness your identity, and its manifestations. Do not 'do' anything with your identity (you cannot, anyway). Simply notice from where it arises. You will eventually attain glimpses that your real nature (true self) is in fact this 'Void' from which the appearance of your identity arises – not the identity itself. Identity is merely a convention that enables us to navigate this world of personalities and bodies. Like everything else, it is ultimately to be enjoyed – not feared, shunned, denied, exaggerated, or indulged in.

C. What is another person, really? The 'other' is merely the projection of the belief in identity. The 'other' is ultimately no other than ourselves. Whenever 'tested' in life – aggravated, angered, betrayed, challenged, judged, and feeling inclined to 'dish out' corresponding behaviors to others – the object is to try to remember that these others are simply us caught in a different reality-tunnel, and different identity-dream.

Probe deeply into these essential questions, either with another person or on your own. Finally, direct your attention to consciousness itself. What is consciousness? Keep looking at it.

When looking directly into the 'I am' consciousness, you'll at first be confronted by the restless, jumpy mind. Persist. In time, the sense of 'I am' will become more consistent. With further practice and sustained attention, the 'I am' awareness will begin to slowly 'expand' (an approximate term) into something else – a vaster presence that is more a pure 'am-ness' with very little (or none at all) sense of an 'I'. Do not fear this vastness. Open to it.

4. Character Purification

Awakening to spiritual truth – whether in a glimpse or in a profound opening that shatters identification with personal, egocentric agenda – does not normally result in immediate purification of all character defects. This latter takes time, usually a whole lifetime, and in some respects is the most important step. The world has known plenty who have undergone some sort of legitimate spiritual awakening, only to not bother to do follow-up work on character purification. The result tends to be a person who does not guide others with anywhere near the degree of skill they otherwise might have been able to.

To 'purify character' essentially boils down to the matter of responsibility. To be truly responsible for our life, actions, communications, and all manner of interpersonal and practical affairs, marks us as a ripe person. To be both awake to our essential nature, and a responsible adult, is to be a true sage.

'Character purification' involves walking a fine line, because it requires a willingness to face life, and the gritty lessons of day-to-day matters. But it also calls for a measure of detachment, and in particular, a willingness to spend some time alone. Avoiding the world is not the answer, because in doing so we inevitably remain blind to our deeper character traits. It is only in relating that we become aware of what we are really capable of.

In order to 'purify' character, we first need to be aware of the unseen elements of our character. These latter usually only surface when we gain some position of responsibility in life – becoming a parent, assuming a leadership position of some sort (anything from a four-star general to the shift leader in a factory) – in general, anything that does not involve playing small or holding ourselves back. To 'step forward' in life is to discover more of what we are capable of. There is no escaping this lesson. A spiritual awakening of whatever sort guarantees nothing in terms of how we comport ourselves in the world. We need to experience ourselves in a variety of situations and positions in order to know the fuller measure of our being. Awakening is merely acquiring a flashlight in a dark mansion. Character purification is to use our newfound light to explore our mansion and put it in order.

5. Tend the Body

The physical body may not be who we ultimately are, but it can be thought of as our temple, our sacred vehicle in which to directly realize our true nature. Accordingly, we are called on to treat it well, like the old and loyal friend it is.

Traditional spirituality (as in classical yoga) regards the process of awakening as one of ascension, whereby the life force is drawn upward, toward the *sahasrara*, or 'crown *chakra*'. Traditional Christian doctrine also points in this direction, with the ascension of Christ.

These views have left a strong imprint on New Age teachings, which regard the process of awakening as fundamentally one of ascension—rising to heaven, or rising to the crown *chakra*. There is, however, an equally valid *descending current* of spiritual awakening, in which we can think of matter being 'spiritualized' rather than shunned or escaped from. In this latter view, the body is regarded not as a mere 'mortal coil' but rather a vehicle, at the innermost level, of light and energy. The body is treated accordingly as a sacred vehicle, and given right nourishment, rest, activity, and grooming. Non-dualism, rightly grasped, ultimately leaves behind ideas like 'ascending' or 'descending', as notions of spatial dimension apply only to conventional reality. In the meantime, though, we eat healthy food, exercise, and get our rest.

6. Keep Going

Long ago I had a mentor who, after I had just completed an intensive training program with him, pulled me aside for some sagely advice. I was expecting a mini-discourse on my character flaws, or wise and detailed advice about the next steps I should take. Instead he looked me in the eyes and firmly uttered two words: *Keep going.* He then dismissed me with a subtle wave of a hand. He was a man of many and articulate words, so his two-word laser beam left an impact. Over the decades it has remained one of my most valued mantras. Few things in life cripple us more than laziness, or the simple and destructive habit of *giving up* before we are complete.

Read the works of other awakened sages. Attend the talks of teachers you feel good about. Learn from them. Never rest on your laurels. Your understanding can always be sharpened, deepened, expanded, yet more. In general, throw yourself into the fires of life. Do not avoid opportunities, what existence presents you with. Face into life, face into yourself. *Keep going.*

7. Give

Remember that you have a unique contribution to make toward the evolution and awakening of the human race. Yes, *you*. Get to it. Let passion be your guiding light. To be awake is not to be a passive stone statue. It is to be a living tree, with fruit, flowers, shade, and branches for others to rest on. You have been given so much. Give back in some way. Complete the circle, finish the sentence, put the last brick in place.

Probably the most crippling facet of the human ego, besides fear, is self-absorption. Most of us have no idea just how deeply self-absorbed we are. We are fascinated with our own story, with how others perceive us. The only real antidote to the spell of Narcissus is to *consider others*. Not just by rote behavior, but by actually considering that they are only vaguely – and *seemingly* – different from us. And more: they *are us*.

Cut open the body of the average mammal and you see an internal anatomy that is basically the same as the anatomy of a human being. (Chimpanzees, for example, are known to have a genetic makeup that is around 96% identical to the genetic makeup of humans.) In truth, we are only marginally different from the average animal. If that is so, then how less so must it be that one human is truly different from another?

8. Create

This existence that you find yourself immersed in is extraordinarily miraculous. It is full of energy and illimitable possibility. Don't wait for someone to present you with something, or for the universe to drop something on you. Rather, bring it forth from within. Your highest calling is always to (seemingly) *create something out of nothing*.

I'm reminded of a scene from Carroll Ballard's 1983 film *Never Cry Wolf*. The main character, a wildlife biologist, finds himself in the remote Arctic (having gone there to observe wolves), hundreds of miles from human contact, in a bleak, vast, empty tundra. After assessing his situation, he pauses, lights his pipe, and reflects on what he can actually do in the immense and utter wasteland he finds himself in.

'The possibilities …' he muses, '… are *many*.'

Notes

1. For my account of Socrates, I rely mainly on Luis E. Navia, *Socrates: A Life Examined* (Prometheus Books, 2007); and *Plato, The Last Days of Socrates* (London: Penguin Classics, 2003).

2. The source material for any wishing to research the 'tripartite Christ' (historical Jesus, Christ of dogma, and the mystical Christ) is, of course, vast. For this chapter, I drew from the following: Robert Funk, *Honest to Jesus: Jesus for a new Millennium* (San Francisco: HarperSanFrancisco, 1996); Uta Ranke-Heinemann, *Putting Away Childish Things: The Virgin Birth, the Empty Tomb, and Other Fairy Tales You Don't Need to Believe to Have a Living Faith* (San Francisco: HarperSanFrancisco, 1994); Burton Mack, *Who Wrote the New Testament? The Making of the Christian Myth* (San Francisco: HarperSanFrancisco, 1995); Ian Wilson, *Jesus: The Evidence* (London: Orion Publishing Group, 1998); Vivian Green, *A New History of Christianity* (Continuum, 2000); Andrew Harvey, *Son Of Man: The Mystical Path to Christ* (New York: Jeremy P. Tarcher/Putnam, 1998); and the works of Bishop John Shelby Spong.

3. *A Course in Miracles* (Glen Ellen: Foundation for Inner Peace, 1992).

4. For this chapter my main sources are Thomas Laird, *The Story of Tibet: Conversations with the Dalai Lama* (New York: Grove Press, 2006), pp. 82–90; and www.kagyu-asia.com/ l_mila_life1.html (accessed September 22, 2010). Selections from Milarepa's poetry are from *The Hundred Thousand Songs of Milarepa*, translated and edited by Garma C.C. Chang (Boulder: Shambhala Publications, 1977).

5. For my account here I rely mostly on *Wild Ivy: The Spiritual Biography of Zen Master Hakuin*, translated with Introduction by Norman Waddell (Boston: Shambhala Publications, 1999);

and *Hakuin on Kensho: The Four Ways of Knowing*, edited with commentary by Albert Low (Boston: Shambhala Publications, 2006).

6. Waddell, *Wild Ivy*, p. 1.

7. Ibid., p. 1.

8. For my account of Ramana's life, I rely mainly on Arthur Osborne, *Ramana Maharshi and the Path of Self-Knowledge* (Boston: Red Wheel/Weiser, 1970).

9. For this chapter I rely mostly on Nisargadatta's famous work *I Am That* (first published in Bombay by Chetana, 1973; most recent reprint Durham: Acorn Press, 1996), as well as several works by Ramesh Balsekar.

10. *I Am That: Talks with Sri Nisargadatta Maharaj* (Durham: The Acorn Press, 1996), p. 354.

11. For this chapter, I am, of course, entirely indebted to Roshi Kapleau's classic work *The Three Pillars of Zen: Teaching, Practice, Enlightenment* (Anchor Books, revised edition 1989; most recent printing, 2000), pp. 299–324.

12. I touch on some of these issues in my earlier book, *The Three Dangerous Magi: Osho, Gurdjieff, Crowley* (O Books, 2010). For an exhaustive study of the matter, see Georg Feuerstein, *Holy Madness: Spirituality, Crazy-Wise Teachers, and Enlightenment* (Hohm Press, 2006).

13. *The Three Pillars of Zen*, p. 299.

14. For an interesting, and in some ways parallel Western story, see Suzanne Segal, *Collision with the Infinite: A Life Beyond the Personal Self* (Blue Dove Press, 1996).

15. *The Three Pillars of Zen*, pp. 299–300.

16. Ibid., p. 303.

17. Ibid., p. 304.

18. Ibid., p. 310.

19. Ibid., p. 313.

20. Ibid., p. 315.

21. Ibid., p. 319.

About the Author

P.T. Mistlberger is a transpersonal therapist, spiritual teacher, and writer who was born in Montreal, Canada in 1959. Since the late 1980s he has privately coached individuals and couples and conducted personal growth seminars in North America, Europe, and Israel. He is the author of two previous works, *A Natural Awakening* and *The Three Dangerous Magi*. He lives in Vancouver, Canada. You can visit him online at www.ptmistlberger.com and at www.ptmistlberger.blogspot.com.

BOOKS

O is a symbol of the world, of oneness and unity. In different cultures it also means the "eye," symbolizing knowledge and insight. We aim to publish books that are accessible, constructive and that challenge accepted opinion, both that of academia and the "moral majority."

Our books are available in all good English language bookstores worldwide. If you don't see the book on the shelves ask the bookstore to order it for you, quoting the ISBN number and title. Alternatively you can order online (all major online retail sites carry our titles) or contact the distributor in the relevant country, listed on the copyright page.

See our website **www.o-books.net** for a full list of over 500 titles, growing by 100 a year.

And tune in to myspiritradio.com for our book review radio show, hosted by June-Elleni Laine, where you can listen to the authors discussing their books.

MySpiritRadio